THE DERRYDALE
GAME COOKBOOK

L. P. DE GOUY

THE DERRYDALE
GAME COOKBOOK

L. P. DE GOUY

THE DERRYDALE PRESS
LANHAM AND NEW YORK

THE DERRYDALE PRESS

Published in the United States of America
by The Derrydale Press
4720 Boston Way, Lanham, Maryland 20706

Distributed by NATIONAL BOOK NETWORK, INC.

First paperback printing 2000

British Library Cataloguing in Publication Information Available

Library of Congress Cataloging-in-Publication Data

De Gouy, Louis Pullig, 1869-1947.
 The Derrydale game cookbook / L. P. De Gouy.
    p. cm.
 Originally published as vol. 1 of: The Derrydale cook book of fish and
game. New York : Derrydale Press, c1937.
    ISBN 1-58667-008-5 (pbk. : alk. paper)
    1. Cookery (Game). I. De Gouy, Louis Pullig, 1869-1947. Derrydale cook
book of fish and game. II. Title

TX751 D358 2000
641.6'91—dc21   00-043110

♾™ The paper used in this publication meets the minimum requirements of
American National Standard for Information Sciences—Permanence of
Paper for Printed Library Materials, ANSI/NISO Z39.48-1992.
Manufactured in the United States of America.

CONTENTS

BEVERAGES, CUPS, AND PUNCHES APPROPRIATE IN
HUNTING

CONTENTS

CONTENTS

· xi ·

CONTENTS

CONTENTS

CONTENTS

CONTENTS

THE DERRYDALE

GAME COOKBOOK

L. P. DE GOUY

INTRODUCTION

IN cookery, as in all other arts, laws must be respected if harmony is to result. I verily believe that in the home where there is harmony in food will be found harmony in domestic relations. And harmony in domestic relations ensures a pleasing adjustment with the world outside, the home representing the unit of social relationship. Basically, without cookery, there cannot be life and without harmonious cookery there cannot be symphonic living.

We know, for instance, that red wine enhances the enjoyment of certain foods. Why? Simply because the wine is rich in certain elements which the food lacks—because tannin associates itself so admirably with albuminoids and our instinct verifies undeniably through the sense of taste the happy result of the wedding of red wine with the dish before us. It is because the salts and acids offered us in so many forms have peculiar properties which are emphasized by the flavor of white wine that the latter is used to such pleasing advantage in certain food preparations, especially fish and game. It is because fats, starches, and sugar are chemical substances of the carbohydrate group that their association, especially in desserts, represents a happy mating, a culinary alliance sanctioned by centuries of practical, instinctive approval, as in the case of the popular and never-tiring dish of French fried potatoes (starch, sugar, and fat); green vegetables with butter or other fat substances (mineral, salts, fat, and sugar); it is because acids attack cellulose and help digest it, attack fat and further its saponification, that salad represents an admirable combination, the desire for which is augmented by its agreeable flavor. For the same reason lemon is mandatory as an accompaniment of fish and certain game or butter sauces.

The very same instinct which appreciates certain combinations discovers certain incompatibilities between this food and that, such as red wine with chocolate, or ice cream, or mustard with pastry.

It will be seen that it is incumbent upon the cook to understand thoroughly the laws which are verified by the instinctive pleasure of taste in certain dishes and their accompaniment, or the instinctive distaste for others. There is a reason for everything. If one were to analyze the story of even the plainest and simplest food preparation, it would be found that long practical experience and research lie behind its evolution into the health-giving and nourishing dish of pleasing taste and flavor. The story of the evolution of any satisfying food preparation is the story of the beginning of man and antedates the dawn of history.

L. P. DE GOUY, *Chef Steward*

WHAT IS GAME?

Under the generic name of game, we understand and include all the animals good to eat which live free in the woods and fields. To the culinary point of view, game is divided in three classes: large, medium, and small.

Game is one of the luxuries of the dinner-table. It is a food healthful, savory, tasty, and easy to digest. But these qualities are not so intrinsic as to be in a great measure independent of the skill of the cook, under whose directions, game, or any other kind of food, undergoes a great number of scientific modifications and transformations, furnishing the majority of the highly flavored dishes on which a transcendental gastronomic art is based.

Take the fragile quail, for example; it is, amongst game properly so called, the smallest and the most agreeable. A very plump quail pleases as much by its taste as by its shape and color. Its flavor is very evanescent and it may be prepared in countless succulent ways.

The woodcock, as another example, is also a bird to be held in high esteem, but few people know it in all its glory when roasted according to all rules and regulations of culinary principles for then the mouth is flooded with delight.

The merit of a pheasant consists in its aroma. But only a few mortals know how to serve it up to perfection. Science has taken into consideration the merit of this aroma, experience has used it, and a pheasant ready for the oven is a morsel worthy of the greatest connoisseur among gourmets. It is a dry-fleshed bird, with a gamy odor that requires tender care during the preparation. Besides it should never be eaten before at least one good week after it is killed, if one wants to enjoy real pheasant.

Many of the wild fowl that lend gustatory elegance to restaurant menus and private tables of true connoisseurs, gourmets, and gastronomes are imported. From the fens and moors of Scotland, we receive tender grouse hen; from Siberia, the hazel hen and snow hen;

from Norway, the wild hen; partridge, black and white plover, come from England; and quails from South America, especially from Uruguay, while the brown-speckled quail comes from Argentina.

The large game or venison is well represented. From Alaska, we have herds of reindeer, which provide delicious stews, tender steaks, succulent casseroles, appetizing roasts, and tempting braised morsels, as will be seen further on.

The widespread American taste for game is not recent; it is a survival from our ancestors, strengthened by repeal of Prohibition, and here to stay. Nowadays, the city dwellers are relieved of the tedious process of curing, marinating, and aging game. That task is done for them by the game dealers and the butchers, and if sometimes the meat may appear or taste too gamy, they may correct this easily at home, and the pungent and sometimes disquieting odor, greatly diminished.

Other than the pheasant and a few minor birds, small game in general should be treated gently, tenderly, and with nice discretion and simplicity, if one wants to enjoy the natural flavor. The generality of wild birds from woodland or shore may be prepared with no extraneous aids of spices or condiments to give them savor, flavor, and piquancy; the larger ones, at least some of them, have to be larded, to "enrich and nourish" the meat, but the main point in game cooking is that any kind of game, small or large, should always be served sizzling hot and cooked just to the indicated point.

REASONS WHY SOME GAME BIRDS AND LARGE GAME ARE "MORTIFIED"

In the state of society which we have now reached, it is difficult to imagine a race living solely on bread, vegetables, and fruits. If such a nation existed, it would undoubtedly have been conquered by carnivorous armies—like the Hindus, who have been successfully and successively the prey of all those who cared to attack them—or else it would be converted by the cooking of their neighbors.

It is gastronomy and cookery that determines the degree of edibility of every alimentary article, for all are not presentable at table under the same circumstances. Some should be eaten before they have arrived at their entire development, as capers, asparagus, spring chicken, squabs, or suckling pigs; others, the moment they have attained all the perfection destined for them and to our taste, as melons, most fruits, mutton, beef, and all animals eaten when full grown; others, when they commence to decompose as certain dried fruits, sour milk, certain cheese, bananas, woodcocks, and especially pheasants; still others after the operations of the culinary art have removed their deleterious qualities, as the potato and the cassava root.

Whatever be the opinion that one may have as regards "mortifying" game, there is, however, a very important point to consider, especially in certain game. Certain birds in their fresh state have a flavor different from the mortified state, some have to be enhanced; the flesh may be dry and must be nourished; some are flavorless; others are tough. Hence the necessity of mortifying them for several days, according to size, which is a kind of marinade, if I may use this term; some are mortified before being plucked and even drawn; others after being drawn, to render the flesh more tender, raising an insipid, ordinary taste to an incomparable height of delicacy.

Only the pheasants, woodcocks, and snipes require this preliminary operation, though sometimes quails and other birds gain in being mortified. All the other game birds are eaten in their fresh state. However, they may be left standing, after being shot, for a day or two to allow them to get "stale," thus adding firmness to the flesh, as well as more tenderness.

TERMS USED IN COOKERY
THEIR DEFINITION

Aspic—Seasoned gelatine mold or meat gelatine.

Au Gratin—Covered either with bread crumbs or cheese or both and browned in oven or under the flame of the broiling oven.

Baked—Cooked in oven, uncovered.

Barde—To surround a fish, a chicken, or a piece of meat with thin slices of pork fat or any other ingredient.

Baste or Basting—To moisten with water, fat, main liquid ingredient, or seasoning fluid and at short intervals.

Bisque—Cullis, gravy, jelly, of shellfish, meat, poultry, vegetables, etc.

Blanch—To whiten, to half cook by heat or cold.

Boil—To cook in boiling liquid.

Bone—Bone means to remove the bones, leaving original shape or otherwise.

Bouquet Garni—Always composed of parsley, thyme, and bay leaves as a foundation and to which may be added various other aromatic herbs, all tied together with a string or thread which should be removed before serving; in formation resembling a bouquet, hence its name.

Braise—To cook either in oven or on the fire, well covered and slowly, so as to obtain a reduction of the liquid gradually. This usually applies to less tender cuts.

Breaded—To envelop an article of food in bread crumbs or cracker crumbs after having been previously dipped in an adhesive liquid.

Brider—To fasten either by sewing or tying with string by means of a special needle a piece of meat, a fowl, or game.

Broil—To cook under direct flame or fire.

Canapé—A round, square, or otherwise shaped small piece of bread or pastry, or plain dough spread with food.

Cassolette—Small fancy individual dish.

CLARIFY—To render clear or limpid; to suppress the solid part; to separate solid and liquid parts.

COLOR—To give a light color, a golden or brown hue to a piece of meat, fowl, fish, game, vegetables, and pastry.

CONSOMMÉ—Concentrated clear soup of beef, fish, fowl, game, or vegetables.

CREAM or CREAMED—To blend, to whip, to soften or thicken according to indications a liquid or a semisolid or several ingredients until smooth or well mixed together.

CROUTON—Cube, square, or triangle of bread, of pastry, etc., toasted or not, or fried in fat.

DISGORGE—To extract what is useless, harmful, or detrimental from a food. *Example:* to remove the drivel from snails; to remove the inedible part of cucumbers or other vegetables; to remove the excess of water or salt.

DRESS—To arrange the fish, the meat, the fowl, the game, or the vegetables; to give an attractive appearance or a symmetrical form.

ENTRÉE—First course which may be the only course of a meal, or a one-dish meal; preceding the roast; between the fish and the roast or between soup and roast.

EXTRACT OF MEAT—Concentrated meat in a solid form.

FINISH—To add at the last minute before serving what is necessary to complete a soup, a sauce, a fish, a meat, or a dessert.

FOUETTER—Consists of whipping cream or solid liquids by means of an eggbeater or wire whip to solid consistency.

FRICASSEE—A combination of sautéeing and stewing.

FRY—FRIED—*Deep fry:* to immerse a food in deep fat brought to the boiling point. *Pan fry:* to cook in fat in a pan cn the range.

GLAZE—To add luster by freezing or by heat. *Example:* to glaze a fish under the flame of the broiling oven, to give the effect of glaze, luster, or polish.

GRATINATE—To place a dish under a direct fire or in an oven to complete its cooking; to make more crisp, of deeper color, to brown.

GRILL—Similar to broil.

· 7 ·

HORS D'ŒUVRES—A titbit usually served before the soup. An appetizer.

JARDINIERE—Combination of vegetables.

JULIENNE—Method of cutting in small strips.

JUS—Concentrated extract of meat in a liquid form.

MARINADE—Preparation containing spices, condiments, vegetables, and aromatic herbs, and a liquid in which food is placed for a certain length of time to enhance its flavor.

MIJOTER—*See* SIMMERING.

MONTER—To cause to rise by means of whipping or stirring when adding another ingredient, a semiliquid or liquid, and render creamy.

MOUSSE—Frozen, perfumed cream or hot or cold creamed food reduced to paste and raised by means of whipping or stirring.

NAPPER—To spread on a food, fish, meat, or cake a light coating of sauce, syrup, or sugar.

NOIR—(French) means black.

PAN BROIL—Cooking in a pan without fat.

PÂTÉ DE FOIE GRAS—Paste made of goose liver.

POACH or POACHED—To cooked a food in liquid brought to the boiling point. *Example:* to poach an egg; to poach a fillet or an entire fish, to poach a fruit, etc.

POÊLER—To cook in butter or any other kind of fat small pieces of fish, poultry, meat, or vegetables, the skillet or saucepan being covered.

PUNCH—Frozen flavored fruit juices, water, or liqueur. Frozen infusion.

PURÉE—Soup—one made of vegetables run through a fine sieve. Vegetables—same operation but dryer. Game—fowl, meat, fish—same operation but dryer.

RAGOUT—A stew (French).

REDUCE—To let a sauce or liquid evaporate slowly or rapidly to give it consistency.

RELEVER—To impart to a sauce or any food a piquant flavor, through seasoning. To season highly.

REVENIR—To give a color to any food by process of heat in a fat substance over a hot or low fire.

RISSOLER—To obtain by means of heat a crackling food. *Example:* to rissole potatoes, to golden brown to crispness in a fat.

SAUTÉED—Cooking slowly with a smile, tossing the pan containing food.

SIMMERING—Cooking very slowly, the liquid smiling.

SOUFFLÉ—A light preparation of food vigorously beaten to a froth, to a paste rather liquid, and cooked in a hot oven.

A FEW IMPORTANT POINTS IN
GAME COOKERY

1. An old guard of a game bird has no other place in cookery but to be used either for stuffing, forcemeat, hash, or preparing stock.
2. It is advisable to "barde," that is to cover with slices of bacon, larding-pork fat, or ham fat, the breast of any game bird to protect it against the intensity of the heat, as well as to enhance its flavor, when roasting it. This also will add to tenderness.
3. A pheasant, when young, has gray feet, the breastbone is flexible, and a sure sign of youth in a pheasant, as well as a partridge, is seen at the very end of the large feather of the wing which should be pointed; if round, the bird is old.
4. As a rule, unless otherwise indicated, the various methods of preparations of "mortified" game birds, may be applied to one another, that is, certain methods of preparing a pheasant may be applied to a woodcock, or a snipe, especially when roasting.
5. A quail which is not plump and with a firm fat, will be tough. Use it for soup, dumplings, hash, or stuffing.
6. A roasted wild duck is always eaten very rare, as in fact are all the dark-fleshed game birds.
7. The roasting of a wild duck, of whatever kind, should be started in a very hot oven (450°) and the bird cooked with a profuse basting. Slices of lemon and a fruit compote are the traditional accompaniment.
8. A wild duck is always singed and drawn, but not washed. Wipe it with a soft cloth (damp) within and without. Cut off the pinions and tie what is left of the wings to the body. A good way to prepare a wild duck is, instead of stuffing, to pepper and salt the cavity of the body, wash out with salad oil and lemon juice and put a scant tablespoonful of currant jelly or a half a dozen cranberries inside.
9. Broiled wild duck should be cleaned and wiped with a soft damp

cloth inside and out. Split down the back and flatten the protuberant breastbone with the broadside of a cleaver; then leave it in a marinade of salad oil and lemon juice for an hour, setting it in a cool place. Without wiping it, broil under clear flame for no more than 20 minutes, turning often.

10. If a prairie hen be tough, put it—trussed as for roasting—into a steamer and set over hard-boiling, salted water for half an hour. While still hot, rub it well with butter and lemon juice, salt and pepper, inside and out, and put a small bit of fat salt pork in the cavity and roast in the usual way, in a quick oven (400–425°) for 30 minutes, basting repeatedly with butter mixed with veal stock. Just before serving rub with butter alone. In this way the dryness and toughness is mollified and you have a fine, tender roasted prairie hen.

11. A few drops of rum, brandy, Madeira or sherry wine, or even applejack, will always enhance a game sauce. Never try using whisky, which does not associate well with food.

12. To prepare "essence" or extract of game bird, usually used to complete and finish a sauce or a stuffing, bones and trimmings are always used with the usual aromates (herbs and vegetables), and it is advisable to use only veal stock to stretch the liquid; being gelatinous it will add unctuosity to the essence, as well as smoothness; then and lastly the wine or liqueur is added according to directions (*see* IMPORTANT POINTS TO REMEMBER IN WINE COOKERY).

13. Game, be it large or small, should be served instantly after being dressed on a hot platter, as it has then the quintessence of flavor enhanced by the heat.

14. A large grouse is best when roasted; a small one may be prepared in many methods and ways. A real gourmet never eats the legs of a small grouse; the second joint may be used for other preparations, such as stuffing, forcemeat, soufflés, or dumpling.

IMPORTANT POINTS TO REMEMBER IN WINE COOKERY

Wine is affected by unfavorable conditions, by changes of temperature. It languishes, it sometimes recovers. When it has reached its allotted span of life, it dies.

Wine is best appreciated in cookery when it is used for flavoring purposes, a trifling amount conferring a subtly pervasive quality to the dish.

The fundamental principle in wine cookery as in ordinary cookery, recognized by all good cooks, is that any introduced flavoring agent must *Never* dominate the flavor of the principal food; each additional flavor or seasoning is merely for the purpose of accentuating the innate flavor of the food to which it must be subordinated and with which it must thoroughly blend (as the flavorings must with each other). When this is accomplished, a simple food becomes an epicurean triumph.

In using wine for flavoring, it is essential to remember that:

(*a*) A few tablespoonfuls of wine can glorify a soup, a fish, a meat, a game, or a dessert if cooked with the food for a considerable length of time at a low temperature. Too much will spoil the food.

(*b*) With soup, a rather semisweet wine is used.

(*c*) With fish, a dry wine.

(*d*) With meat, a rather dry red wine, or Madeira, or sherry.

(*e*) With game, large or small, red or white wine may be used, according to directions.

(*f*) With dessert, a semisweet or sweet wine.

(*g*) Wine should never be combined with acid foods.

(*h*) If eggs, milk, or cream are to be added or butter to smooth a sauce, it should *Always* be done after the wine.

(*i*) To get the full benefit of a little spirits (brandy, for example) in certain dishes, it is advisable to pour it over the cooking food, touch a match to it and shake until the flame dies out. The flavor of the spirits will permeate the food subtly, raise the flavor, and instil aroma.

(*j*) To hold every bit of the aroma of the wine or spirits, the cooking utensil must be kept closely covered as in braising.

(*k*) In chilling wine- or liqueur-flavored foods, the dish must be kept covered, even in the refrigerator.

(*l*) When braising foods into which wine enters, the wine must be added with the meat, or fish, or game, or vegetables.

(*m*) More wine *Must Not* be added to the food after it has been served. This would entirely spoil the dish.

MARINADES

The word MARINATE comes from an old Spanish word meaning "to pickle," and it is the acid of the marinade that does the work, adding new flavor, softening tough fibers, increasing their natural sapidity through the action of penetration, lifting ordinary foods out of the commonplace and in most cases ensuring their preservation.

There are several kinds of marinades:

THE LIGHT MARINADE—Usually used for small game, fish, meats, vegetables, and fruits. It is also called instantaneous marinade. It may be plain and consist of only a little lemon juice, vinegar, mixed with a little oil, and a few spices and seasonings.

Tomato juice, French dressing, vinegar, fruit juices, spicy sauces (cooked or uncooked), and sour cream are the most used in cookery.

A few drops of prepared sauces, such as Worcestershire sauce, chili, mustard, or Madras.

INGREDIENTS FOR A LIGHT MARINADE

1 small lemon, sliced fine	2 small bay leaves
1 small raw carrot, sliced fine	3 whole cloves, slightly bruised
1 tablespoon vinegar	1 large sprig parsley, or parsley root
1 tablespoon of oil	
1 sprig of thyme or thyme leaves	12 peppercorns, slightly crushed
	Salt to taste

All the above ingredients are placed in a flat-bottomed dish, usually of earthenware; then the meat, fish, or game is placed in it, stirred gently once in a while and turned over often. The meat, fish, or game should always be completely subjected to the marinade, lest the action of the air decompose the exposed part. Keep in a cool place.

ORDINARY MARINADE—This kind of marinade may be made hot or cold, according to indications, but it is more often made hot and for the same kind of meat, fish, or game. The ingredients are almost all the same as for LIGHT MARINADE, and are prepared in the same way, except that they are heated up, nearly cooked, then poured cold over the meat, fish, or game to be marinated.

The purpose of cooking is to precipitate more rapidly the essences, aromas, and extracts from the ingredients used, thus producing a stronger effect. Keep in a cool place.

MARINADE FOR LARGE PIECES OF MEAT, GAME, *but seldom fish*—This marinade may be hot or cold according to indications in the recipe. It is employed mostly for large pieces of game such as wild boar, deer, and bear. In it are included additional aromatic herbs, such as rosemary, sarriette, sweet basil, salt, mace, and sage. The directions are the same as for LIGHT MARINADE and ORDINARY MARINADE, except that the proportions are larger, according to the size of the piece of game or meat; and if the meat or game is to remain several days in the marinade, the vinegar is less in proportion to the other liquids; if of short duration the vinegar is equal or thereabouts. Keep in a cool place and covered with a cheesecloth.

DIFFERENT METHODS OF COOKING

BRAISING—Is a combination of stewing and baking meat through immersion in a covered vessel containing a solution of vegetable and animal juices called "braise," hence its name. The meat is exposed to a strong but not boiling temperature and is self-basting. This is for less tender cuts.

BROILING—Consists of cooking meat over, under, or in front of direct heat. The meat is turned often during the cooking process to ensure an even browning and cooking. This method is for tender cuts.

DEEP FRYING—Consists of cooking food in deep fat at a temperature of 350 to 375° for uncooked food, and 380 to 400° for cooked food. In meat, this method is for tender cuts.

PAN BROILING—Consists of cooking meat or any other food in a skillet or frying pan with little or no fat. In meat, this method is for tender cuts.

PAN FRYING—Consists of cooking food in a frying pan or skillet with a small amount of fat. In meat, this method is for tender cuts.

POT ROASTING—Consists of cooking meat on top of the stove, using direct heat, browning or searing the meat first, then placing it in a covered kettle, pouring over a little liquid, and adding some vegetables according to directions. This method is for large and less tender cuts.

ROASTING—Consists of cooking meat in the oven by the application of indirect dry heat, using an uncovered pan. It is usually used for large tender cuts.

SEARING—Cooking the surface of the meat in a very high heat to caramelize or brown the surface. Meat may be seared in a hot oven, a hot skillet, or under the broiler while the oven is preheating. This method enhances its flavor and appearance and applies to any kind or size of cut.

SIMMERING—A method of cooking food slowly in liquid below the boiling point. This, done over direct heat, enhances the flavor and softens tough cuts.

STEAM ROASTING—Consists of cooking meat in the oven in a covered roaster, using indirect moist heat. A little water, stock, wine, or milk is added to the pan to assure enough moisture for steam. This method is for large tender cuts.

STEWING—Stewing differs from boiling in the fact that the juices of the meat or vegetables are dissolved in the heated liquid, whereas in boiling, the juices are kept from passing out into the water by the coagulation of the external surface of the food mass produced by immersing it suddenly into boiling water. The proper temperature for stewing is between 135 and 160°. This method is for less tender cuts.

For further explanations see Volume II, FISH.

TIMETABLE FOR COOKING GAME

According to size

Venison ....Well done	30 to 40 minutes
Venison ....Rare	20 to 30 minutes
Large Game ....Roasted	20 to 40 minutes
Large Game ....Broiled	15 to 20 minutes
Small Game ....Roasted	20 to 30 minutes
Small Game ....Broiled	15 to 25 minutes
Large Birds ....Roasted	40 to 75 minutes
Large Birds ....Broiled	15 to 25 minutes
Small Birds ....Roasted	10 to 15 minutes
Small Birds ....Broiled	10 to 15 minutes

Game should be cooked and served at once.

All dark meats are served rare—white meats well done.

In general, all wild game should be hung some time before cooking—to improve the flavor, and to make it more tender. Birds should be drawn, but need not be plucked until just before using. Birds should *Never Be Scalded* before plucking. To more easily remove the down from birds, especially ducks—which are the most difficult to "de-feather"—pour hot paraffin over the bird, allow it to harden, and then pull it off, the down coming with it. Other birds may be handled about the same way chickens are.

Duck, especially, should be almost raw next to the bone, or at least it should be decidedly underdone.

For the smaller birds, such as pheasants, 15 to 20 minutes at the utmost for roasting or broiling.

Canvasback, mallard, teal, or any of the other varieties are prepared by first plucking, drawing, and singeing to remove pin feathers, then the heads are removed, and the birds wiped well. Next they are seasoned slightly with salt and pepper and are, when roasted, placed in a very hot oven (500°) to cook and sear at the same time. If no stuffing be used, it is advisable to place either an onion, slices of apples, a small grated carrot, a few stalks of celery, a few loganberries, cranberries, or juniper berries, in the cavity, removing when serving. This absorbs some of the wild flavor.

The time-honored sage dressing is excellent with wild duck, but there are many other dressings for this delicate bird. These delicious dressings will be found under DRESSING AND STUFFING FOR WILD BIRDS. Ducks, especially wild ducks, seem to have an affinity for wild rice and orange slices, the latter placed over the cooked wild rice surrounding the cooked bird.

Game in general should be treated gently, tenderly, and with nice discretion and simplicity. Our wild birds from woodland and shores need no extraneous aids of spices or condiments to give them savor and piquancy; they should be aged and ripened just about as much as are the common meats of the market, except pheasants and a few others.

All birds of the air, field, and forest put on plump layers of muscle, pure lean meat, and have little of the fatty tissue of farm-raised ducks and chickens and they should always go to gridiron, spit, or oven well fortified with added fat.

Wild pheasant, grouse, and quail should be properly larded and blanketed over the breast with a thin sheet of sweet larding pork, held in place by the trussing of the fowl. Quail will roast or broil in 15 minutes, and grouse and pheasant take about 40; and the blanket of larding pork must be removed when the bird is half done, so the breast may be delicately browned.

Canvasbacks or mallards love celery, so it is advisable to use it freely with these birds.

HOW TO BONE A WILD BIRD

Clean the bird as usual and singe. With a sharp-pointed knife, begin at the extremity of the wing, and pass the knife down close to the bone, cutting off the flesh from the bone, and preserving the skin whole; run the knife down each side of the breastbone and up the legs, keeping close to the bone. Lay flat on a clean towel; fill with whatever stuffing or filling indicated; roll up, restoring the bird to its natural form, and sew up all the incisions made in the skin.

HOW TO CARVE WILD BIRDS

Like all masters of an art, the carver of distinction makes no secret of his methods; rather, longing to see the world bettered, he seeks to impart his skill to others. The duck, for example, has a bad reputation of many years' standing as a carvee. Many a promising meal has gone to wreck because, when the duck is set before the head of the family, confusion is brought upon him by a shrill voice uttering these lines, "We all of us prepare to rise when father carves the duck." However, the method of carving a duck or goose or pheasant is a little more complicated than that of a chicken, although it is very easy after a little practice.

Have the duck on a platter with the tail to your left. Insert the fork between the right drumstick and thigh. Now run the point of a sharp knife around the leg, cutting the skin, using the fork to raise the leg toward yourself. Then place the knife underneath the leg and cut straight toward the tail, raising the leg until you find the joint with the point of the knife. Cut across the joint and remove the leg. Now insert the point of the fork in the bottom of the right wing, and carve from the top of the breast down to the wing joint, which you then easily sever with the point of the knife. Remove the left leg and wing in the same fashion. If the duck or goose is large enough slice the breasts. If it is small, split it from tail to neck and then cut across it, providing four portions. Proceed without haste, but with speed. The duck does not grow cold under such ministrations. Use no violence, for violence tears and disfigures. From point to heel the knife blade has its uses, which should be adapted to the task at hand.

Because the goose is more fatty, the carving is easier. After removing the legs as indicated for duck, the breast slices are made directly from the top of the breastbone downward to the end of the wing.

The carving of a wild turkey is accomplished exactly as for chicken. However, since the wings and legs of a wild turkey are more fleshy, slices may be carved from them.

Small wild birds are carefully split in two lengthwise from the breastbone downward. Then the legs and second joints are removed.

DRESSING AND STUFFING FOR WILD BIRDS

BROWNED WILD RICE STUFFING

(For Wild Duck, Pheasant, Wild Turkeys and the Like)

PROPORTIONS FOR A WILD TURKEY

2 cups uncooked wild rice	2 cups game stock, or meat stock
½ cup cooking oil	2 teaspoons salt
1 cup chopped celery	½ teaspoon Worcestershire sauce
1 cup chopped onion	½ teaspoon Tomato Catsup
½ cup button mushrooms	1 generous tablespoon parsley,
½ cup green pepper, minced	minced

4 juniper berries (optional)

Wash the rice. Dry. Heat oil in heavy skillet. Add the rice, celery, and onion, stirring constantly until rice is golden browned. (You may have soaked the wild rice an hour in tepid water to soften the bran coats and shorten the cooking period.) Add the game stock or meat stock and cover tightly. Let simmer for 30 minutes after adding all the remaining ingredients.

STUFFING FOR CANVASBACK, MALLARD, AND SIMILAR DUCKS

1 slice of onion	½ cup bread crumbs
2 tablespoons butter	¼ cup chopped tart apple
½ cup chopped celery	Salt and pepper to taste

Brown onion in butter and add celery, bread crumbs, apple, and seasoning, heating well. Mix thoroughly and stuff into duck.

SAUERKRAUT DRESSING

(*For Wild Fowl of Any Kind*)

Sauerkraut counteracts the "wild flavor" of game birds, and also imparts a distinctively delicious taste. For each wild fowl, be it grouse, partridge, prairie hen, and even turkey and wild duck (except canvasback, mallard and the like), use:

One cupful of sauerkraut, parboiled for 5 minutes in enough of its own juice, over a low fire. Drain thoroughly and combine with a teaspoon (scant) caraway seeds, no salt, but plenty of black pepper to taste. Stuff the bird, and roast as directed.

SAGE STUFFING

(*Polish Method*)

Mix 1 scant cup of cracker crumbs, 1/3 cup of butter melted in 1/3 cup of meat stock, and salt and black pepper to taste. Add ½ generous teaspoon of powdered sage, a blade of summer savory or marjoram. Mix well and fill the bird. A fine sage dressing for duck, prairie hen, and even partridge.

Other dressings will be found under appropriate recipe.

HOW TO SKIN A RABBIT

The best way to skin a rabbit or a hare is to hang it by its hind-legs, on hooks. Cut the skin at the full length of the belly. Now proceed to remove the skin on either side, first, up to the first joint of the hindlegs. Make incisions on the back of the leg but do not remove the skin as yet. Skin the tail the same way and then continue skinning the head and the back. Cut off the ears at the base and leave the skin on the forelegs. Cut the skin round the eyes and hips. In this way the skin comes off in one piece. Then draw, and clean. Squirrels may be skinned in the same way, as well as all other haired game.

It is a well-known fact that the flesh of the hare or rabbit is much better in winter than in summer, and that a freshly killed hare or rabbit is tender if cooked when the animal has not had time to stiffen and stretch, providing, of course, that the animal is young. Never attempt to prepare an old hare or rabbit otherwise than in loaf shape, or similar preparations.

GAME RECIPES

"Dans l'air qui s'éclairait, l'alouette légère,
De l'aurore, au printemps, active messagère,
Du milieu des sillons monte, chante, et sa voix
A donné le signal au peuple ailé des bois."

BOISGELIN

THE CURLEW

The different methods of preparation of all the small birds: thrush, lark, etc., may be applied to this fine small bird.

THE GROUSE

(*Ruffed, Sand, Snow, and all other Grouse*)

The best method, the one universally accepted and recognized by gourmets and connoisseurs for this fine morsel is the roasting method. However, all the different methods of preparation of the pheasant may be adapted to the larger grouse and the small grouse in all the different methods of preparation for the partridge and quail. In most cases, the grouse should be eaten in the fresh state, unless otherwise indicated. The flesh of the female is more delicate, the aroma more exquisite.

ROAST GROUSE

1 recipe of browned wild rice stuffing	6 slices larding pork
6 grouse	2 tablespoons olive oil
2 teaspoons salt	1 tablespoon flour

Prepare rice stuffing as indicated under DRESSING AND STUFFING WILD BIRDS. Wipe birds clean with a damp cloth, inside and out. Sprinkle inside lightly with salt. Fill to 2/3 with rice stuffing. *Do Not Sew Opening*. Cover entire fronts of birds with slices of thin larding pork, fastening with string or toothpicks. Place on rack in roasting pan. Add 1/2 cup boiling water (veal stock is much better, if available). Bake in hot oven (450°) for 15 long minutes. Reduce the heat to moderate (350°) and cook 20 short minutes longer, or until birds are tender. Remove the fat. Rub lightly with olive oil. Dredge lightly with flour. Return to hot oven (450°) and let brown for 10 long minutes.

Serve with your favorite jelly and breadsauce.

ENGLISH JUGGED GROUSE
(*A Very Old Recipe Much Used in England*)

Have 6 grouse of the same size, plucked and cleaned, and stuff each bird with the following forcemeat:

2 cups fresh bread crumbs	2 hard-cooked eggs, rubbed
½ lb. chopped fat pork	through a sieve
½ cup cooked celery, chopped fine	1 generous teaspoon onion juice
	Salt, pepper to taste, and a blade of mace

Truss the birds. Tie wings and legs close to the bodies and pack in an agate-iron pail with a close top. Plunge this into boiling water deep enough to cover the pail almost to the top, but not to float it. Put a weight on the top to keep the pail from turning over as the boiling becomes more vigorous, and cook for 3 hours. Dish the birds, and serve with Hunter sauce, to which has been added, at the last minute, a generous tablespoon of catsup, and pour over the grouse. Serve with a side dish of stuffed oranges made as follows:

6 oranges	Butter
6 small sweet potatoes	Salt
Orange slices for garnish	Pepper (white)

Cut a slice off the top of each orange and scoop out the pulp. Pare and boil sweet potatoes. Mash and mix with some of the orange pulp, using good judgment, season with salt, white pepper, and butter to taste. Fill the orange shells with this mixture and place in the oven to heat (350°). You may place the stuffed oranges around the grouse after pouring the sauce over them. Just before serving, top each orange with slices (using 3) of fresh orange and place in center a nice plump cranberry, a red cherry, or a pompon of whipped cream.

SPINACH IN OVEN

After washing 4 lbs. of fresh spinach in several cold waters, shake them, then press through a clean kitchen towel to extract all the water, then place on a clean board and chop raw, as fine as possible, or still better put them through food chopper. Place on a board, 1 cup of flour, arranging a well in center, and in this well, sprinkle salt, black pepper, and nutmeg to taste, ¼ lb. of butter and 1 cake of cream cheese (pot cheese may be used if desired). Break 3 fresh eggs over all this and mix the whole thoroughly, so as to obtain a paste, adding the raw chopped spinach gradually. Place this mixture in a generously buttered baking dish and set in a moderately hot oven (350–375°) for 30 minutes, or until a crust is formed on top. Unmold this over a hot platter and arrange the dumplings neatly on the top. Garnish the base of the spinach with slices of hard-cooked eggs and serve with a side dish of rich curried sauce, to which may be added a scant teaspoon of "Fumet" (*see* recipe, How To PREPARE GAME STOCK, page 45).

BROILED GROUSE

Grouse are usually broiled in the same manner as squabs. They are also nice and appetizing when dressed on a piece of freshly made toast, dunked in brown gravy, melted butter, or any other kind of sauce and a thin slice of broiled ham placed between the toast and the bird.

Singe, clean, wipe well, split down the back and lard the breast of each bird with 4 sticks of larding pork, or fat salt pork, drawn through the skin for an inch and out the other side with a larding needle. Or if they are decidedly tough, steam for half an hour and lay until cold in a marinade of lemon juice and oil. Pepper and salt to taste and broil for 15 short minutes. Serve upon squares of toasted bread, or upon oblongs of fried hominy. Sprinkle generously with melted butter before sending to the table.

ROAST GROUSE HUNTER STYLE

Test the birds, after cleaning and wiping, and if they are tough, put them—trussed as for roasting—into a steamer and set over rapidly boiling water for half an hour. While still hot, rub them well with butter and lemon juice, salt and pepper to taste, inside and out, put a bit of fat salt pork in each and roast, covered, in a quick oven for half an hour, basting frequently with butter and hot water, and, just before taking them up, with butter alone. They are dry birds and need mollifying. Serve with currant jelly and bread sauce.

GROUSE PIE

(*Cold*) (*English Recipe*)

One of the few exceptions, this recipe has to be highly seasoned. Cold leftovers of grouse are delicately prepared in this method.

2 turkey livers	½ teaspoon cloves
6 legs of grouse	½ teaspoon cinnamon
1½ lbs. of forcemeat	Salt, pepper, and cayenne to
½ teaspoon thyme leaves	taste
1½ cup bread crumbs	Special pot pie pastry

Chop the turkey livers very fine, or rather grind them, also the meat of the grouse legs; add the bread crumbs which should be fine, salt, pepper, cayenne to taste, and the remaining spices. Mix all together and moisten with a little veal stock. Put in a pan and cook for 30 long minutes, keeping it moist and turning over often. Turn the mixture into a deep pie dish and cover with pastry and bake 35 long minutes in a moderately hot oven (350°). Cool before serving.

SPECIAL POT PIE PASTRY

¾ cup lard or other shortening	1 teaspoon salt
2 cups sifted flour	5 tablespoons of water
1 egg, separated	

Chop shortening coarsely into sifted flour and salt. Mix the egg yolk with the water, and add to the dry mixture. Gather the dough together, roll to ½-inch thickness. Cut into a round shape and adjust on top of the dish. Make several slashes to allow the steam to escape and brush with egg white.

SALMIS OF GROUSE

(*German Method*)

Cut neatly into joints a pair of underdone grouse and divide the breasts into two pieces each. Put a cupful of good veal stock in a saucepan, season highly, add a medium-sized minced onion, a chopped small carrot, and a small stalk of celery, with a teaspoon of minced parsley and allow this to simmer for a long hour. Then rub through a colander, stir in a tablespoonful of brown roux, bring to a boil and put in the grouse. After this is done, the grouse should not be allowed to boil, but set it in a saucepan of boiling water just where it will keep at the scalding point for ½ hour. At the last moment, add ½ scant cup of button mushrooms, heated in their own liquor, and serve at once.

If you have preserved the cooked giblets of the grouse, mince them fine, work them to a paste with butter, season with salt and pepper to taste, and spread this mixture on generously buttered toast upon the dish intended for the salmi before serving. The toast will absorb the gravy and be delicious.

> *In addition to the above recipes the various methods employed in the preparation of small game birds, such as Land Rail, Quails, and the like may be adapted to this universally popular bird.*

GROUSE IN AUSBRUCHE

(*Hungarian Recipe*)

Ausbruche is one of the most rare and expensive, as well as the most delicate of the Tokay wines family. However, other Tokay wine (less expensive) may be used if desired.

Clean as many grouse as required, singe carefully and rub inside and out with a damp cloth, moistened with cold water, to which a few drops of good wine vinegar has been added; then rub with salt mixed with a finely pounded juniper berry and a few grains of pepper. Fill the cavity with its own liver, mixed raw with 2 table-spoons of finely chopped green celery leaves, 2 small shallots chopped fine, 1 scant teaspoon of chives, also chopped fine, and seasoned to taste with salt and pepper. Sew and lard through and through with 8 or 10 small strips of larding pork. Set the bird in a braising kettle and add a braise or mirepoix (*see* TERMS USED IN COOKERY) made as follows:

BRAISE or MIREPOIX

Sauté in plenty of lard, one very small carrot, one small onion, both minced fine, and add ¼ cup of fresh lean pork, diced, 1 table-spoon of diced small raw lean veal, 4 sprigs of parsley tied with a bit of bay leaf and 1 small sprig of thyme, a small whole clove, crushed, a bit of garlic, bruised, and salt and pepper to taste, until well browned (about 10 short minutes), stirring frequently. Pour over this vegetable mixture, 1 generous cup of Ausbruche wine and ½ pony glass of fine champagne, ½ cup of rich veal stock, salt and pepper and 1 generous teaspoon, yes 1 generous teaspoon of real paprika, found only in certain stores in our country. Allow this to simmer 10 long minutes to mellow, then add the prepared bird, ad-just the cover tightly, and set the braising kettle in a moderate oven (350–375°) and do not disturb for 30 long minutes. If the braising kettle is of suitable appearance to be presented at table, so much the better. Serve in the kettle, if not, dress the bird on a hot platter, and surround with the vegetables and gravy. A side dish of Brussels sprouts, made as follows, is the usual accompaniment for this fine and delectable dish:

BAKED BRUSSELS SPROUTS HUNGARIAN METHOD

Put 3 cups of thoroughly washed and cleaned Brussels sprouts in a saucepan with boiling salted water, ½ medium-sized onion coarsely chopped, 3 sprigs parsley tied with 1 small bay leaf and 1 small, very small, whole clove of garlic, and boil until pierceable (about 10 short minutes). Drain, saving the liquid for other uses. Turn the sprouts into a buttered baking dish; cover with a sauce made of 2 fresh eggs well beaten, ½ cup grated Swiss cheese, and salt, pepper, and paprika to taste. Bake in a moderate oven (350°) for 10 long minutes.

A side dish of gooseberry jelly with fresh-made toast is passed around.

GROUSE À LA MOSCOVITE

Clean, singe, then remove all bones from a plump grouse. Fill the cavity with 4 chestnuts, ½ cup bread, soaked in Smitane sauce (*see* SAUCES) and slightly squeezed, the liver of the bird, mashed with a fork, and 2 tablespoons of ground pistachio nuts, the whole seasoned to taste with a pinch of dried tarragon herbs, salt and pepper (black) to taste. Sew, blanket the bird with a thin layer of fat salt pork, rubbed with vodka or rather sprinkled with this spirit, using good judgment, then with 1 tablespoon of finely chopped chives spread all over the blanket of fat pork. Truss and roast in the usual way, keeping the bird rather underdone. Occasionally pour over, that is baste, with a sauce made of crumbs, brandy or vodka, and hot butter. Dress the bird as is, without removing the blanket of pork, simply garnished with artichoke bottom, sautéed in butter, interspersed with small triangles of bread fried in butter. Of course the traditional side dish of red currant jelly should be passed around.

GROUSE SICILIENNE

Prepare a risotto as indicated in recipe for RISOTTO OF QUAIL, page 108, adding a pinch of curry powder to taste, 2 small truffles, first cooked in Madeira wine for 5 short minutes, then minced fine, and 3 chicken livers, sautéed in butter for 3 short minutes, then minced fine.

Meantime, prepare a plump grouse, or as many as required, as for roasting, filling the cavity with 2 small sprigs of fennel and the liver of the bird. Sew and truss after blanketing the bird with a thin slice of fat ham, with a little lean meat on it. Roast in the usual way.

Dress on a hot platter with a garnishing of mushroom cutlets made as follows:

MUSHROOM CUTLETS

Chop fine, half pound of vegetables (altogether), consisting of green pepper, celery, and carrots in equal parts; then add 1 pound of fresh mushrooms, 2 large onions, chopped, 2 tablespoons of olive oil, 1 scant cup of fresh bread crumbs, 2 eggs and 1 egg yolk, salt, pepper, a small clove of garlic, chopped very fine, and mix thoroughly, and shape into small cutlets or rather chops. There should be 6 cutlets or chops. Place in a generously olive-oiled earthenware baking dish and bake 25 short minutes in a moderately hot oven (375°).

Serve the risotto as a side dish, with a rich Madeira sauce, to which has been added 1 tablespoon of tomato paste.

A fine, delicious, and substantial meal, which does not require any additional dish, but a generous piece of your favorite cheese, and a bottle of good red Italian wine, such as an Asti Spumante.

Apples are supposed to have been the biblical fruit of temptation and a succession of Eves have been adding to their tempting qualities ever since. A flick of spice on an apple will make anybody fall.

PUNCH MARQUISE GLACÉ

Prepare a Sauternes Punch Marquise as indicated in recipe on page 83. When the wine is hot, that is, is covered with a fine white foam, throw into it a tablespoon (generous if a strong flavor is desired) of good tea and let infuse, covered for 10 long minutes. Strain through a fine cloth, and add one orange and one lemon, peeled, and sliced thin, 1 scant cupful of good rum, heated, then a match touched to it, allowing the flame to die out of itself. Allow to cool and place in a hand freezer. The punch will be like snow. Serve in sherbet glasses.

GROUSE À LA MODE DE DÜSSELDORF

Select a nice plump grouse, pluck, singe, and rub the inside and out with lemon juice mixed with white wine (Moselle). Fill the cavity with cooked rice, to which has been added the bird's liver, a tart apple, cored, after being pared, then diced very small, and soaked in brandy for a few seconds, seasoned to taste with salt, black pepper, and a little nutmeg. Sew and blanket with a thin slice of fat larding pork, rubbed with minced parsley and chives, using a scant tablespoon of equal parts. Truss and roast in the usual way. Dress the bird over a layer of red cabbage cooked with apples as follows:

RED CABBAGE DUTCH STYLE

Wash, core, and chop 1 medium-sized red cabbage. Parboil in slightly salted water for 5 short minutes. Drain, add 2 apples pared and cored, then sliced thin as for apple pie, 1 tablespoon of minced onion, 1 generous tablespoon of goose fat, a very scant teaspoon of salt, 2 tablespoons of vinegar, a pinch of mace, ½ teaspoon sugar, and ¼ teaspoon of black pepper; then add enough good chicken stock to about half cover the cabbage. Cook over a gentle fire for 30 minutes or until tender, tossing the cabbage mixture about occasionally to expose evenly to the heat.

The bird should be placed in the cabbage on the platter as in a nest. Garnish the edge with small triangle of bread fried in goose fat, alternating with small mushroom, placed over a fried slice of tomato, fried in goose liver. Serve a side dish of Cherry sauce (*see* SAUCES).

ROAST GROUSE JUGOSLAVIA STYLE

Prepare a grouse in the usual way as for roasting not forgetting to blanket the bird with a thin slice of fat larding pork. Do not stuff. Cook it rather underdone, about 12 to 15 minutes will do, in a hot oven, basting often with melted butter, to which have been added a few drops of onion juice and a teaspoon of finely chopped parsley (chervil is much preferable if available). Remove the bird from the oven and while piping hot, cut in four pieces (serving portions), then place in a sauerkraut prepared as follows:

JUGOSLAVIAN SAUERKRAUT

Mince 3 medium-sized onions and fry in goose fat until slightly colored; do not be niggardly with the goose fat, use about ½ cup. Then add 1½ lbs. of young sauerkraut, thoroughly drained, tossed carefully, and 2 large tart apples, peeled, cored, and sliced as for apple pie. Cook this, uncovered, over a medium flame, shaking the kraut, occasionally, so that the goose fat will permeate every particle of kraut, for 15 minutes. Add the bird. Cover and set in a hot oven (400°) for 30 long minutes. Serve in the casserole with a side dish of currant jelly and another of giblet gravy (*see* SAUCES).

GROUSE À LA PAVLOVA

(*Russian Recipe*)

The following recipe used to be the favorite dish of the famous, indisputably the greatest dancer in living memory, of the Ballet Russes, Anna Pavlova.

Select a plump grouse left standing unplucked for 3 days. Clean, after plucking carefully, singe over the burning flame of good vodka (Russian spirit), setting aside the liver and giblets. Rub with allspice, slightly salted and peppered and to which has been added a large juniper berry, ground fine. Fill the cavity of the bird with a stuffing made of bread crumbs soaked in Smitane sauce (*see* SAUCES), then squeezed, and equal parts of mashed goose liver, plus the liver of the bird, leaving enough room for the swelling, during the cooking process. Spread a thin slice of fat larding pork with a mixture of chopped chives, using half teaspoon, ½ teaspoon of finely chopped black truffle, 1 small shallot, minced fine, the whole thoroughly mixed, and blanket the bird with it. Secure and truss. Roast in the usual method, keeping the bird *vert-cuit* (French expression meaning well underdone), basting often with buttered bread crumbs also flavored with vodka, using very little (a few drops only). Dress the bird in a small earthenware casserole, the bottom of which has been spread with 4 leaves braised lettuce. Pour over ½ cup of good Smitane sauce (*see* SAUCES). Cover and set in a hot oven (450°) for 15 long minutes. Serve with a side dish of bread sauce, a side dish of white currant jelly, and a side dish of Saratoga chips. The casserole should be ornamental enough to be presented at table, and should not be uncovered until ready to carve. The bird is left blanketed as it was cooked.

BRAISED LETTUCE À LA RUSSE

Wash 2 or 3 leaves of spinach and cook in good chicken stock 2 or 3 minutes with a sprig of parsley or two, tied with a bit of bay leaf, and a small sprig of thyme. Drain. Discard the parsley–bay leaf–thyme bouquet, and mince, then force through a coarse sieve, with 1 teaspoon of good goose fat, to ease the rubbing and grease the spinach, seasoning meanwhile with a few drops of onion juice, and cayenne pepper, using your own taste. Set aside in a cool place. Wash a small head of iceberg lettuce, separate the leaves, and make 4 mounds (separately), placing the lettuce leaves one over another. Secure with a string, and cover (barely) with good chicken stock. Cover hermetically and let boil for 5 long minutes. Drain. Place the lettuce roll in a skillet and cover with good brown gravy, add the spinach mixture, cover hermetically and braise in a hot oven for 25 minutes (the oven set at 450°).

GROUSE BRAISE SCOTTISH STYLE

The grouse should be fat, and freshly killed, that is, from a day's bagging. Pluck, singe over the gas flame, rub inside and out with a little Scotch whisky, oh, very little, mixed with a little lukewarm water, then with very little salt and plenty of black pepper. Fill the cavity of the bird with a mixture made of ½ cup bread crumbs, profusely buttered, and an equal part of raw mashed goose liver, 1 scant teaspoon of parsley, and a few drops of onion juice, the whole thoroughly mixed and seasoned with a few grains of allspice and a tiny blade of mace. Sew. Blanket with a thin slice of fat larding pork. Truss. Place in an earthenware braising kettle, the bottom of which contains a scant cup of braise, or mirepoix (*see* recipe for GROUSE IN AUSBRUCHE, page 29, for MIREPOIX). Arrange, on top, 4 thin slices of black truffles, adjust the cover hermetically and braise for 25 long minutes, in a hot oven (450°). Remove from the oven; dress the bird on a hot platter; surround with fresh large mushrooms peeled, stems removed (the stems may be used for the mirepoix) and sauté in brown butter, place the casserole in which the bird has been cooked over a hot fire; reduce the liquid to nearly nothing, add then a wineglass of white wine. Boil 2 or 3 times, strain through a fine sieve, and pour over the bird. Serve with a side dish of fried bread-crumb sauce, another side dish of red currant jelly, and one of Apple Sauce Swedish Method (*a fine sauce to be served with goose, duck, and any kind of game birds*).

APPLE SAUCE SWEDISH METHOD

Mince and cook over a small flame in an enameled saucepan, having a tight-fitting cover, 1 lb. of tart apples, adding a few drops of lemon juice, and ¼ cup of good dry white wine, a few grains of salt. (*The cooking process is really a smothering by concentrated steam rather than a stewing.*) Throw the apples over a fine sieve or hair sieve, and rub until all is strained. Return the sauce to the fire (very low) and allow to reduce a little, or rather thicken a little. Cool and when very cold, add half volume of mayonnaise, and 1 tablespoon of prepared horseradish, well drained, and chopped very fine; still better, put through food chopper.

GROUSE EN COCOTTE À LA AYRSHIRE
(*Scottish Recipe*)

Clean a plump grouse, pick, then rub with lemon juice. Do not salt, nor pepper, the inside, but only the outside. Fill the cavity with bread crumbs, softened in good chicken stock, and mixed with the mashed bird's liver, 2 tablespoons of cooked lean ham, minced fine, ½ teaspoon parsley, minced fine, a few drops of onion juice, and 1 teaspoon of green pepper, chopped fine, the whole thoroughly mixed and seasoned with salt, cayenne, and a few drops of Worcestershire sauce (about ½ teaspoon). Sew, blanket the bird with first, a very thin slice of cooked ham, then with a thin slice of fat larding pork spread with a thin layer of goose liver, mashed with a fork, and slightly salted. Secure carefully, then truss. Place the bird in an earthenware casserole having a tight-fitting cover, and add 4 canned artichoke bottoms, diced small, 4 mushrooms, peeled, then sliced very fine, using stems and caps, 4 thin slices of small carrot (raw) and 1 medium-sized onion, cut in thin rings and raw. Pour over 1 generous half cup of game stock, flavored with a teaspoon of Madeira wine, and highly seasoned, and add also a bouquet garni (4 sprigs of parsley, 1 small bay leaf, and a small sprig of thyme tied securely together). Cover and set in a hot oven (450°) for 25 long minutes. Serve in the casserole, after removing the excess of fat, and adding 1 tablespoon of tomato paste. A side dish of bread-crumb sauce, and one of red currant jelly should be passed around. The bird should be carved right at the table, and a portion of the blanketing served on each plate by the hostess.

The following recipe has been contributed by Chef Kinjiro Kojima (Executive Chef of the Fujiya Hotel):

PUNCH AU RHUM FLAMBE

Throw 2 tablespoons of good tea into a quart (4 cups) of rapidly boiling water, and let infuse for 10 long minutes. Place in a punch bowl, 1 lb. of sugar (2 cups) and strain the tea over it, stirring to dissolve the sugar completely. Place a large piece of ice in the tea and add 2 small lemons, sliced thin, and seeded. Pour over this 2 generous cups of good rum, touch a match and allow to burn, alimenting the flame by stirring gently with a long punch ladle. Lastly, add 1 cup of fresh pineapple, peeled and cubed small. Serve in glass cups with a slice of lemon and 2 or 3 pineapple cubes in each cup.

KITCHEN WIDOWER

*". . . In gingham apron he explores
The shelf of canned and potted stores,
And wonders in what daft condition
He wed a lecturing dietitian . . ."*

VIRGINIA BRASIER

GROUSE PRINCE PUSHKIN

Clean a grouse, singe, and rub inside and out with a little fine champagne, then with a mixture of allspice, salt, and black pepper. Fill the cavity with finely chopped green celery leaves, mixed with the liver of the bird, and 2 chicken livers, raw, and mashed with a fork, then seasoned with a few drops of lemon juice, salt and pepper to taste. Sew. Spread all over the bird part of the stuffing mixture reserved for this purpose, and blanket over with a thin slice of fat larding pork, sprinkled with a little allspice mixed with a little sage, sprinkling over this, a few drops of lemon juice. Truss, place in an earthenware casserole, and add: 6 small white onions, peeled, then parboiled 10 minutes in salted water, 6 small mushrooms, peeled, the caps whole, sautéed 5 short minutes in lard, pouring the lard and mushrooms into the casserole, add the stems, sliced, but raw, 1 single sweetbread, parboiled and cubed small, 4 sprigs parsley tied with a small bay leaf, 4 whole peppercorns, gently bruised, 1 whole clove and 1 sprig of tarragon herb (dried). Pour over this 2 pony glasses of good brandy and place the casserole over a very hot fire, so that the brandy will catch fire of itself through the intense heat. Remove aside and let the alcohol burn out. Then pour over the whole, 1 cup of tomato juice, heated and to which has been added 1 teaspoon of calf's foot jelly (a generous teaspoon) and 1 teaspoon of "Fumet" (*see* recipe, How To PREPARE GAME STOCK, page 45). Cover and place the casserole in a hot oven for 25 minutes (oven at 450°) without disturbing at all. Just before serving, add 1 tablespoon of kneaded butter (equal parts of butter and flour kneaded to a smooth paste).

Let stand 5 minutes over a low flame, to mellow and allow the kneaded butter to melt and mix. Serve in the casserole, with a side dish of plain boiled rice, and another of quince jelly.

KIRSCH PUNCH À LA FRANÇAISE

Throw 2 tablespoons of good tea into 1 quart of boiling water and let infuse for 10 minutes. Place in a large punch bowl, a half pound of sugar, stir until sugar is dissolved, then place in the liquid a large piece of ice. Allow to cool for 15 minutes, then pour over 2 cups of good kirsch, and 1 bottle of maraschino cherries (red or green). When thoroughly cold, serve in glass cups with 2 cherries in each cup.

GROUSE EN CASSEROLE À LA HENRI HOCQUART

Select 2 plump grouse, which have been bagged 48 hours before. Pluck, clean and bone thoroughly, reserving the livers for later use. Rub with lemon juice, then with salt and black pepper. Lay the birds flat on a clean board and spread each one with a thin slice of lean, cooked Virginia ham, then over spread a thin layer of stuffing made of the livers of the birds, 3 chicken livers (raw), ½ cup of bread crumbs, soaked in tomato juice, then squeezed and tossed; then add 1 scant teaspoon of shallots, minced very fine, and 1 scant teaspoon of white truffles, cooked first in champagne for 5 short minutes, then ground. Rub this mixture through a fine hair sieve, then season to taste with salt, black pepper, and a little nutmeg. Roll the birds and surround them with a blanket of fat larding pork, brushed with a little "Fumet," slightly melted (*see* recipe, How To PREPARE GAME STOCK, page 45), truss securely. Place the birds in an earthenware casserole in which you will have cooked ¼ lb. of fresh pork, cut in small dices, ¼ lb. of pork liver, also diced small after removing the tubes and nerves. Lift out the pork and liver after 10 short minutes of cooking, and squeeze out, that is press them with a spoon to extract all the juice and fat possible. Pour over this, ½ cup of game stock made from the trimmings and bones, ½ cup of thick cream, 1 small clove of garlic, whole, 2 small cloves, and a bouquet garni (parsley tied with a small bay leaf), seasoning to taste with salt and pepper and a generous pinch of paprika. Cover and set in a hot oven for 20 short minutes. Remove the casserole from the oven; place on a medium flame over the range, uncover and burn over a generous tablespoon of brandy, letting burn until exhausted. Cover at once and let simmer, rather mellow, on the side of the range for 5 long minutes. Correct the seasonings and serve in the casserole, without any other accompaniment than a side dish of candied pears (*see* GARNISHINGS).

GROUSE SAINTE ANNE

Take ¼ lb. of pork liver and mash it raw with a fork, removing the tubes and nerves carefully. To this, add 1 tablespoon of finely ground cooked ham, 1 scant teaspoon of chives minced, 1 teaspoon of truffles, chopped fine and raw, but peeled, ½ teaspoon of shallot, minced fine, salt, black pepper, and a pinch of allspice. Fill the cavity of a plucked, singed, cleaned grouse, rubbed with a damp cloth, sprinkle with a few drops of vinegar, then rub with salt and black pepper, and sew, then truss, after blanketing the bird with a thin slice of fat larding pork, spread with a little of the stuffing set aside for the purpose. Truss and roast in the usual way. Dress the bird on a hot platter. Garnish the border of the platter with 4 broiled lamb kidneys, interspersed with 4 large mushrooms, peeled, stems removed and broiled under the flame of the broiling oven, after being dipped in melted butter, flavored with a few drops of lemon juice, and seasoned to taste. Serve at once with a bread sauce and currant jelly.

MAY CHAMPAGNE CUP

1 medium-sized fresh pineapple
½ cup sugar (more or less according to taste)
   Sugar syrup to raise the sweetness
½ bottle good white wine
1 small bunch aromatic woodruff (wild forget-me-not,
   found at drug stores)
1 bottle good dry champagne

Wash pineapple thoroughly, pare it, taking out the center, and save parings and core. Cut the best part of the pineapple meat into small dices, taking care there is no core included, and place in a large punch bowl with powdered sugar. Keep on ice or in refrigerator. Chop up finely the parings and the core and then pound in a mortar or put through meat chopper. Make a syrup with ½ cup of water and 1 cup granulated sugar and add to this syrup the pounded or ground parings and core, then the white wine and aromatic woodruff. Let infuse for about 1 hour; strain through a very fine cloth. Place in ice-cream freezer, and freeze halfway, using the handle freezer. Open the freezer and add the diced pineapple, alternating with the champagne. Finish freezing. Serve in sherbet cups.

LAND RAIL

The different methods of preparation of the quail may be adapted to this fine and delicate bird, sometimes called the "King of Quails."

MOOR HEN

The different methods of preparation of the quail as well as of all the other wild hen, such as prairie hen, may be adapted to the moor hen.

PARTRIDGE

As a general rule roasted and broiled partridges are always dressed on buttered toast or still better on bread fried in butter. A slice of lemon and a small bunch of crisp watercress are the only garnishing, unless otherwise indicated for special recipes. It is advisable to envelop the bird to be roasted first with a thin slice of larding pork, then with a vine leaf, generously buttered.

BRAISED PARTRIDGE BOURGUIGNONNE

Prepare as many partridges as required. Color each bird in butter, that is, lightly golden brown in heated butter over a medium fire. Put it in a buttered baking dish, having a tight-fitting cover (earthenware preferably), with, for each partridge, half a dozen small white onions, glazed, and 6 small mushrooms (omitting the stems) sautéed in butter. Season to taste with salt and pepper and place in a moderately hot oven (350°) for 20 short minutes tightly covered. The bird being done, lift it out with onions and mushrooms and keep hot. To the butter in the baking dish, add gradually a scant wineglass of Burgundy wine, place the baking dish over a hot fire and deglaze, stirring rapidly until the liquid is reduced to 2/3 volume. Then add the size of a small walnut of extract of meat (beef). Strain through a fine sieve. Remove the excess of fat. Return the partridge, onions, and mushrooms to the baking dish; pour over the sauce and bake, covered, 10 minutes longer. Serve in the baking dish.

A side dish of fried hominy may be served at the same time (optional).

BRAISED PARTRIDGE WITH JUNIPER BERRIES

Clean, wipe with a damp cloth, and truss a partridge or as many partridges as required. Sear in 1 tablespoon of butter until delicately colored on all sides. Place in a buttered baking dish, having a tight-fitting cover and add for each bird: 2 raw carrot balls, 2 small round white turnip balls, 3 small white onions, glazed, 1 tablespoon of celery, minced and parboiled, 2 small mushrooms, peeled, stems removed, the stems chopped fine, 1 scant half teaspoon of sugar, 2 crushed juniper berries, 1 teaspoon of good gin, and salt and pepper to taste. Pour over this ¼ cup of veal stock. Season to taste with salt and pepper. Cover tightly and bake in a moderately hot oven (375°) for 30 minutes. Serve in the baking dish.

BRAISED PARTRIDGE WITH SOUR CHERRIES

First roast a cleaned, wiped partridge, or as many as required, seasoned inside and out with salt and pepper, for 15 minutes in a hot oven, basting generously with melted butter. Remove from the oven and turn the bird into a generously buttered baking dish. Add half a dozen red or white sour cherries (canned), 2 tablespoons of cherry juice, and 3 medium-sized mushrooms, cooked in butter. Adjust the cover as tightly as possible, bake in a moderately hot oven (375°) for 20 minutes. Serve in the baking dish.

CASSEROLE OF PARTRIDGE À LA KOTSCHOUBEY

The original recipe requires the larding of the bird with small sticks of black truffles. This is optional. Cook a cleaned, wiped dry partridge in 2 tablespoons of butter, in a casserole placed over a medium-sized fire, until golden browned on all sides, for 30 minutes and covered, turning the bird often (the bird should be trussed as you would an ordinary chicken). Turn the bird in an earthenware casserole. Surround it with a generous half cup of cooked Brussels sprouts, first parboiled then cooked in brown butter; add also ¼ cup of small dices or cubes of salt pork, rather lean, sautéed also in butter. Pour over 3 tablespoons of Demiglacé sauce (*see* SAUCES).

Adjust the cover and set the dish in boiling water for 5 long minutes to mellow. Serve in the casserole.

CASSEROLE OF PARTRIDGE
(*Polish Method*)

For each partridge make a stuffing as follows:

The partridge's liver	The size of a large pinhead
1 tablespoon of grated salted	of garlic
pork fat	1 small leaf of tarragon herb
	Salt and coarse pepper to taste

Chop the liver fine and combine with all the remaining ingredients, mixing thoroughly. Fill the bird with this mixture. Truss. Line a casserole with a thin slice of cooked ham and sprinkle over the ham 2 tablespoons of raw veal, ground. Place a thin slice of larding pork around the breast of the partridge; tie with string and arrange the bird over this unctuous bed. Place over a low flame, covered, and allow to cook slowly for 15 minutes. Lift out the cover and pour over the bird a small pony glass of gin or brandy, according to taste. Cover and set the casserole in a hot oven (400°) for 20 minutes. Lift out the bird. Keep hot. Remove the excess of fat from the baking dish and strain through a fine sieve. To the sauce thus strained, add 2 tablespoons of sweet butter, little by little, beating vigorously after each addition, alternating with 2 tablespoons of clear meat stock, in which has been dissolved ½ tablespoon of flour. Bring to a rapid boil; season then, and only then, with salt and coarse pepper, the juice of a small orange. Return the bird and ham slice to the sauce and serve in the casserole.

PUNCH BOURGUIGNON

A fine and delicate winter punch in which the bouquet of this delicious Burgundy wine predominates, fortified by good brandy. Chablis wine may be substituted by Pouilly, another fine Burgundy wine, or by the king of the kings of the white wines, namely Sauternes. In that case, reduce the sugar in proportion of the sweetness of the wine.

1½ cups granulated sugar (more or less according to taste)
2 bottles of Chablis wine
1 two-inch stick cinnamon bark
2 or 3 whole cloves
1 scant pint of good brandy
Grated rind of 2 medium-sized lemons and juice

Place first the grated lemon rind in a punch bowl with the lemon juice and sugar. Stir well to melt the sugar. Cover. Meanwhile, heat up the wine to which is added the cinnamon bark and cloves, until mixture whitens. Strain over the lemon rind, juice, and sugar. Mix well.

Bring the punch which is not quite ready, into the dining room; strike a match and light 2 lumps of sugar placed on a punch ladle with a little brandy poured over the sugar. Have the lights in the room turned out. Feed the flaming punch with the rest of the brandy, adding gradually. Let the flame die out and wait a few minutes before pouring into glass cups, to mellow, and also lest the glass suffer from the heat.

HOW TO PREPARE GAME STOCK

One of the most important operations in game cookery is to know how to prepare game stock, also called "Fumet" (raciness) which is much used in this particular section of cookery. This is very simple and easy to make.

Place in the bottom of an earthenware casserole 3 tablespoons of chopped, uncooked, rather fat ham, with 1 medium-sized onion, minced, 2 small shallots, minced, a pinch of thyme leaves, 1 bay leaf tied up with 4 sprigs of parsley. Add to this all the trimmings of game that you may have, and add 2 tablespoons of butter. Heat gradually and slowly, and cook stirring often until mixture is delicately colored. Then pour over this 2 tablespoons of Madeira wine, and allow this to reduce to nearly nothing, stirring very often to prevent scorching. Then pour over 1 cupful of good brown sauce (chicken or veal stock may be used if desired), and allow to simmer very gently for 20–25 minutes. Strain through a fine sieve. Return the strained liquid to the saucepan and allow to reduce again to nearly nothing, that is to a kind of glaze. A teaspoon of this extract is quite enough to add game flavor to any kind of sauce used for game. This will keep a long while in a refrigerator.

CASSEROLE OF PARTRIDGE LADY CLIFFORD

Cook the partridge in butter in a casserole until ⅔ done. Then add 1 generous tablespoon of truffles, sliced very thin, 1 pony glass of good brandy touched with a match and allowed to burn out and ½ teaspoon of game glaze "Fumet." Cover and continue cooking over a low flame for 20 minutes longer. Serve in the casserole with a side dish of Onion sauce (*see* SAUCES).

CASSEROLE OF PARTRIDGE

(*Italian Method*)

Cook 6 cleaned, trussed partridges, wiped with a damp cloth, inside of which has been placed a slice of bacon rolled around a large black olive, and secured with a toothpick, in a casserole with ½ cup of butter, covered, for 30 long minutes, turning the bird occasionally to allow to brown on all sides. Lift off the cover and add 4 generous tablespoons of good champagne, rather sweet, 1 pony glass of good brandy, 2 dozen large, pitted black olives, and ¼ cup (generous) of tomato paste. Stir gently but carefully; then add 6 tablespoons of rich veal stock, and 1 teaspoon of "Fumet" (*see* recipe, How To PREPARE GAME STOCK, page 45). Cover and cook 10 long minutes more. Dress the bird over a layer of freshly made chestnut purée. Boil the sauce once, then pour over the bird. Serve at once.

CHARTREUSE OF PARTRIDGE
(*Old Method*)

Braise an old partridge in the usual way for 30 minutes after having seared it in plenty of butter (using ¼ cup) with 2 cups of shredded green cabbage, 6 whole peppercorns, slightly bruised, 1 or 2 juniper berries, slightly crushed, 1 whole clove, and ½ cup of veal stock, seasoning with salt to taste. Dress the partridge on a hot platter over a bed made of the cabbage. Garnish with 1 slice of bacon on each side. Serve with a side dish of onion and bread sauce and another of steamed white rice. A side dish of currant jelly may also be served aside if desired.

CREAMED PARTRIDGE
(*Russian Method*)

Cook a cleaned, trussed partridge in 3 tablespoons of butter over a medium fire, turning the bird occasionally so as to brown on all sides for 20 minutes, with 1 small onion sliced. Then add 6 generous tablespoons of sour cream, or fresh cream to which has been added 1 teaspoon of lemon juice, 1 scant teaspoon of "Fumet" (*see* recipe, How To PREPARE GAME STOCK, page 45), salt, pepper, and a generous teaspoon of real paprika. Cook, uncovered, for 15 minutes longer, turning the bird frequently. Serve in the casserole with a side dish of plain boiled white rice.

GRILLED PARTRIDGE
(*English Style*)

Clean, singe, cut off the legs, split open from the back without separating and flatten with a cleaver, as many partridges as required. Marinate in olive oil for at least 30 minutes to which is added salt, pepper, 1 large bay leaf, a small clove of garlic, 4 sprigs parsley and a few drops of Tabasco sauce. Grill under a very hot flame, turning twice during the cooking process. Dress on a hot platter on which has been spread maître d'hôtel butter, sprinkle with a little lemon juice, and serve at once with a side dish of remoulade sauce.

PETIT BRÛLÉ PUNCH

As many oranges as there are guests
As many whole cloves as there are guests
As many bay leaves as there are guests
As many small sticks of cinnamon bark as there are
    guests (1-inch, or thereabouts)
As many lumps of sugar as there are guests
One bottle of very good brandy

For this delicious punch which is also a delight to the eyes, and which may also be considered as an after-dinner cordial, since it should be served with the coffee, select thick-skinned oranges, one for each guest. Then cut the top of the orange with a spoon handle, loosen the peel from the orange almost to the end, and turn it inside out, making a cup, leaving half the fruit pulp with the cup on top. Place each orange in a dessert plate; into the cup put:

> 1 whole clove
> A tiny bit of bay leaf
> A very small stick cinnamon bark
> 1 lump of sugar

Pour over each cup 2 tablespoons of the best brandy. Bring the oranges to the table. Light the brandy and let it burn away. Pour the liquid thus obtained into the demitasse cups of coffee, brought during the operation.

The burning of the brandy in the orange peels, which contain essential oils, gives a most delicious flavor accentuated through witnessing the preparation on the dining table.

PAN FRIED PARTRIDGE WITH GRAPES

Pan fry 6 young partridges, previously cleaned, singed, and wiped with a damp cloth, then trussed, in ½ cup of sweet butter, rubbing them with salt and pepper to taste, over a gentle fire, for 35 long minutes, turning the birds often to color on all sides, the pan covered after the first 15 minutes. Dress the birds on a hot platter covered with fried-in-butter toast, and garnish with grains of large green grapes, skinned and seeded, rolled in melted butter. Serve with a side dish of giblet gravy (*see* SAUCES) and another side dish of fried hominy squares.

PARTRIDGE CASSEROLE BENNETT TOUSLÉY

Clean, singe, fill the inside of 6 partridges with a tablespoon of pâté de foie gras, mixed with the liver of the bird, after rubbing the inside and outside with lemon juice, then with salt and coarsely ground peppercorns to taste. Then truss and cook in an earthenware casserole with ½ generous cupful of sweet butter for 20 long minutes, turning the bird often to color on all sides. Remove aside and add 1 cup of cubed salt pork, previously tried over a gentle fire and slightly golden browned, 1 dozen of small potato balls, previously parboiled, 12 small mushrooms, peeled, stems removed, and sautéed in butter. Pour over this a cupful of Italian sauce (*see* SAUCES), 1 pony glass of good gin, and 2 dozen of small white onions, glazed. Cover tightly and finish cooking in a hot oven (400°) for 20 long minutes. Serve in the casserole.

PARTRIDGE CASSEROLE
MADAME P. V. METZELTHIN

Lard 6 young partridges, after cleaning, singeing, and stuffing them with 1 small onion and 1 juniper berry with thin strips of cooked tongue, using 6 strips for each bird. Surround the breast with a thin slice of larding pork. Place them in a braising kettle, the bottom of which is spread with the usual vegetables for braising. Pour over 1 cup of brown sauce, and 1 pony glass of good brandy, to which you may touch a match to add flavor. Add also 1 large bay leaf, 1 small pinch of thyme leaves, 1 dozen of small white, raw, peeled onions, and 1 dozen of fresh mushrooms, cut in two after peeling and removing the stems. Cover tightly and braise in a hot oven (400°) for 40 minutes without disturbing. Serve in the braising dish with a side dish of plain boiled wild rice.

PAN FRIED PARTRIDGE MOTHER PULLIG

Select 5 young partridges; clean, wipe with a damp cloth, rub with orange juice, then with salt and black pepper, then cut as you would for a chicken fricassee, discarding the pilon. Sauté, in plenty of butter in a heavy skillet, over a low fire, stirring occasionally to brown on all sides, for 30 short minutes. Dress, well drained of butter, on a hot round platter and garnish around the pieces of partridge, in small mounds, with:

6 artichoke bottoms, sautéed in brown butter;
2 dozen of small potato balls, first parboiled, then cooked in butter;
2 dozen of small white onions, glazed rather brown;
6 small molds of steamed wild rice;

separating each mound with a small bunch of fried parsley, preferably the curled. Serve with the following sauce:

Deglaze the skillet in which the partridges have been sautéed with 1 cup of veal stock, to which is added a small wineglass of sweet white wine, 1 scant teaspoon of "Fumet" (*see* recipe, How To Prepare Game Stock, page 45). Decorate with thin slices of lemon, dipped in paprika. Serve as hot as possible.

PAN FRIED PARTRIDGE
(*Viennoise Method*)

Select young partridges. There should be 6. Split open in two from the back, discarding the pilon. Season to taste with salt and pepper; dredge the pieces with flour, then dip them in beaten eggs, and in freshly made soft bread crumbs. Cook in plenty of butter or lard, as slowly as possible, using a heavy skillet, turning the pieces once in a while to brown on all sides. Dress on a hot platter, covered with a fancy folded napkin and surround with crisp fried curled parsley and quartered lemons. A side dish of melted butter to which may be added a few drops of onion juice, may be served aside.

PANNED PARTRIDGE PORT WINE SAUCE

Select 6 young partridges. Clean, wipe with a damp cloth, rub the inside and out with a good gin, then with salt and pepper. Put inside of each 6 sections of tangerine. Truss as you would a roasting young chicken. Cook in plenty of butter in a casserole, over a medium fire, covered, turning occasionally so as to brown on all sides, for 25–30 minutes. Dress on a hot platter (round) in circle. Garnish the center with potato chips, and serve with a side dish of Port wine sauce (*see* Sauces).

As a rule all kinds of feathered game are, besides the indicated sauce, served with an extra sauceboat of bread sauce and a side dish of freshly made potato chips, called also Saratoga chips.

PANNED PARTRIDGE IN SAUTERNES WINE

Prepare 6 young partridges as indicated in recipe for Panned Partridge Port Wine Sauce, above, substituting tangerine sections and using the size of a large walnut of pâté de foie gras (goose-liver pâté), mixed with a little heavy cream. Cook. Dress. Serve as directed, with a side dish of the following sauce:

Place in a saucepan 2 cups of Sauternes wine and let reduce to half over a hot fire; add when reduced, a generous tablespoon of tomato purée, stirring well until very smooth. Add then 1 teaspoon of "Fumet" (*see* recipe, How To Prepare Game Stock, page 45) and stir. Remove from the fire and stir in 1 scant tablespoon of kneaded butter (equal part of butter kneaded with equal part of flour). Return to the fire. Boil once. Season to taste with salt and white pepper. Allow to simmer a few minutes before serving.

PARTRIDGE À LA GOMBERVAUX

Bone 6 partridges (*see* How To Bone a Wild Bird). Have an extra old one which you will boil in salted water until the meat leaves the bones. With the meat of this boiled partridge make a stuffing with equal parts of parboiled sweetbreads and ¼ lb. of fresh mushrooms, peeled, and chopped very fine, stems and caps, seasoning to taste with salt, pepper, and a little nutmeg.

Before rolling and tying the birds, place a little of this stuffing in the center. Roll up and tie securely. With whatever left, spread around the birds; then place a thin slice of larding pork and tie securely. Place the birds thus dressed in a large casserole in which has been melted ½ cup of sweet butter. Cover and let cook very gently, turning the birds once in a while to brown on all sides, for 25 minutes. Now lift out the bird, place on a hot platter and keep hot.

Into the butter remaining in the casserole, put 1 cup of lean ham, chopped fine, ¼ cup of salt pork, chopped fine, 1 medium-sized onion, chopped fine, 1 small carrot, sliced fine, 1 bay leaf, and 6 sprigs of parsley tied up together (called bouquet garni), 6 peppercorns, bruised, 1 clove, and salt and pepper to taste. Cook this slowly, stirring often until mixture begins to brown, or about 15 minutes, then pour over 1 cup of good champagne, and ½ cup (generous) of consommé, 1 teaspoon of "Fumet" (*see* recipe, How To Prepare

GAME STOCK, page 45). Bring to a boil, reduce the heat and allow to simmer very gently for 15 minutes. Return the partridges in this unctuous sauce. Let simmer 15 minutes longer. Lift out the birds. Dress on a hot platter, a piece of toast under each bird. Strain the sauce through a fine sieve over the partridges and place on each bird a thin slice of black truffle. Serve at once. A side dish of fried hominy and one of potato chips should be served.

PARTRIDGE À LA TOUSSENEL

Roast 6 young partridges in the usual method after stuffing them with the following stuffing:

One tablespoon of finely chopped truffles, the livers of the partridges, mashed with a fork, then heated with a few drops of champagne, but not boiled, 2 tablespoons of ground, cooked lean ham, salt and pepper to taste, 1 shallot, finely chopped, 1 teaspoon parsley. The whole thoroughly mixed, then divided equally among the 6 partridges. Roast only 15 minutes. Remove from the oven and very carefully, very gently lift out the legs and wings, without separating from the body, and between the body and each member spread the following stuffing:

½ cup of fresh bread crumbs	1 teaspoon of chives, finely
½ teaspoon of coarse black pepper	chopped
per	1 scant half teaspoon parsley,
2 tablespoons of sweet butter	minced
A blade of nutmeg	

The whole gently but thoroughly kneaded. Reshape the birds. Place them in a large casserole, with 4 tablespoons of butter, 1 pint of champagne and allow this to simmer, "to smile" over a very low flame for 30 minutes, uncovered. Dress the partridges on a hot platter, over freshly made toast. Add to the sauce in the casserole, ½ teaspoon of grated lemon rind, 1 tablespoon of grated orange rind, 1 pony glass of good brandy. Bring to a rapid boil, let reduce a little and pour over the partridges. Serve at once with the traditional bread sauce and potato chips.

PARTRIDGE DUMPLINGS

5 tablespoons butter
5 ozs. ground cooked old partridge
2 whole eggs

2 egg yolks
Salt, pepper, and a few grains of nutmeg to taste
Bread crumbs

Cream butter. Add the 2 eggs and the egg yolks, salt, pepper, and nutmeg to taste. Mix well and add ground cooked partridge and enough bread crumbs to thicken. Shape into small balls, the size of a small walnut. Allow to stand a while (about 30 minutes) to mellow, and drop in boiling meat stock (if bird game stock is available, it is much better and may be made out of all the bones and trimmings). Cook 8 to 10 minutes. Serve on a bed of mashed potatoes. Garnish with triangles of bread fried in butter. These dumplings are delicious with game soup, and also dressed over cooked spinach or mashed potatoes.

SNAP-DRAGON

(*Serves 6 People*)

Put 4 bunches of cluster raisins into hot water and let stand half an hour. Drain and dry carefully, and remove the seeds, inserting half a toasted almond in each raisin. Arrange the clusters in the middle of a silver tray, strew some finely shredded peel of tangerines over them, and pour half a cup of heated brandy over all. Heat an extra tablespoonful of brandy, set fire to it, and pour over the raisins, thus igniting the remaining brandy. With a long-handled spoon keep ladling the blazing brandy over the raisins, until the flames mount high.

This is half game and half dessert. The tray should be placed in the middle of the table, and while the brandy is still burning, the trick is to have the guests pull out the raisins and pop them into their mouths.

PERDREAUX AUX CHOUX I
(*Modern Method*)

Pick, clean, singe, and truss 6 partridges. Color, that is, brown delicately in ½ cup of butter, for 10 short minutes, turning the birds often so as to obtain an even browning on all sides, sprinkling a generous tablespoon of flour over the birds. Moisten with 3 cups of good meat stock; add ¼ lb. of salt pork, cubed small, 6 sprigs of parsley, tied with 1 large bay leaf; allow this to simmer gently for 15 long minutes. Meanwhile parboil 3 green cabbages after removing the ribs, for 5 long minutes. Lift out the cabbage with a perforated skimmer and add to the partridges with 1 lb. of lean fresh pork, adding more meat stock to cover. Adjust the cover tightly after seasoning to taste with salt and black pepper, and set in a moderately hot oven (350°) for 30 long minutes. The length of time of braising may be longer according to age of the birds. When ready to serve, dress the cabbage on a hot platter in nest shape. Place a partridge into each nest and surround each one with 2 or 3 small pork sausages, cooked slowly in butter.

PERDREAUX AUX CHOUX II
(*Old Method*)

Prepare 6 partridges as indicated for PERDREAUX AUX CHOUX I, above, as far as cooking the cabbage, which in the old method is quite different and more delicious. While the partridges are simmering, place in another saucepan 3 lbs. of green cabbage, after removing the large ribs, with ¾ lb. of bacon and 2 tablespoons of lard. Cook this 15 minutes. Now take 4 carrots and slice thinly, and one French cervelas or Bologna sausage, which slice also thinly. Butter a large braising kettle, arrange on the bottom, first the sliced carrots, then the sliced Bologna. Cut the salt pork into slices, which was cooked with the cabbage and line the sides of the kettle. Drain the cabbage and arrange one layer over the carrots and Bologna sausage. Place the partridges over the layer of cabbage and between each partridge arrange a slice of lean pork, using about 1 generous pound; cover with the remaining cabbage, moisten with enough stock in which the partridges were first cooked. Cover tightly and set in a hot oven (400°) for 30 minutes. When ready to serve, place a large round platter over the braising kettle, turn upside down very gently and all at once. Serve immediately.

PARTRIDGE PIE
(English Method)

Line the bottom and sides of a deep pie plate with thin slices of bacon, and sprinkle bottom and sides with ¼ scant cup of very finely chopped shallots. Arrange 3 partridges, or more, according to size, cut into 4 pieces, skin removed, and seasoned with salt, pepper to taste and a little parsley, minced. For each partridge, add 1 hard-cooked egg yolk cut in two. Moisten with a scant ½ cup of good game stock, made from the trimmings. Cover with a rich pie crust, or puff paste; brush with beaten egg yolk diluted with a few drops of milk or cream; make a few slits in center to allow the steam to escape. Bake in a moderately hot oven (350°) for 1¼ hours. Serve hot.

Many additions and variations may be made, such as adding small button mushrooms, glazed onions, or small potato balls, if desired.

PARTRIDGE STEWED IN RED WINE

NOTE: Many so-called connoisseurs and gourmets will be horrified. "What partridge in red wine! This surely is too great a liberty to take with partridge!" But why not? Will this not equal, indeed surpass, the Hare Civet of classic fame? However, the main point is that you must not be niggardly when selecting the wine; it must be of the best quality claret. No substitute will answer the purpose. Try.

4 partridges, cut up as for fricassee, the blood set aside and a few drops of vinegar or lemon juice added to it to prevent coagulation.

18 small white onions, blanched	1 bay leaf, tied with
½ lb. lean bacon, diced small	6 sprigs parsley
4 tablespoons butter	2 small cloves of garlic, bruised
18 small fresh mushrooms, peeled then quartered	1 bottle of good red wine
	Salt and pepper to taste

Cook the onions with the butter, adding the diced bacon, until delicately browned. Lift out. Keep hot. In the fat remaining in the skillet, sauté the cut-up birds until brown or well seared. Return onions and bacon to the birds in the pan, adding the mushrooms, bay leaf, and parsley, and the bruised garlic. Cook, stirring very gently for 15 short minutes, over a very gentle fire. Then and only then pour over the red wine; cover and allow to cook gently over a medium fire for 25 minutes, or until wine is reduced to nearly half. Remove from the fire and add the blood of the partridges, then the liver. Stir gently one short minute. Dress rapidly onto a hot, deep, round platter and garnish with triangles of hominy, fried in plenty of butter, alternating with a small triangle of bread, also fried in butter. Dust the top with parsley chopped fine. Serve at once with guava jelly.

PARTRIDGE À LA CREOLE

First prepare a Creole sauce as follows: For 6 partridges use:

¼ cup butter	6 sprigs parsley
1 cup sliced (not chopped) onions	1 large can tomatoes
1 cup sliced green pepper, seeds and white ribs removed	1 cup small green olives, stones removed, then split in two
1 cup button mushrooms (canned)	2 cups meat stock mixed with ½ cup sweet white wine
1 large bay leaf tied up with	Salt and pepper to taste
	2 cloves

A small pinch thyme leaves

Melt butter in a large skillet; add onions and cook 10 long minutes, stirring frequently. Do not brown. Add green pepper, mix well and cook 5 long minutes, stirring very often, then all the remaining ingredients. Mix well and gently and allow to simmer very slowly over a gentle fire, stirring occasionally.

Now prepare 6 partridges as for roasting, and arrange neatly, as in a nest in the Creole sauce. Cover tightly and place in a hot oven (400°) for 30 minutes. Lift out the birds. Arrange the Creole dressing nestlike on a large platter and into each nest place a bird. Surround the edges of the platter with small triangles of fried hominy. Serve with either currant, grape, or guava jelly, and freshly made dry toast. To serve: Place a piece of toast on each plate; cover with the Creole sauce and place over a partridge.

It is advisable when roasting a partridge and using a coal or wood stove (for hunters to) place the back of the bird toward the fire side; this is very important, especially if the bird is mortified, as it is always the back of the bird which is the most touched by mortification and should be cooked first, and rapidly.

WASSAIL PUNCH

3 quarts good beer
1 lb. loaf sugar, or granulated sugar if pound sugar is not available
½ teaspoon grated nutmeg
½ teaspoon powdered ginger
4 cocktail glasses Sherry wine
3 to 4 slices lemon peel, thinly pared
3 slices of freshly made toast
  More sugar if necessary

Place one quart of the beer in a saucepan and set over a gentle fire, allowing to simmer until a white foam rises to the surface; then add the sugar, nutmeg, ginger and mix well, until sugar is entirely melted. Add the Sherry wine, mixed with the remaining beer and lemon peel, adding more sugar if necessary. Set aside on the range to infuse. Pour into a punch bowl, place the toasted bread floating in it. Serve in small deep punch cups or dessert plates.

SAUTÉED FILLET OF PARTRIDGE

Pluck, clean, singe, wipe with a damp cloth, remove the skins of 6 partridges. Carefully lift out the breasts, removing all the nerves. Melt ½ cup of sweet butter in a heavy skillet, roll each fillet into the melted butter, then arrange neatly the fillets or breasts side by side; dust with salt and white pepper to taste; cover with a round buttered paper, exactly fitting the skillet. Set aside. With the trimmings make a little stock (there should be 2 cups). Let this reduce to half, then add half a small can of tomato paste, 1 teaspoon of "Fumet" (*see* recipe, How To PREPARE GAME STOCK, page 45), and season to taste with salt, coarsely ground peppercorns, 1 small bay leaf, 1 clove and 1 tarragon leaf, let simmer gently while placing the breasts or fillets of partridge over a gentle fire for 10 short minutes, turning them once. Drain. Dress in circle on a hot platter, over a freshly made piece of toast, the size of the breast or fillet, and fried in butter. Strain the sauce. Heat to the boiling point and just before serving, beat in ¼ lb. sweet butter, bit by bit, and pour over the breast. Place over each fillet a thin slice of black truffle. Serve at once with a side dish of steamed wild rice, a side dish of currant jelly, and another one of potato chips.

PARTRIDGE EN SALMIS

Select 6 young partridges, and prepare for roasting, first wrapped in a green vine leaf, then in a thin slice of larding pork, held to-

gether with string or skewers. Roast in the usual method, but well
underdone (15 long minutes only). Remove the slice of larding
pork, then the vine leaf from each bird. Lift out the legs and breasts.
Trim neatly, remove the skins and arrange neatly in a large heavy
skillet in which has been melted ¼ generous cup of butter, ½ cup
of mushroom stock, or mushroom soup (canned), 4 small mushroom caps and 2 thin slices of black truffle for each partridge. Keep
hot while preparing a Salmis sauce (*see* Sauces). Then add this
sauce to the partridge pieces in the skillet. Heat well, but do not
boil. Dress the pieces of partridges on a hot round platter. Pour the
sauce over and garnish with small hearts of bread fried in butter.
Serve with a side dish of currant jelly and a green lettuce salad with
French dressing.

FOGOLY LIBAMAJSZELETEKKEL

(*Hungarian Recipe*)

Clean, wipe with a damp cloth, place a small piece of cooked
celery in the cavity of 6 young partridges before trussing, and lard
through and through with sticks of larding pork (using 4 sticks for
each partridge). Roast in the usual method for 20 long minutes in a
hot oven (400°). Dress on a hot platter, over a piece of toast, covered with goose-liver sausage, in circle, and garnish the center with
slightly heated goose-liver pâté slices. Serve with a rich Madeira
sauce in which has been added cooked, sliced mushrooms, another
side dish of bread sauce and currant jelly.

SIMMERED PARTRIDGE LUMBERJACK

Select very old partridges. There should be 6. Clean, singe, wipe
with a damp cloth, then rub with lemon juice, inside and out, and
rub with salt and coarse black pepper. Place in the cavity a medium-
sized white onion, and a small sprig of parsley. Truss or sew. Heat
½ scant cup of bacon drippings and place the birds in it. Allow to
brown on all sides, over a medium fire, turning often, for 20 min-

utes. Lift out the bird and turn into a large casserole, the bottom of which is lined with 1 cup of raw ham, chopped fine. Into the butter remaining in the skillet, pour 1 wineglass of white wine, and as much mushroom stock. Stir from the bottom of the skillet with a wooden spoon, and allow the mixture to reduce to ⅔. Then add a full small can of tomato purée, bring to a boil, add 1 cup of brown sauce, bring to a boil, and return the birds to the sauce, with 1 small can of button mushrooms, ¾ cup of bacon, coarsely chopped, 1 dozen of small white onions, glazed. Correct the seasoning, cover and continue cooking over a gentle fire for 25 minutes longer. Dress on a hot round platter, the birds in circle; pour the sauce and vegetables in center; surround with small mold of plain boiled rice, interspersed with small triangles of bread fried in butter. Serve a side dish of grape jelly.

SIMMERED PARTRIDGE ROTHSCHILD

Pluck, clean, singe 6 young partridges. Fill the cavity with the following mixture: ¾ cup fresh mushrooms, finely ground after being peeled and coarsely chopped, the livers of the 6 partridges, 1 small truffle, finely chopped, 2 egg yolks, salt and pepper to taste. Mix these ingredients thoroughly, moistening with a few drops of good, fine champagne, fill the cavity of the bird equally, then sew and truss. Melt ½ cup of butter in a large casserole and arrange the birds neatly in the bottom. Cook over a medium fire for 10 long minutes, turning the birds occasionally to color on all sides. Then add 6 artichoke bottoms, 2 crushed juniper berries, 1 cup of small fresh mushrooms, and 2 dozen of small white onions, previously glazed, lastly add 1 whole green pepper, seeds removed and cut in small strings, or circles. Season to taste with salt and pepper, and pour over 1¾ cups of Salmis sauce (*see* SAUCES) to which has been added 1 pony glass of good brandy. Cover and set in a moderate oven (375°) for 30 minutes. Serve in the casserole with a side dish of currant jelly, and another of sauerkraut.

SIMMERED PARTRIDGE TIVOLI

Pluck, clean, singe, fill the cavity of each bird with 1 slice of onion, 1 small piece of celery, and 1 crushed juniper berry. Truss and sew. Melt, for 6 partridges, ½ cup of butter and cook the birds in it for 15 minutes, turning frequently to color on all sides. Add 1 full large can of tomatoes, 1 small can of button mushrooms, and 1 large green pepper, seeds removed, and coarsely chopped. Season to taste with salt and pepper and add 1 large bay leaf tied with 3 sprigs of parsley and 2 sprigs of fennel. Cover and let simmer for 25 minutes, over a gentle fire. Open the casserole and add 1 tablespoon of kneaded butter (equal part of butter kneaded with equal part of flour), cover again and let simmer for 5 long minutes. Serve in the casserole, with your favorite jelly and Saratoga chips.

SIMMERED PARTRIDGE PIEDMONTESE

Consists of cooking 6 partridges prepared as indicated for SIMMERED PARTRIDGE TIVOLI, above, and served with a side dish of risotto.

GLOW WINE PUNCH

2 bottles red Bordeaux wine
1 cup granulated sugar (more or less)
6 whole cloves
    The whole peel of a large lemon, thinly pared
2 or 3 oranges, sliced and seeded

Pour the claret into a saucepan and bring slowly to the boiling point, or until a white foam forms on the surface. Remove from the fire and add sugar, cloves, and lemon peel. Stir well, cover and let stand a few minutes to infuse. Serve in glass cups, adding a slice of orange to each glass.

THE PHEASANT

The pheasant is a mystery of which the key is only revealed to the initiated; they alone can taste the bird in all its perfection. Each substance has its highest point of succulency; some arrive at it before their entire development, as capers, asparagus, gray partridges, and green pigeons; others arrive at it the moment when they are as perfect as they ever can be, such as melons, nearly all fruits, mutton, beef, venison, red partridges; others, finally, when they begin to decompose, as medlars, the woodcock, and especially the pheasant.

This bird, when it is eaten within three days after it has been killed, is not so delicate as a pullet, nor so sapid as a quail. When eaten at the right time, its flesh is tender, sublime, gamy and tastes of chicken and of venison. The right time is when the pheasant begins to decompose; then its aroma is developed, and combines with an oil, which to become developed requires a slight degree of fermentation, just as the essential oil of coffee is only obtained by roasting the bean.

This right moment reveals itself to the senses of the uninitiated by a slight odor, and by a change in the color of the belly of the bird; but the *Born* gourmand divines it by a sort of instinct which shows itself on many occasions, so that, for example, a first-class cook can tell in an instant whether a fowl should be taken from the oven, or be allowed to remain a few minutes longer. When a pheasant has arrived at this stage, it ought to be plucked, but not before, and larded carefully with the freshest and firmest pork fat.

It is not a matter of indifference to pluck a pheasant too early; very careful experiments have taught us that those kept in their feathers are *More* highly perfumed than those plucked some time ago, either because the contact of the air has neutralized some part of the aroma, or that a part of the juice for nourishing the feathers is absorbed again, and serves to give more flavor to the meat.

The pheasant is the king of the game birds. Through the aroma and fineness of its flesh, the male carries it with a high hand against the female, already so distinguished. Finer than the domesticated, the wild pheasant deserve a profound veneration.

The pheasant is a native of Asia. Reascending the Phase to reach the Colchis, the Argonauts saw for the first time this magnificent bird, which they first brought to Greece, endowing Europe thus with a conquest more precious than that of the Order of the Golden Fleece (Toison d'Or). Most certainly and undoubtedly, these brave Argonauts did not realize that later on humanity would have delicious dishes. The Order of the Golden Fleece! Bah, a trifling matter indeed when compared to a pheasant.

One may serve it: En Chaud-Froid, Minced, in Cutlet, in Gallantine, in Pie form, in Loaf with a soft sweet-sour cream added, in Dumplings, à la Hongroise or à la Tartare. The pheasant is always himself, a regal dish, a marvel, an ideal: the pheasant!

First introduced from its birthland, China, into the United States near Portland, Oregon, in 1881, whence it has been brought in nearly every state of the Union, where it may be found on the markets, during the season, this splendid game bird has not escaped censure on the score of its damage to crops, and it is undoubtedly true that it has a keen appetite for corn, peas, grain, and even potatoes.

The pheasants are naturally hardy and prolific, and once established in a region, need only reasonable protection to ensure their perpetuation for all time—and our tables.

BRAISED PHEASANT CREOLE

Follow the same directions as indicated in recipe for PARTRIDGE À LA CREOLE, page 57, substituting pheasant for partridge. Cook, dress and serve as directed.

BRAISED PHEASANT SOUWAROFF

Cook for 5 short minutes 6 small black truffles in ½ cup of Madeira wine, to which has been added 1 teaspoon of "Fumet" (*see* recipe, How To PREPARE GAME STOCK, page 45), using an earthenware dish. Dice ½ lb. of goose liver and add to the saucepan with the Madeira wine and truffles, and cook 2 short minutes, over a gentle fire. Lift out truffles and goose liver and fill the cavity of a mortified pheasant, previously cleaned, rubbed inside and out with lemon juice, then with salt and pepper, with the goose liver and the black truffles. Truss. Arrange a thin slice of larding pork around the breasts of the bird, secure with a string, and place in a heavy skillet with 3 tablespoons of butter. Cook for 25 minutes, turning the bird often to golden brown on all sides. Turn the bird and butter into the earthenware baking dish in which remains the Madeira wine; cover hermetically and set in a hot oven (400°) for 20 minutes longer. Serve in the casserole.

BRAISED PHEASANT À LA MODE AU MARSALA

Select an old bird for this delicious recipe.

1 pheasant, cleaned, mortified
    4 to 5 days, larded
1 dozen small fresh mushrooms,
    caps only, sliced
3 small shallots, chopped
2 ounces butter
1 small peeled orange

1 scant tablespoon flour
1½ wineglasses of Marsala wine
4 tablespoons lard
    Salt, pepper, and a sprig of
    fennel
2 juniper berries, bruised

Place the small peeled orange (a tangerine may be used if desired), and the liver in the cavity of the bird. Sew and truss. Heat up the lard and roll the bird in it, then cook for 15 long minutes, turning the bird often, browning all sides. Baste the bird often with the lard. Lift out the bird and transfer to a casserole. Keep hot. In the fat remaining in the skillet, cook the mushrooms, sliced. Warm the butter, add the minced shallots, do not brown, stir in the flour and blend well, then pour in the Marsala wine, slowly, gradually, stirring the while. Season to taste with salt, pepper, and the sprig of fennel. Turn the bird into an earthenware casserole, add the wine sauce, the 2 juniper berries, crushed, cover hermetically, and set in a hot oven (400°) for 25 minutes without disturbing. Serve in the casserole, with fried hominy, currant jelly, and a green salad.

MOSELLE CUP MAITRANK

(Very Old German Recipe)

¼ lb. granulated sugar
½ cup cold water
1 pinch of woodruff, called also "wild forget-me-not" and may be purchased in drug stores
1 bottle Moselle wine
(Rhine wine may be substituted)

Melt the sugar in a punch bowl with the cold water. Place a large piece of ice in center of the bowl. Pour over it the Moselle wine. Add the woodruff. Stir gently. Cover and let stand to infuse for at least half an hour. Serve in glass cups.

FILLET OF PHEASANT ARCHIDUC RODOLPHE

Select a young pheasant. Lift off the breasts. With a sharp knife remove the skin, operating as if you were slicing thin slices of larding pork, or removing the skin from a ham without taking any meat with the skin. Pound them slightly with a cleaver. Trim neatly. Melt ¼ cup of sweet butter in a skillet and roll the pheasant fillets in it. Dust with salt and coarsely ground or rather pounded black peppercorns. Arrange flat in the skillet; cover with a round buttered paper. Remove the meat from the legs, and grind it. Place this ground meat in a saucepan. Set aside. With the trimmings and bones make a "Fumet" (see recipe, How To PREPARE GAME STOCK, page 45). This fumet will be used for glazing the fillets, at least part of it. Sauté the fillets in the usual way, over a very gentle fire, turning often to cook on both sides to a golden brown. To half the fumet, add 2 tablespoons of tomato paste, 1 tablespoon of butter (scant) and moisten with ½ scant wineglass of red wine. Stir and bring to a boil; to this sauce, add the ground legs, and cook 15 long minutes, stirring occasionally. Remove aside and stir in 1 or 2 egg yolks, season to taste with salt and pepper; set aside and keep hot. Do not boil any more. Spread the remaining fumet over the fillets and glaze under the broiling oven. Dress in a casserole, over freshly made toast, and surround with part of the sauce. Serve in the casserole, with the remaining sauce aside.

FILLET OF PHEASANT SCHNITZEL
(*Hungarian Method*)

With a sharp knife, lift out carefully and neatly the breast of a very young pheasant. Pull out the skin; slice in thin wafers. Lay each wafer on a board, rub it with salt and coarsely ground black pepper, then pound fiercely with the back of a cleaver or the edge of a heavy carving knife. Turn the thin fillets over and sprinkle with pepper and salt and continue the pounding. Fiber will be broken down and the fillet slices will expand under the punishment, which should not cease till the thickness has been reduced to ⅜ of an inch. Dip each wafer or fillet carefully in flour, then in beaten egg, and lastly in sifted biscuit or cracker crumbs. Sauté in a frying pan with plenty of butter or olive oil, turning each piece till it is well and evenly browned. Serve on a hot platter, garnish with fried hominy triangles, alternated with thin slices of lemon dipped in paprika, with a side dish of Cumberland sauce (*see* SAUCES).

OLD-FASHIONED PHEASANT POT PIE
(*British Recipe*)

Select an old pheasant, slightly mortified (4 days). Clean, singe, and cut into serving pieces as you would a chicken fricassee, removing the skin as you go along. Parboil the pieces in enough water to cover with a small onion, sliced, 1 bay leaf, 2 cloves, a sprig of thyme, a small carrot cut into thin slices, salt and pepper to taste, for 25 minutes. Drain, reserving the liquid, and reduce to half over a hot fire. Make a light biscuit dough, and plenty of it; roll out the dough not very thin, and cut most of it into long squares. Butter the bottom and sides of a deep pie dish, and line bottom and sides with slices of fat and lean ham, then the pieces of pheasant, interspersed all through with squares of dough and potatoes, pared and quartered. Pour in the reduced stock, 1 pony glass of Madeira wine, a large bay leaf, and (optional) 1 small can of button mushrooms. Cover the whole with a lid of dough, having a slit or two in the center through which the gravy will bubble up. Bake steadily for 1 long hour in a moderate oven (325°). Remove from the oven, and through the hole in center of the crust, put in some bits of butter rolled in flour, to thicken the gravy. Serve as hot as possible with the traditional currant jelly, fried bread-crumb sauce, and thin slices of lemon.

PAN FRIED PHEASANT WITH SAUERKRAUT

Select a young pheasant, and let mortify for 4–5 days. Pick, clean, wipe with a damp cloth, place 2 juniper berries and a small white onion in the cavity. Truss and sew. Cook in a casserole for 35 minutes (the pheasant should be a little rare)—in plenty of butter, turning the bird often to color on all sides. Dress on a hot platter, covered with a layer of sauerkraut, generously greased, with, if possible, goose fat, then well drained. Surround the edges of the platter with small squares of cooked fresh pork, cooked in the sauerkraut. Serve with a side dish of sauce made as follows:

To the butter left in the casserole, add 1 scant cup of game stock made from trimmings, and bring to a boil, stirring from the bottom of the casserole; add 1 teaspoon of "Fumet" (*see* recipe, How To PREPARE GAME STOCK, page 45). Stir, bring to a boil. Serve.

PHEASANT À LA MODE D'ALCÁNTARA

HISTORICAL NOTE

This recipe was found in the famous Convent of Alcántara, Spain. Napoleon by his "Decree of Berlin" issued in that conquered city in November, 1806, declared the British Isles under blockade, and prohibited commerce between England and France and all the latter's allies. To refuse to accept the blockade, to have the least intercourse with Britain, was practically to invite war with Napoleon. What continental prince dared risk it?

". . . I desire . . .," announced the Emperor, ". . . to conquer the sea by the power of the land. . . ." The Corsican, in his efforts to gain control of the sea by means of irregular and unusual devices, was only anticipating the more desperate expedients of Germany (1915–1918) with her unlimited submarine policy. To enforce such a drastic decree was, however, impossible even for the victor of Austerlitz and Jena. Despite the unpopularity of the decree, Napoleon adhered to it and sharpened it. Russia, Austria, Prussia, and Denmark all kissed the rod, and joined the blockade against Britain. When Napoleon's own brother Louis Bonaparte (whom he had made King of Holland) refused to ruin his subjects by a strict application of the system, the Emperor forced him off his puppet throne and annexed Holland to the already swollen Empire of France (1810). Earlier he had laid a like hand on Italy, and in 1807 had overrun Portugal, because "that *weak* kingdom had vainly talked of *neutrality*."

It was then at the beginning of Napoleon's campaign in Portugal, in 1807, headed by General Junot's soldiers, that the famous Bibliothèque of the Convent of the Monks of Alcántara was ransacked of many precious manuscripts, some of which were sent to the Imperial Bibliothèque, in Paris, but unfortunately many valuable manuscripts were used to make cartridges or burned at the pyre. Among those happily saved, figure many culinary concoctions, of which the following is one which, primarily intended for partridges, has been successfully applied to pheasant (THE AUTHOR).

Recipe

Clean a plump, plucked pheasant, removing the breastbone (as you would for a small broiler), without damaging the bird. Stuff the well-cleaned and lemon-rubbed bird (inside and out) with a whole duck liver, mixed with ⅓ volume of coarsely chopped black truffles, previously cooked in port wine for 5 long minutes. Sew carefully. Truss, and marinate for 3 or 4 days in a bath of port wine to cover, seeing to it that the bird is constantly submerged with the wine. Drain and cook in a casserole as you would an ordinary chicken, with plenty of butter (about ¼ cup). Take 1½ cups of the marinade, place over a hot fire and reduce to half volume. Add ½ dozen of small black truffles to the reduced port wine and 1 teaspoon of "Fumet" (*see* recipe, How To Prepare Game Stock, page 45) and allow to simmer gently, to smile imperceptibly, for 15 short minutes. Dress the bird over the port wine sauce and the truffles. Serve at once.

No mention is made of a garnishing. However it is to be presumed that the Monks, who had a reputation as gourmets and connoisseurs, must have served the bird of birds with the usual garnishing, which is a side dish of bread-crumb sauce, and jelly, and the writer suggests one of the following garnishings: Grilled grapefruit au sherry, glazed cranberry apples, stuffed oranges, baked oranges, apple rings, purée of red pimentos, stuffed green peppers, Spanish garnishing, broiled peaches, etc., which will be found under Garnishings.

This recipe was found in the "Mémoires of the Duchesse d'Abrantes," and is probably the only thing worthwhile that the French garnered from this disastrous war.

PHEASANT À LA SAINTE ALLIANCE

When the bird has been mortified, prepare a stuffing as follows: Remove the bones of two woodcocks, set aside the entrails and livers. Mince the meat and add to it 1 generous tablespoon of cooked beef marrow, 1 generous tablespoon of minced raw bacon, a pinch each of sage, chives, parsley, and tarragon herb finely chopped, 1 scant teaspoon onion, finely chopped, 1 teaspoon of black truffle, chopped very fine, salt and coarse black pepper to taste. Mix thoroughly and fill the cavity of the bird. Sew carefully. Truss. Now, pound the entrails and livers with 2 small black truffles, the size of a large hazelnut, 1 whole anchovy fillet, washed, then sponged, 1 teaspoon of scraped raw bacon and a generous teaspoon of sweet butter to a paste. Spread this unctuous paste on a slice of freshly made toast, and put it under the stuffed pheasant, so that it may receive all the gravy dripping while roasting. Roast 25 to 30 minutes in a moderately hot oven (350–375°). When the bird is done to the desired point (it is advisable to have it very rare), serve on a hot platter, lying gracefully on its toast. Garnish with sweet-sour sliced oranges round it.

". . . A pheasant prepared in this manner," says Brillat Savarin, "is worthy of being served to angels, if these were still travelling on this earth, as they did in the days of Lot. This highly flavored dish ought to be washed down, preferably, with some of the best Burgundy wine, such as 'Clos de Citeaux,' a wine produced from stocks of more than 1000 years and planted by the famous Monks of the Abbaye de Citeaux, Côtes d'Or, France, a wine meriting the endorsement of the most discriminating. It has a wonderful bouquet, is generous and possesses fruitiness."

PHEASANT LIEUTENANT COLONEL NELSON MORRIS

Select a young pheasant with gray feet. The extremity of the breastbone as well as the beak should be flexible and soft. Allow to mortify 4 long days, then and only then pluck, clean, singe, and rub inside and out with orange juice; then with salt and coarsely ground peppercorns to taste. Make a paste of the liver scraped with the back of a knife, adding 1 crushed juniper berry, 1 generous tablespoon of sweet butter, a very tiny pinch each of thyme leaves, sage, ground mixed allspice, 1 small shallot, chopped fine, ½ teaspoon of chervil, or parsley if chervil is not available, 1 teaspoon of scraped raw bacon, a small black truffle, chopped very fine, after being cooked 5 short minutes in a tablespoon of sherry wine, and 1 tablespoon of pâté de foie gras, and ¼ teaspoon of grated lemon or better tangerine rind. Fill the cavity of the bird with this thoroughly mixed, appetizing paste. Sew. Truss, and place in a casserole with 4 tablespoons of butter. Cook 15 minutes, over a gentle fire uncovered, turning the bird often to color on all sides. Turn the bird into an earthenware casserole, having a tight-fitting cover. Pour over the butter from the cooking, and 1½ cups of Malaga wine, reduced to half over a hot fire; then add 1 teaspoon of "Fumet" (*see* recipe, How To PREPARE GAME STOCK, page 45). Cover tightly; set in a moderately hot oven and do not disturb for 20 minutes. Serve in the casserole with a side dish of plain cooked wild rice, and side dish of guava jelly, as well as a fried bread-crumb sauce.

This recipe was dedicated to Lieutenant Colonel Nelson Morris because of his appreciation of the culinary art, of which he is one of the foremost patrons in America.

HIS CHEF, *the Author.*

CLARET CUP JACQUELINE

½ lb. granulated sugar
1 generous cup cold water
1 generous cup Curaçao
1 generous cup of Kirsch
Juice of 3 medium-sized lemons, and rind of one
2 bottles of red Bordeaux wine

Place all the ingredients but the Bordeaux wine in an ice-cream freezer, and freeze halfway. Open the freezer and pour in the 2 bottles of wine. Close the freezer and turn until the mixture has the consistency of snow. Serve in champagne *coupe* with ladyfingers.

PHEASANT DEMIDOFF

Let a young pheasant mortify for 4 days; then pluck, clean and place a juniper berry and a small piece of celery in the cavity of the bird after rubbing inside and out with a little lemon juice; then season with salt and black pepper to taste. Sew and truss. Place the bird in a casserole, containing 4 tablespoons of melted butter and golden brown on all sides, turning the bird often, until the bird is done halfway (about 20 minutes). Then add ½ generous cup of small young carrots, first parboiled, then cooked in a little butter for 5 short minutes, but not browned too much; ½ generous cup of white turnips, parboiled, then cubed and sautéed in a little butter for 5 short minutes, 12 small white onions, the smallest possible and of the same size as far as possible, thinly sliced, and raw, and ¼ cup of cooked celery, diced small, 1 small truffle, sliced thin and a generous ½ cup of game stock. Cover and set in a moderately hot oven (350–375°) for 20 minutes. Serve in the casserole without any other accompaniment. You may cut the vegetables in shapes, such as half-moon, circles, balls, etc., if desired, using the small, fancy French cutters.

PHEASANT À LA PERIGUEUX

It is optional to mortify the bird, but it is imperative that the bird be young. If the bird is mortified, pluck it at the moment it is to be cooked. In either case (fresh state or mortified state), rub inside and out with orange juice, then with salt and pepper to taste. Place 4 small truffles, previously cooked in Madeira wine for 5 long minutes, in the cavity of the bird (you may lard it with truffles if desired, larding only the breast). Sew, then truss. Melt 4 tablespoons of butter in a casserole, add the bird and let sear thoroughly on all sides for 15 minutes over a hot fire; then reduce the heat and add 4 tablespoons of good Madeira sauce (*see* SAUCES). Cover and allow to simmer very gently for 20 to 25 minutes longer. Lift out. Dress the bird on a hot platter, pour the sauce over and surround the bird with small dumplings made of any kind of game bird, operating as indicated for PARTRIDGE DUMPLINGS, page 54, adding to the mixture, before dropping into hot stock, a little chopped black truffle. Serve with an extra dish of Perigueux sauce (*see* SAUCES).

PHEASANT À LA GALITZIN

Bone 2 nice snipes, reserving the entrails and livers; and chop the meat of the two birds fine, adding gradually and alternately the same amount in weight of cream (fresh) and butter (sweet); then salt and black pepper to taste. Cook the entrails and livers 2 short minutes in a teaspoon of butter, remove from the fire and mash with a fork; then add this to the first mixture, mixing well and thoroughly. With this unctuous mixture, fill the cavity of a young pheasant, mortified 4 to 5 days, then plucked, cleaned, singed, and rubbed inside and out with lemon juice and then with salt and pepper to taste. Sew. Truss. Place in a roasting pan or still better in an earthenware shallow pan, and roast for 30 minutes in a moderate oven (350–375°), basting often with melted butter kept aside in a cup. Five minutes before removing from the oven, baste with 1 generous teaspoon of melted "Fumet" (*see* recipe, How To PREPARE GAME STOCK, page 45), made from the trimmings and bones of the snipes. Serve a side dish of bread-crumb sauce and another of currant jelly. Decorate the platter with small triangles of bread fried in butter, alternating with thin slices of lemon dipped, one-half in minced parsley and the other half in paprika (optional).

PHEASANT À LA BOHÉMIENNE
(*Bohemian Method*)

Season a goose liver with salt and pepper to taste; lard it through and through with small sticks of black truffles (raw) and poach it in plenty of butter, over a very slow fire (300°) for 20 short minutes. Remove from the butter. Cool. When cold, put it into the cavity of a young pheasant (unmortified), plucked, cleaned, the inside and outside rubbed with lemon juice, then with salt and pepper to taste. Sew. Truss. Melt 3 tablespoons of butter, or, still better, use the butter in which the goose liver was poached (there should be 3 tablespoons at least). Place the bird in it (an earthenware casserole is advisable) and cook very slowly, as slowly as possible, over a low fire, turning very often to color on all sides, for 45 minutes. Then remove half the butter from the casserole, pour over the bird a pony glass of good brandy, touch with a match and let burn out, nourishing, that is ladling the liquid occasionally all over the bird. When the flame has burned out, add 3 or 4 tablespoons of rich game stock and serve at once without any other accompaniment.

PHEASANT À LA VATEL

Author's Note

The following recipe is taken from the immortal pages of Edmond Richardin, poet and member of the French Academy of Science and Letters, who at the beginning of the recipe says: ". . . Puisque le bronze sur les places publiques ne perpétue pas le souvenir de ta mort héroïque, je te dédie un mets nouveau, qui portera ton nom et consacrera ta gloire. . . . Tu resteras, O Vatel! pour toutes les générations futures, l'éternel honneur du grand ART culinaire." (Since then a statue to the celebrated and famous Vatel has been erected in his native village, in the South of France.)

Recipe

Mortify a young pheasant for 4 days; pluck, clean, rub the inside with tangerine juice, then with salt and pepper, likewise the outside. Make a mixture with 3 black truffles, peeled and thinly sliced, the mashed raw liver and the entrails, salt and pepper to taste, and fill the cavity of the bird with this. Sew and truss. Place 4 duck livers in a casserole, larded with small sticks of black truffles and pour over 1 cup of boiling Marsala wine. Season to taste with salt and pepper, and place the pheasant over this savory bed. Set the casserole in a moderate oven (350°) and roast for 30 minutes. Lift out the bird. Dress the duck livers on freshly made toast, dipped into the Marsala sauce in the casserole and arrange the bird over the livers. Pour the reduced sauce over; garnish with thin slices of lemon and serve at once with a side dish of currant jelly.

PHEASANT À LA LECZINSKI

Author's Note

During the reign of its last Duc, Stanislas, King of Poland, the Lorraine Duchy, among others did not only keep a distinguished rank in Letters and Arts, but also asserted herself an incontestable authority in Culinary Art. Amiot, who was intendent or in charge of the King's Commissary, had gathered at the Court of Lorraine the pick of the Masters of cookery, who at the death of King Stanislas were scattered among the most illustrious houses of the Duchy, where they perpetuated the traditions of the Culinary Art. It was at a famous feast given by the King, in his castle of Luneville that the delicious Pheasant à la Leczinski was served for the first time.

Recipe (*modernized*)

Bone 2 snipes, take the meat, the liver and entrails and pound all in a mortar with 3 duck livers and 5 ounces of cooked ham fat, moistening with a wineglass of Moselle wine, and seasoning to taste with salt and pepper. Take half of this unctuous stuffing and fill the cavity of a young pheasant, mortified (5 days), plucked, cleaned, singed, rubbed inside and out first with brandy, then with salt and pepper, then sew and truss. With the remainder of the stuffing, spread a piece of freshly made toast. Place this toast in a dripping pan, place the bird over, right in the center, and set the dripping pan on a hot fire (400°), basting often with melted "Fumet" (*see* recipe, How To Prepare Game Stock, page 45). Dress the toast and bird as is on a hot platter and serve at once, without any accompaniment.

PHEASANT EN COCOTTE LAKEWOOD FARM INN

Do not mortify. Clean, singe, wipe with a damp cloth, and fill the cavity of a young pheasant with the following mixture:

3 chicken livers, ground with
1 slice of rye bread, cut in small
  pieces
1 juniper berry
½ teaspoon sherry wine

Enough cream to moisten
Salt and pepper to taste
½ teaspoon chives, minced
½ teaspoon parsley, minced

Mix all the above ingredients thoroughly to a paste, and fill the cavity of the bird, after rubbing inside and out with lemon juice, then with salt and pepper to taste. Sew, then truss. Place the bird in a casserole with 4 tablespoons of butter and cook slowly, very slowly, covered, for 45–50 minutes, turning the bird occasionally to brown on all sides. Dress the bird on a hot platter, over a piece of freshly made rye-bread toast. Garnish with small green peppers, stuffed with hominy and combined with equal parts of leftover cooked chicken, topped with buttered bread crumbs and baked in a moderate oven alternating with thin slices of lemon, topped with a green olive.

PHEASANT À LA CREOLE

(Braised)

Proceed as indicated for PARTRIDGE À LA CREOLE, page 57, substituting a pheasant for partridge. Cook and serve as directed.

PHEASANT LOAF

(Austrian Method) (Cold)

Mortify a pheasant for 4 days. Pluck, singe, clean, and separate in two, but do not separate entirely. Bone carefully and entirely. Lard the breast and legs with thin strips of larding pork. Prepare a filling as follows: Grind together, alternating with each kind of meat: ¾ lb. lean pork; ¾ lb. lean veal, and ½ lb. pork or ham fat, previously cut into small cubes. Place this mixture in a mixing bowl. Heat 6 tablespoons of bacon drippings and cook in it 1 medium-sized onion, chopped very fine, for 2 short minutes and add to the mixture, the ground, or mashed pheasant liver, salt and coarsely ground black pepper to taste, 1 small pinch of marjoram and 1 small pinch each of sweet basil, cloves, sage, and allspice, using good judgment. Pour over this 1 wineglass of dry white wine and cook, stirring constantly until mixture dries up almost entirely; then transfer to a mixing bowl and add 1 ordinary roll, soaked in cream, then squeezed and tossed to loosen and ¼ scant cup of grated Parmesan cheese. Mix thoroughly and pass through food chopper to ensure smoothness. Use half this filling for stuffing the pheasant. Sew securely and place the pheasant in a roasting pan. Add 1 scant cup of game stock (well strained), made from the bones and trimmings, and 1 generous tablespoon of butter. Roast in a moderate oven (350–375°) until half done (about 20 short minutes). Remove from the oven. Pour the gravy from the pan over the remainder of the filling. Line a loaf mold with pastry crust. Add 1-inch thickness of the filling, then a layer of fresh mushrooms, thinly sliced. Place the half-roasted pheasant in center of the loaf pan and fill the cavities on the sides all around with the remainder of the filling. Adjust the top crust; make a few slits here and there to allow the steam to escape; brush with milk or beaten egg yolk. Set in a moderate oven (350°) and bake for an hour, brushing twice with milk or beaten egg yolk, covering the top with a buttered paper if browning too fast on top and removing the paper after 50 minutes of baking. Cool in the pan overnight before using.

You may unmold the next day; then place it in a larger loaf pan and fill the space between the loaf and the pan with aspic, meat jelly, or gelatine. If meat jelly is used, it should be very clear. You may also, when pouring the chosen jelly, decorate with small fancy-cut hard-cooked egg whites, truffles, capers, olives, etc. This will keep several months in a refrigerator.

PHEASANT TYROLIAN METHOD

After the pheasant has been hanging for a whole week, pluck it, leaving the feathers on the head and roll the head in a buttered paper, so that during the roasting process the feathers will not burn off. Sprinkle or rather rub with salt and pepper after cleaning, singeing, rubbing it first with lime juice, then with salt and coarsely ground black pepper. Fasten the feet with string. Lard here and there with thin strips of fat larding pork, using 6. Rub the bird with butter and roast in a moderately hot oven (350°), basting often with melted butter or with the fat dripping from the bird. Dress on a hot platter, over a thick slice of toast. Remove all the fat from the roasting pan. Pour in a pony glass of fine champagne, then 1 cup of good, rich mushroom sauce. Stir from the bottom of the pan; boil once, correct the seasoning. Pour part of it over the bird and serve the remainder aside. Garnish the platter with a crisp bunch of young watercress and thin slices of lemon dipped in paprika. Serve at once.

FLAMING TEA PUNCH

Green tea
½ pint of brandy
½ pint rum
½ lb. granulated sugar (more or less according to taste)
Juice of a whole large lemon

Make an infusion of the best green tea (about 1 ounce to each quart of boiling water). Meanwhile heat the punch bowl; then pour in the rum, brandy, lemon juice, and sugar. Now set the liquid aflame and then pour in the tea slowly, mixing it thoroughly with a ladle. The mixture will continue to burn for a short while, and should be poured flaming into glass cups.

PÂTÉ CHAUD DE FAISAN À LA FRANÇAISE
(*Pheasant Loaf, French Method*)

AUTHOR'S NOTE

This dish is unusually delicious and is frequently served in France. Its usual accompaniment, because pheasant has an affinity for old Burgundy wine, such as a robust Corton with its warmth, its agreeable flavor and delicious aroma, or a Chambertin, be it Charmes, Varoilles, Clos Saint Jacques, Clos de Beze, or Clos Mazin (a wonderful wine with many first cousins), but all with a complete quality that a real Burgundy wine must possess. This wine, described as the king of wines and the wine of Kings, has something of the mellow maturity of Autumn and owes its precious and incomparable qualities of richness and color to the soil in which the vines are grown, as well as the method of cultivation; the pheasant is also excellent accompanied by Fleury wine, the Beaujolais nectar of Châteauneuf-du-Pape, an outstanding valley of the Rhône wine with a special "ester" (bouquet) of its own. Beaujolais is a wine to be proud of and is beautiful to look upon because of its lovely garnet color.

RECIPE

Roast a young pheasant (unmortified) in the usual way. Cool a little, carve as follows: Remove the legs, then the entire skin, recovering the bird. Cut the breasts into thin strips and do likewise with the legs. Line a charlotte mold with either puff paste or rich pie crust. Spread a layer of fine smooth stuffing made as indicated under FISH FORCEMEAT AND FISH STUFFING (Volume II), substituting the meat from the legs and the trimmings of the bird, adding, if necessary a little cold cooked chicken. Over this smooth stuffing, arrange a layer of pheasant strips, then a layer of cooked mushrooms, minced, then a layer (thin) of thinly sliced black truffles. Repeat until the mold is full. The top layer should be forcemeat. Over this last layer of forcemeat, sprinkle a little allspice. Adjust the cover, after brushing the rim with milk or water, pressing the edge tightly to rim. Make a small opening in center to let the steam escape. Set in a moderate oven (350°) and bake one hour. Simple, indeed, but how good. Now to serve:

Remove the mold from the oven and turn upside down over a hot platter. Lift out the bottom crust carefully, which now is the top layer, and cut it into small triangles and arrange around the loaf. Pour over the forcemeat, thus left on top, with several tablespoons of good Madeira sauce. Place in the center an extra large fresh mushroom, cooked in butter (the mushroom may be carved around if desired and for effect) and surround the mushrooms with a ring of thin slices of black truffles. No other garnishing is necessary. Serve with an extra side dish of rich Madeira wine sauce.

PHEASANT À LA KOTSCHOUBEY

Operate exactly as indicated in recipe for CASSEROLE OF PARTRIDGE À LA KOTSCHOUBEY on page 43, substituting pheasant for partridge. Cook, dress and serve as directed.

PHEASANT REGENCE

AUTHOR'S NOTE

You may or may not allow the bird to mortify, this is left to your own discretion, but it is advisable to let it mortify a little as it will add to the flavor and mellowness of the bird. There are parties, cliques, and rugged individuals who will grow violent at the mere broaching of the subject; and, such is the fanatic devotion of partisans to their respective cults that they will vow by bell and book that a pitiful burnt offering done according to formula is pure ambrosia from Olympus. Some hold that all wild pheasant, grouse and quail should be properly larded, after being left to mortify awhile, others are of the opposite opinion; some say that the same birds should be properly larded and blanketed over the breast with a thin sheet of sweet larding pork, held in place by the trussing of the fowl. And certain it is, that a bird so prepared for immolation comes to the table sizzling and bubbling with richness, trailing clouds of glory and sweet savors.

Still others claim that stuffing and spicing such birds is like gilding the lily, and nothing less bland and mild than a purée of cabbage, chestnuts, and the like, or an old-time bread sauce should ever be used. This used to be so, years ago, but today taste and appetite are quite different, and progress in cookery has demonstrated that we can mix several different ingredients, if properly done, without the least endangering the basic flavor and savor of the main ingredient, and without exaggeration, while taking into consideration the proper balancing of the meal.

RECIPE

Assuming that you choose to have your bird mortified for 4 or 5 days. Pluck it, clean it, place in the cavity a juniper berry, sew and truss, after blanketing it with a thin sheet of sweet larding pork. Cook in 3 generous tablespoons of butter, preferably, turning often to golden brown on all sides, for 35 minutes, in a casserole. Dress the bird on a hot platter on a slice of bread, fried in butter on both sides, and garnish as follows:

Four small dumplings made as indicated in recipe for PARTRIDGE DUMPLINGS on page 54, using pheasant meat instead (from an old bird preferably), 4 scallops of pâté de foie gras, the size of a teaspoon bowl, slightly heated in butter, and 4 small black truffles, cooked for 5 short minutes in Madeira wine. Serve with a side dish of Salmis sauce (*see* SAUCES).

PHEASANT SOUFFLÉ MODERNE

Pound 1 lb. of raw pheasant in a mortar (or pass twice through fine food chopper); add gradually 3 ounces of butter, 4 egg yolks, and salt and pepper to taste. Pass this mixture again through food chopper or rub through a hair sieve, adding meanwhile 2 unbeaten egg whites, one at a time. Whip 3 egg whites to a stiff froth; whip halfway 2 cups (generous) of heavy cream and stir the beaten egg whites alternately with the cream whipped halfway into the mixture. Turn mixture into a generously buttered large soufflé dish, set in a pan of hot water, and bake 40 to 45 minutes in a moderately hot oven (375°). Serve at once wth a side dish of Gloucester sauce (*see* SAUCES).

PHEASANT TITANIA

Prepare a young pheasant as for roasting. After being trussed, place in a casserole with 4 tablespoons of butter and cook slowly for 20 long minutes. Transfer the bird to an earthenware casserole, pouring the butter over it and add 1 scant cup of seedless black grapes, skinned carefully, 8 to 10 sections of seedless oranges, all the white parts and skin removed. Pour over this 2 or 3 tablespoons of Salmis sauce (*see* SAUCES) and about 3 tablespoons of pomegranate juice and pulp, kernels removed. Allow to simmer 10 short minutes to heat the fruits and mellow and serve at once in the casserole, with only a side dish of fried bread-crumb sauce.

SAUTERNES PUNCH MARQUISE

> 1 bottle of good Sauternes wine
> 2 scant cups granulated sugar
> The whole peel of a large lemon
> 3 whole cloves, heads removed
> ½ cup of good brandy
> 12 thin slices of lemon, seeded
> 12 Maraschino cherries (green or red)

Pour the Sauternes wine in a copper pan (do not use aluminum) or in an enameled pan, add the sugar, lemon zest, and cloves. Heat until the wine is brimming with a fine foam. Pour immediately into a large crystal punch bowl through a very fine sieve. Place one or two lumps of sugar in a punch ladle, pour over a little of the brandy, touch it with a match, pour over the rest of the brandy

gradually, feeding constantly, and carry into the dining
room flaming. If the lights are turned out, the spectacle
of the bluegold flame reflecting through the crystal glass
of the punch bowl is simply beautiful. Let it burn thus
until exhausted. Place a slice of lemon into each glass
cup and serve.

PHEASANT COMTE POCTOCKI

When you have an old pheasant, this recipe is an excellent way
to prepare it.

Arrange 1 quart of sauerkraut in a casserole. Do not use aluminum. Add enough meat stock, not colored, just enough to cover, or
still better, half meat stock and half goose fat; pour over this 1 cup
of good white wine. Let this simmer gently for an hour, after adding 2 juniper berries, chopped coarsely, 6 whole peppercorns, gently
bruised, and 2 whole cloves stuck into a medium-sized onion.

Meanwhile—the pheasant should be mortified for a whole week—
pluck, clean, singe, rub the inside and out with good gin, real gin,
then with salt and black pepper, coarsely ground. Sew and truss after
blanketing the bird with thin slices of larding pork. Place the bird
in a casserole with 3 tablespoons of goose fat and golden brown on
all sides for 15–20 minutes. Add the bird thus colored to the sauerkraut mixture with 1 lb. of lean fresh pork. Cover with a buttered
or greased paper, set in a moderate oven (350°) and cook for 1½
hours. Fifteen minutes before serving, drain the sauerkraut; carve
the bird, return to the casserole with the sauerkraut; sprinkle over a
wineglass of champagne (dry) and allow to simmer 10 to 15 minutes. Dress the sauerkraut on a hot platter; dress the carved pheasant
over, and the lard, sliced around. Garnish the border with slices of
carrots, which may be cooked with the sauerkraut. This dish used
to be one of the favorite game dishes of the late Emperor Francis
Joseph of Austria.

The addition of a few small juniper berries, gently bruised, to
the sauerkraut enhances the flavor.

PHEASANT À LA RUSSE
(*Pheasant, Russian Method*)

Prepare a young mortified pheasant as for roasting, after placing in the cavity 1 dozen small cranberries, previously parboiled for 10 long minutes, but not mashed. Sew. Blanket with a thin slice of fresh larding pork, then with a layer of fine forcemeat made with breast of chicken, and over this a blanket of thin slices of Virginia ham (the recipe calls for Bayonne ham). Now dress the bird in a cheesecloth, and sew carefully. Place the bird in a casserole lined with 1 cup (scant) of finely chopped fresh mushrooms and cover entirely with Smitane sauce (*see* SAUCES). Cover. Set in a moderately hot oven (350°) for 45 minutes without disturbing. Serve in the casserole.

SAUTÉED PHEASANT WITH BLINIKI
(*Russian Recipe*)

IMPORTANT. *Unless cooked slowly, and thoroughly watched, pheasant, when sautéed, is always dry. This is one of the main reasons why one should always select a young bird, cook slowly over a low fire and in plenty of butter, turning the pieces often, so that they will be always enrobed with fat.*

Cut a young pheasant, which has been marinated 4 or 5 days, as for chicken fricassee, removing the small end of the legs. Season to taste with salt and black pepper—the pheasant loves it—and sauté as you would an ordinary chicken, until the pieces are underdone, or about 20 short minutes (*Pheasant as a Rule Should Be Eaten Rather Rare, if One Wishes To Enjoy Its Full Wild Flavor. This Applies to Almost All Wild Birds*). Lift out the pieces. Keep hot. To the butter left in the skillet, add 1 pony glass of good vodka and deglaze, that is stir from the bottom of the skillet, set over a gentle fire, until all the gelatinous particles of food are removed from it. To the deglazing of the skillet, add 1 generous cup of Smitane sauce (*see* SAUCES). Return the pieces of pheasant to this sauce, stir and dress on a hot platter. Garnish with a border of Bliniki (*see* GARNISHINGS), interspersed with thin slices of oranges (raw).

SAUTÉED PHEASANT CATALANE

Operate as indicated for SAUTÉED PHEASANT WITH BLINIKI, above, as regards preparing and cooking the bird. Dress the pieces on a hot platter. Keep hot. To the butter left in the skillet, add 1 small wineglass of Valdepenas wine, which, if we are to believe the immortal author of "Don Quixote," is of a handsome body, abundant vinosity, with a slightly pleasing sour taste, similar to the French wines of the Rhône Valley and the white Jurançon. This delicious wine is produced in the magnificent vineyards which cover the whole picturesque plains of La Mancha, the site of the exploits of the witty Sancho Panza, and the illustrious Don Quixote, Knight of Sad Figure. Stir from the bottom of the skillet until all the particles of gelatinous matter adhering to it are loosened, and the wine bubbles gently; then, and only then, add ½ teaspoon of lemon juice. Pour over the pheasant pieces, garnish rapidly with small lozenges of wine jelly (*see* GARNISHINGS), interspersed with thin slices of oranges spread with sugar and slightly glazed under the broiling oven. Serve immediately.

> *Of course the usual jelly should not be omitted with any kind of pheasant preparation, as well as the traditional fried bread-crumb sauce, and (optional) the Saratoga chips.*

SPARKLING CIDER PUNCH

(*Serves 25 Easily; for Less or More Diminish or Raise Accordingly*)

½ cup water
1 cup sugar
4 tablespoons good gin

1 tablespoon (generous) rum
1 tablespoon (generous) curaçao
   Juice of a small lemon and grated rind
   Juice of 2 small oranges and grated rind of one
1 cup grapefruit juice
1 cup strong black tea
1 quart sparkling cider
   The rind of a small cucumber cut in spirals
1 cup cubed pineapple (fresh or canned)

Prepare a syrup with the water and sugar. Combine all the remaining ingredients, except the rind of cucumber and cubed pineapple, adding, however the sparkling cider at the last minute. Add sugar syrup to the combined ingredients and pour in a large punch bowl, in which a large piece of ice has been placed. Decorate with the rind of cucumber cut in spirals and the cubed pineapple. Serve.

STEWED PHEASANT BUDAPEST

2 young pheasants
1 cup chicken stock
   Salt and pepper

1 cup red wine
1½ cups (generous) brown sauce
   Slices of freshly made toast

Select 2 young pheasants and prepare as for roasting in the usual way. Cool. Cut them up into 6 pieces each: the legs, the wings, with the small end of the wing removed, the breast split in two, lengthwise. Remove the skin from the pieces. Trim neatly. Remove the bones. Pound the bones and trimmings and add to it the chicken stock and wine with a cupful of coarsely chopped vegetables (such as carrot, onion, celery, turnip), seasoning to taste with salt and pepper. Place on a hot fire and boil to half of its quantity; skim off the fat and scum and strain through a fine sieve. Divide this into two parts. Pour one half over the pheasant pieces; heat, but do not boil.

Arrange on a hot platter; pour over it the other half of the sauce. Encircle with slices of toast and serve with a side dish of fried bread crumbs, and another dish of your favorite jelly.

SCHNEIDER'S PHEASANT PIE

(*Bavarian Cuisine*)

Select a young pheasant and allow to mortify for 5 long days. Pluck, singe, clean, rub with white wine, inside and out, then with salt, pepper, and allspice mixed together, using good judgment. Cut into 6 pieces, as indicated for STEWED PHEASANT BUDAPEST, above. Lard the breast and legs with small strips of fat fresh pork. Line a deep-dish pie with slices of bacon; arrange in the bottom 1 dozen small white onions, previously parboiled 10 short minutes; place or rather arrange a layer of pheasant pieces over the onions; over this sprinkle 2 juniper berries, ground fine, then 1 dozen small fresh mushrooms, peeled, adding stems and caps. Top this with the remaining pieces of pheasant. Pour over the mixture enough Moselle wine to cover the pheasant entirely; sprinkle with mace (a tiny blade will do) and again allspice and thyme leaves. Cover the whole with generously buttered bread crumbs. Place in a moderate oven (350–375°) and bake for 35 minutes or until tender and delicately browned. If the top browns too fast, cover with a buttered paper, removing it 10 minutes before serving. The usual accompaniment of this delectable dish, which is the acme of Bavarian cuisine, is Moselle wine.

STEWED PHEASANT WITH DUMPLINGS

Select an old pheasant, and allow to mortify for at least 6 days. Then pluck, singe, clean, rub inside and out wth lemon or lime juice, then with salt only. Cut into pieces as indicated for STEWED PHEASANT BUDAPEST, page 87, and cook as directed. Meanwhile you will have prepared small dumplings as indicated for PARTRIDGE DUMPLINGS, page 54, using only chicken livers. Dress the pheasant on a hot deep platter, and surround with the dumplings. Serve with a side dish of fried bread-crumb sauce, and your favorite jelly.

SUPREMES OF PHEASANT

(*Their Meaning, Their Cooking*)

The words: "Fillets," "Breast," or "Supremes" are synonymous in poultry and game-bird cookery. They include the whole breast, which may be sliced in two according to directions, sizes—or economy. They may be stuffed or left plain. Their cooking is usually done with very little butter or whatever the shortening indicated, because the least boiling may toughen them irremediably. When the recipe calls for a Poached Fillet, Breast, or Supremes, the whole bird is usually boiled, then the breast removed according to indications.

SUPREMES OF PHEASANT BERCHOUX

(*Modernized*)

Split open, but do not separate, as many breasts of pheasant as required, and lifted in their raw state from slightly mortified pheasant (3 to 4 days). Spread all over with a stuffing made of the trimmings, the liver, and equal amount of the two together of fried bread crumbs, also 1 scant tablespoon of chopped black truffles. Fold the breast. Secure with toothpick, and arrange in a heavy skillet which contains 1 tablespoon of butter for each breast and ¼ scant cup of good chicken broth. Cover with a buttered paper and allow to simmer very, oh, very gently for 15 short minutes, turning once during the cooking process.

Just a few minutes before serving, sprinkle the breast or breasts each with a sprinkling of good brandy, a few drops of lemon juice. Serve aside with Demiglacé sauce (*see* SAUCES). This recipe has been modernized and the author has omitted the garnishing, which is too elaborate. However, the garnishing may consist of crusts of puff paste filled with a stuffing made with the legs and equal parts of minced mushrooms, but this, too, may be omitted if desired.

SUPREMES OF PHEASANT WITH
DIVERS SAUCES

If desired, one may prepare breast of pheasant according to directions indicated for SUPREMES OF PHEASANT BERCHOUX, page 89, or one may omit spreading with the stuffing. One may then poach the breast in a little butter for 5 short minutes, then dip into a Villeroy sauce (*see* SAUCES), to which has been added a scant teaspoon of "Fumet" (*see* recipe, How To PREPARE GAME STOCK, page 45), then in fresh bread crumbs, when the sauce is cold, then color (golden brown lightly) in butter, heated in a skillet, and over a gentle fire, and serve with a side dish of either one of the favorite sauces found in the Index. This is mentioned to prevent tedious repetition.

AUTHENTIC HISTORIC MENU

The following menu was given at Gomberveaux, near Vaucouleurs, birthplace of Joan of Arc, in 1367, in the castle of Sire Guerard de Gomberveaux, at the sealing of an alliance between Charles V, King of France, and Jean, Duc de Lorraine, for the purpose of repressing the numerous acts of banditry and ferocity, as well as depredations, perpetrated by bandits and adventurers who desecrated, at that epoch, the duchies of Lorraine and Champagne provinces, in France.

The following menu was prepared by the famous author and Esquire of Cuisine, Guillaume Tirel, alias Taillevent, who was the Chef of the King. Here a word is necessary to introduce this legendary Cook Guillaume Tirel, better known under the name or alias Taillevent. He learned cookery in the cuisine of Queen Jeanne of Évreux (Orleans dynasty); later he is found as Head of the Kitchen of Philippe de Valois, then of Monsignor the Dauphin de Vienne, then of the Duc of Normandy. In 1373, he was appointed First Cook of Charles V of France. It is then that he began the writing of his voluminous cook book "Le Vivandier" (Canteen-man).

Charles VI, successor to Charles V of France, made him his First Esquire of Cuisine and, in 1392, Master of the Cuisines of the Garrisons of the Kingdom of France. He died around 1395, and was buried near Saint-Germain-en-Laye, a well-known suburb of Paris, always visited by Americans when traveling in France, at the Convent of Notre Dame d'Hennebont, where he had founded a chapel. His tomb, richly sculptured, is an object of intense interest to visitors today. He is pictured in stone, dressed as "Homme d'Armes" with his two wives, Jeanne Bonnard and Isabeau le Chandelier; on the shield which he holds, three kettles are represented, surrounded with roses.

Legend says, according to the historian Froissart, that it was Taillevent who was delegated to carry to the King of England a challenge to arms from the King of France, Charles V, the Sage, who was fortunate in finding a very able captain—Bertrand du Guesclin, a valiant Breton knight who never shunned battle when it promised advantage, but who understood clearly the folly of trying to ride down the English archers by serried lines of horsemen. "Never was there a king of France who fought less," spoke Edward III of England, angrily, "and yet never one that gave me so much trouble." The Black Prince sickened and returned to England to die (1376). By 1380 the islanders held only the coast towns of Calais, Cherbourg, and Brest in the north, and Bordeaux and Bayonne in the south. The first great English attack on France was over. Charles the Sage of France died at the age of only 43. His passing was a national calamity.

All Taillevent's manuscripts are today at the Vatican Bibliothèque and have been published through the interest of Baron Pichon and the famous food historian and gastronome George Vicaire. Here is this historical menu:

FIRST COURSE
{
Potage of Head of Wild Boar, Venison Savory
of Spring Chicken
Roasted Hare in Spit, Coulis Sauce Wild Geese
Pâté
}

SECOND COURSE { Swan, Heron, Pheasant, and Peacock Roasted
Trimolectes of Partridges

THIRD COURSE {
Most Jehan of Capon
(The capons are first roasted, then simmered in
thin cream perfumed with aromatic herbs)
Blackbird Loaf in Crust
Roast Squabs

FOURTH COURSE {
Darioles de Crème Frites
(Almonds chopped fine and mixed with a thick
cream batter, then fried)
Pastes de Poyres
(Baked stuffed pears covered with custard
flavored with saffron)

FIFTH COURSE {
Almonds, Hazelnuts, Fresh Pears
Jonchée
(Highly seasoned cream cheese strewn with
candied and fresh flowers)

Assorted Wines—Liqueur of the Visitandine Nuns—Candied An-
gelica—Orange-Flower Cake from the Sisters of Château Thierry—
Walnuts preserved in sugar from the Ursuline Nunnery of Belley,
etc., and, to finish, the usual hippocras highly spiced with cinnamon,
clove, and numerous other spices. This kind of wine punch was
usually served after each meal, at feasts and banquets, until 1789.

The French poet, Edmond Richardin, using valuable and authen-
tic documents preserved at the Bibliothèque of Nancy, France, has
described this magnificent and Gargantuan feast of the Middle Ages
in a lengthy and beautiful poem; a brief sketch of it runs as follows:

The royal retinue ascended the hillsides by the flowery lane lead-
ing to the castle of Gomberveaux, traveling through the thickly
shaded forests to arrive finally at the drawbridge of the feudal castle.
The lookout man from the drawbridge proclaimed the return of the
royal hunt.

Surrounded by countless and active valets and handsome troubadours, heroes of all the court functions, and always invited to the feasts of the lords, the Dame de Gomberveaux, dressed in a magnificent golden robe, her hair dressed in hennin, greets the royal visitor.

Into the large dining room of gothic splendor, moves forward Charles the Fifth, called *le Sage* (the Wise) and Jean de Vaucouleurs, followed by the Duc of Bar, Robert and the Duchesse Marie, wearing a golden shawl embroidered with lilies of the valley, Du Guesclin and Clisson, the Baillif of Chaumont, the Sir Jehan de Longe, the Chevalier de Ville, and Guillot de Hamel, etc. Hundreds of pages, of heralds, and many a minstrel, dressed in gorgeous tunics.

The somber walls of the large dining room were spread with Aragon leather, booty of long combats, brought from beyond the mounts; helmets and shields hang on the portico, telltales of heroic deeds, animating with strong glimmers the fresco of the arches.

Flowers, golden fruits, bundles of gladioli, mingle on the royal table with branches of the linden tree. Handsome pages followed by diligent valets pour the hippocras into silver goblets, while the numerous Maître Queux (chefs) carve whole wild boar and deer, and others serve herons, swans, pheasants, and wood pigeons, preceded by trouvères, dressed in velvet doublet, who harmonize their songs with the lute, oboes and bass-trombone players.

The feast is in full swing; peasants, common people, frolic freely under the paddocks, the echo of their joyous clamors resounding through the night in the valley.

.   .   .   .   .

It is all over! The lords go down the slope of the flowery lane of Gomberveaux, riding their palfreys through the sinuous valley in the luminous twilight of the day.

AUTHOR'S NOTE

One should not believe that the use of the swan is a sign of ignorance or alimentary heedlessness of our forefathers. The flesh of a young swan, and especially the wild one, is much more tender and highly delicious than that of many other palmmipeds, including the young wild ducks.

Mention of succulent and nutritious dishes, such as pie, roasts, patties, and so forth, is often encountered in stories of feasts and banquets in the Middle Ages. Even today young swans are eaten on a large scale in the North of Holland and the Ost-Frize, where many a fine and delectable dish is made in the fashion of the famous Pâté d'Amiens, that is, encased in a piecrust made of rye flour, profusely mixed with melted lard. This is a kind of pastry which does not date from yesterday, but it is found in many manuscripts dating back from the fourteenth and fifteenth centuries, some of which are easily accessible at the Royal Bibliothèque of Amsterdam, the Bibliothèque Royale of Antwerp, the Bibliothèque Nationale of Paris and also at the Vatican Bibliothèque.

Of course, this does not mean that we should destroy our domestic swans, far from it. As to these, there are, unfortunately, not enough of them to adorn our parks and private mansions, but it is recommended to sportsmen and hunters who, during a severe winter, are lucky enough to bring down a young wild swan not to give it to their dogs, but save it for their own table; by doing this, they will afford themselves a fine dish and also follow the sage advice of Palmerin des Gaules and that of the Comte de Foix, given in their famous treatise of "Chasse & Nutrition Giboyeuse" (Manuscript No. 7097, Bibliothèque Nationale, Paris, France).

PRAIRIE HEN

The different methods of preparation of the quail and even the partridge may be adapted to the prairie hen, as in fact to any kind of wild hen. However, they are at their apogee when prepared in the roasted method. Wild hens are always eaten in their fresh state and seldom mortified. Without any exception, when wild hens are prepared in stew forms or even in salmis forms, the skin should be always removed.

QUAIL

Quail are always prepared in their fresh state; however, they may be left to stale for a couple of days, but seldom more than 3 days, when they may reach the mortification state, which does not belong to these fragile birds. Only partridges, pheasant, and woodcock as well as snipe among the game birds are allowed to mortify.

Quail should be plump, with a white and firm fat. Roasted, they are delicious, especially when the spit method is used, which unfortunately is impossible today, the oven having supplanted the spit. However, quail may be prepared, besides the following methods of preparation, in all the different methods adapted to the partridge, prairie hen and all the wild hens.

The quail seems to have an affinity for veal, especially veal stock, so it is advisable always to have some on hand when preparing quail.

When roasting quail, it is absolutely "de rigueur" to surround first the bird, cleaned, singed, then trussed with a vine leaf, then with a thin slice of fat larding fresh pork. The leg extremities are always removed, as well as the neck.

As for almost all kinds of game birds, bread sauce and a kind of jelly should be served as a side dish, even if there is already another sauce indicated.

BAKED QUAIL
(Methode Normande)

Cut in two, lengthwise, 6 large apples, scoop the inside, being careful not to break the skin or peel. Clean 6 quail (killed at least 48 hours before) and truss, after introducing into the cavity of each quail, the size of a large walnut of butter. Place the quail in a casserole containing 3 generous tablespoons of melted butter and color, that is cook until lightly browned on both sides, for 5 long minutes, over a medium flame. Place one quail into each scooped apple. Sprinkle each quail with half teaspoon of good eau de vie (cider spirit, similar to applejack). Adjust the other parts of apple, also scooped on top. Envelop each apple thus stuffed with a quail with rich piecrust, operating exactly as if making a turnover or apple dumpling. Arrange the apples thus enveloped onto a buttered baking sheet; brush each apple with beaten egg yolk, milk, cream, or milk and egg yolk and bake 30 short minutes in a hot oven (400°), brushing occasionally with butter to prevent burning. Serve dressed on a hot platter. Garnish (optional) with a bunch of watercress. Serve at once.

BRAISED QUAIL
(*Methode Normande*)

Clean, wipe with a damp cloth and truss as many quail as required. Color each bird in butter, that is lightly golden brown in heated butter over a medium fire. Meanwhile sauté slightly 3 small crab apples, pared, cored, and minced. The bird is then colored to the desired point. Arrange a layer of apples in the bottom of a baking dish, having a cover fitting tightly. Place the quail over this delicious bed, and cover with the remaining sautéed apples. Sprinkle over 2 or 3 tablespoons of fresh cream, season to taste with salt and white pepper, and set in a moderately hot oven (350–375°) for 25 to 30 minutes to complete the cooking process. Serve as is without any sauce or garnishing, and from the baking dish, which by the way should be of earthenware.

> *Like almost all the game birds, quail should*
> *be cooked rather rare if one wants to enjoy*
> *the full gamy flavor of the bird.*

BRAISED QUAIL À LA STANISLAS

The following recipe used to be one of the favorites of King Stanislas of Poland, Duc of Lorraine, and has been discovered in the Library of Montbéliard, France, by the author, during his research work for the preparation of this book.

You may prepare as many quail as required, but the following is for one person.

Bone a plump quail from the back, leaving the legs and feet on. Spread the inside with a little of your favorite forcemeat (*see* FORCE-MEAT AND STUFFING, Vol. II), and in the center of the breast, 1 scant walnut size of raw goose liver, and a thin blade of truffle, the whole highly seasoned with salt, allspice, coarse pepper to taste, and a few drops of good Madeira wine. Close the bird and place breast downward on a piece of thin, rich piecrust (puff paste would be better), of the exact size to envelop the bird, as for an apple dumpling; dampen edge with water and press edges firmly together. Prick with the tines of a fork to allow the steam to escape. Butter a piece of unglazed white paper and surround the crust to prevent a too fast cooking of the dough. Place on a buttered baking sheet and bake 30 minutes in a hot oven (400°). Serve without any accompaniment or garnishing.

BERMUDA PLANTER'S PUNCH

1 oz. lemon juice	2 oz. Barbados rum
1½ oz. Falernum	1 dash Angostura bitters

Shake well after combining all the above ingredients and pour into a tall glass, filled with cracked ice. Top off with seltzer and stir well. Garnish with a slice of orange and one cherry. (Serves one.)

BRAISED QUAIL WITH QUINCES

Two days in advance, place as many quail as required, previously cleaned from the back, singed, then trussed, in an earthenware casserole having a tight-fitting cover, with, for each quail, ½ teaspoon (scant) of brandy and 3 or 4 peelings of quinces, well yellowed and ripened. When ready to cook, remove the peeling, and for each bird 1 teaspoon of sweet butter, season to taste with salt and pepper, close the casserole hermetically and braise in a very hot oven (450°) for

20 short minutes. Serve in the casserole, with a side dish of quince jelly, and a side dish of fried bread-crumb sauce.

BRAISED QUAIL GOURMET
(*Also Called "Quail in Bird's Nest"*)

Prepare a dozen quail (or less according to number of birds required) as for roasting, trussing and sewing after filling the cavity of each bird with the size of a small walnut of pâté de foie gras, mixed with half its size of black truffles, chopped fine. Line a casserole, having a tight-fitting cover, with thin strips of bacon, using 2 for each bird. Arrange the birds over this lining, add a bouquet garni (6 sprigs parsley tied with 1 large bay leaf and a sprig of thyme), ½ cup of good veal stock, and ¼ cup of good Madeira wine, seasoning to taste with salt, black pepper, and a pinch of allspice. Adjust the cover tightly and set in a hot oven (400°) for 20 long minutes. Meanwhile, you will have prepared as many artichokes of the same size. Cut in two, lengthwise, remove the choke carefully. Form into nest. Line the bottom with a thin layer of chicken forcemeat, or, still better, with a quail or two sacrificed for the purpose, which, as you will see, is worthwhile. Arrange the artichoke thus prepared in the bottom of another casserole, lined with strips of bacon, or ham; pour over ½ generous cup of veal stock, seasoned to taste with salt and pepper; adjust the cover hermetically and braise in a hot oven (400°) for 15 long minutes. Lift out the artichoke nest. Place one quail in each nest, pour over a little melted "Fumet" (*see* recipe, How To PREPARE GAME STOCK, page 45) and serve at once on a hot platter, simply garnished with a crisp young watercress dipped in paprika and well shaken, and as many slices of lemon as there are of quail.

BRAISED QUAIL ARCHIDUC RODOLPHE

Allow the bird to stale for 48 hours after being shot; then pluck, singe, clean, rub the inside with a few drops of fine champagne then rub with salt and pepper. Place a small black truffle, cooked 5 minutes in Madeira wine, inside the cavity, sew and truss. Cook the bird in an earthenware casserole, with 1 tablespoon (scant) of butter, and the size of a small pea of anchovy paste, cover and set in a hot oven (400°) for 20 long minutes. Remove the casserole from the oven, place the bird on a platter and keep hot while deglazing the bottom of the casserole with a small wineglass of Sauternes wine, stirring from the bottom of the casserole to loosen the gelatinous particles which may adhere, the casserole placed over a hot fire, stirring occasionally until the wine has been reduced to half volume. Then add a scant half teaspoon of "Fumet" (*see* recipe, How To Prepare Game Stock, page 45), stir, add the quail liver, let stand a short minute, lift it out and spread over a piece of freshly made toast, pour over the liver on the toast part of the sauce, dress the bird over it and pour the remainder of the sauce over the bird. Serve with a garnishing of 1 small stuffed pimento and a candied pear made as indicated under Garnishings.

BRANDIED QUAIL

Clean as many quail as desired, singe, rub the inside and out with olive oil, then with salt and black pepper. Place in the cavity of each bird a small truffle, cooked in fine champagne 5 short minutes, sew and truss. Place the bird in a casserole with ½ teaspoon of sweet butter and ½ teaspoon of olive oil. Cover hermetically and set in a hot oven for 20 short minutes. Lift out the bird. Keep hot. Remove the excess of fat and place the casserole over a low flame. Fill a tablespoon with good brandy, touch with a match and pour over the remaining butter in the casserole, allowing to burn out; then stir from the bottom of the casserole to loosen all the gelatinous particles which may adhere to the dish; then pour ½ cup of good Madeira wine over, bring to a rapid boil, place the bird in the sauce. Cover and set aside to mellow for a few minutes. Now dress the bird over a piece of toast, spread with the quail liver, cooked 2 short minutes in the sauce with the bird. Dress the bird over, pour the sauce all over, and serve at once, garnished with fried hominy, and serve also a side dish of currant jelly, and a side dish of fried bread-crumb sauce.

BROILED QUAIL BOURGEOISE

Clean, singe 6 plump quail. Split from the back, but do not separate. Marinate in 2 scant cups of olive oil, to which is added: 1 large bay leaf (crumbled), 2 whole cloves, 1 tiny pinch of thyme leaves, 1 tablespoon of parsley (minced), 1 clove of garlic (minced), 1 teaspoon allspice, 12 whole peppercorns (crushed), 1 teaspoon salt, and 3 tablespoons of lemon juice, for at least 3 hours, turning occasionally. Lift out dripping, cover each bird with a strip of fat larding pork, and broil very slowly, as slowly as possible, for 15 short minutes. Now, remove from the broiler, roll the birds into freshly made bread crumbs and return to the broiler and continue broiling, turning often, for 20 minutes, that is, altogether 35 long minutes, basting often with a little of the marinade, using solid and liquid ingredients. Dress each quail over a piece of toast, spread lightly with a film of anchovy paste. Garnish with watercress and quartered lemon. Serve with a side dish of Hussarde sauce (*see* SAUCES).

BROILED QUAIL HUNTER STYLE I

Clean as many quail as required, split from the back, rub with brandy on both sides (the birds should not be separated), then with salt and coarse black pepper; then spread the inside of each bird with a smooth stuffing made from the flesh of two extra birds (raw), thoroughly boned, the meat put through a food chopper, with 3 tablespoons of ground bacon, salt and pepper and allspice to taste, and moistened with enough heavy cream to make a smooth spread; then close the bird to its natural shape. Now surround the birds with a vine leaf, and over this a thin blanket of fat larding pork. Secure with string, and over this place 1 sheet of buttered paper (the paper should be heavy, or else use two also buttered, placing them one over another). Tie with string.

You will have previously prepared a camp fire, collecting enough embers and ashes entirely to cover the birds, having on top about 5 inches of embers and ashes. Allow to stand thus for 35 long minutes, renewing the embers and ashes from time to time. To serve: remove the paper, which, of course, is maculated, the two sheets if two have been used, and serve as is, leaving on the other envelopes. A very fine dish to be prepared right on the field.

BROILED QUAIL HUNTER STYLE II

This second method is more elaborate, but the labor brought to its preparation is amply repaid.

The birds should be plump, or else do not start the work. Pluck, clean, and singe 6 quail. Split from the back, separating the bird entirely. Make a stuffing with their livers, equal weight of grated fresh lean pork, 1 tablespoon of parsley (minced), 1 tablespoon of chives (minced), 3 large fresh mushrooms (minced fine, after peeling, using caps and stems), 1 large bay leaf (chopped very fine), 3 shallots (minced fine), salt and coarsely ground black pepper to taste. Mix this thoroughly to a smooth paste and spread thickly on one side of the bird. Top this with the entrails (optional). Envelop first with a vine leaf, then with a blanket of fat larding pork, and still again with two sheets of buttered paper, one above the other and secure solidly with string. Cook as indicated for Broiled Quail Hunter Style I, page 100. Meanwhile line a camping kettle with 6 thin slices of raw ham; cover the ham with thin slices of raw lean veal, and on top of the veal place a lining of thin slices of fat larding pork. Pour over this enough veal stock to cover. Cook over an open fire, hanging to a spit or direct over bright embers for 30 minutes. Remove the slices of larding pork carefully, add to the liquid a generous cup of white wine and bring this to a boil; then let reduce to half, or until of the consistency of an ordinary thick sauce. Remove the excess of fat with a ladle, correct the seasoning with salt and pepper if necessary. Strain over the quail which have been disrobed of their different blankets. Squeeze a lemon over the whole. Serve at once.

CASSEROLE OF QUAIL PRINCE OF WALES

Prepare 6 plump quail as for roasting, that is clean, rub the inside and out with brandy, place in the cavity their own liver with 2 blades of black truffles. Sew and truss. Do not roast, but pan roast in plenty of butter, in an earthenware casserole, turning the birds frequently so as to color on all sides, for 20 short minutes. Sprinkle over the birds 4 or 5 juniper berries, finely ground. Turn the bird so as to impregnate them with the flavor of the berries, mingled with the butter, which in turn has been impregnated with the flavor of the bird. Lift out and dress the birds on a small tartlet made from puff paste, the bottom of which is lined with a thin layer of pâté de foie gras mixed with finely chopped truffles. To the butter in the casserole, add 1 generous wineglass of champagne, and 1 tablespoon of "Fumet" (*see* recipe, How To PREPARE GAME STOCK, page 45) and stir from the bottom of the casserole, placed over a hot fire until the mixture foams and is reduced to nearly nothing; then add 2 cups of Port wine sauce (*see* SAUCES). Heat to the boiling point. Return the birds to the sauce, turning them in to enrobe them with it. Arrange a bird anew into each puff-paste tartlet. Pour a tablespoon or two over the birds, and serve the remainder aside, with the traditional fried bread-crumb sauce and quince jelly.

CASSEROLE OF QUAIL WITH CHERRIES

Prepare 6 plump quail as for roasting, without any blanket of larding pork, simply trussed after cleaning. Pan roast in plenty of butter in an earthenware casserole, for 25 minutes. Lift out and keep hot. To the butter remaining in the casserole, add 1 generous teaspoon of brandy and 3 tablespoons of good port wine, and stir from the bottom of the casserole until the mixture boils once. Then add 1 tablespoon of grated orange rind, 5 tablespoons of good veal stock,

2 tablespoons of currant jelly, 5 dozen English cherries (sour), stoned, and cooked in a light syrup, then cooled and thoroughly drained before being added. Return the quail to this fine sauce. Cover and heat to the boiling point. Serve in the casserole. In case the sauce is too sweet, you may add a few drops of lemon juice before serving and after tasting. Serve with a side dish of bread sauce and no jelly.

SWEDISH GLUG

(A Fine Punch)

- 1 bottle of red Bordeaux wine
- 2 cups of good brandy
- 8 whole cloves, heads removed
- 4 cardamon seeds (slightly bruised but not enough to allow seeds to come out)
- 1 two-inch stick cinnamon
- 1 cup of seedless raisins previously plumped in hot water and well drained
- ½ scant lb. sugar (more or less according to taste)
- A dozen blanched whole almonds

Place all the above ingredients into an enameled saucepan, except the sugar, and bring slowly to a boil; then lower the flame as low as possible and touch the mixture with a match, sprinkling immediately with a scant teaspoon of sugar, stirring occasionally with a long ladle, and let this burn for a short minute (longer if you desire the mixture strong). Extinguish by placing a cover over the saucepan. Remove from the fire. Serve hot in cup glasses with a few raisins and at least one almond in each.

CASSEROLE OF QUAIL GRAND MÈRE

After cleaning and rubbing 6 plump quail with lemon juice, rub with salt, pepper, allspice, mace to taste, mixed together. Fill the cavity of each bird with 1 tablespoon (scant) of sweet butter, mixed with equal parts of minced parsley, chives, shallot, tarragon herbs, the whole thoroughly blended (you may add a little truffles also finely chopped). Sew and truss. Place in a large casserole in which has been heated 6 tablespoons of butter, and add 1 small clove of garlic (minced), ½ lb. fresh mushrooms (peeled), caps whole and stems sliced, 1 dozen small white onions (very small), peeled and raw, salt and pepper to taste, 1 bay leaf tied with 6 sprigs of parsley. Cover and allow to simmer very gently for 25 long minutes. Then lift up the cover and add 1 tablespoon of kneaded butter, and 1 pony glass of good Madeira wine. Cover and continue to simmer for 10 long minutes. Serve in the casserole without any other accompaniment but freshly made toast on which the birds will be served.

CREAMED QUAIL À LA NORMANDE

Clean, singe, and rub inside and out, 6 quail with lemon juice, then with salt (you may rub with Calvados instead of lemon juice if desired) and pepper to taste. Truss. Pan roast 15 minutes in an earthenware casserole, in which has been melted and heated 6 tablespoons of butter. Meanwhile pare, core, and slice, as for apple pie, 6 medium-sized tart apples, and cook in 2 tablespoons of butter for 2 short minutes. Arrange a layer of apples in the bottom of an earthenware casserole. Over the apples, arrange the quail, then add the remainder of apples. Pour over 1 generous cup of rich fresh cream. Season to taste with salt and white pepper. Adjust the cover hermetically, and place the casserole in a hot oven (400°) for 20 long minutes. Serve in the casserole without any kind of accompaniment, but freshly made toast on which the birds will be served.

ENGLISH JUGGED QUAIL

Clean 6 plump quail, singe, rub with a damp cloth, then with lemon juice and again with a mixture made of salt, pepper, allspice to taste, and stuff with a forcemeat of bread crumbs, chopped fat pork, the yolks of two hard-cooked eggs, rubbed to powder, and a tablespoon of minced celery boiled tender, a little onion juice to taste, and pepper and salt, using good judgment. Sew and truss. Tie the wings and legs close to the bodies and pack in an agate-iron pail with a close-fitting top. Plunge this into boiling water, deep enough to cover almost to the top. Placing a weight on the top to prevent the pail from turning over during the boiling process, and cook for 2½ hours. Dress the birds on a hot platter, over a piece of toast. Serve with a side dish of orange-mint sauce, another side dish of bread-crumb sauce and an extra one of red currant jelly.

PANNED QUAIL

(Greek Method)

Clean 6 plump quail, singe and rub with lemon juice, then with salt and black pepper. Sew and truss. Cook in plenty of butter in an earthenware casserole over a gentle fire, turning the bird often to brown on all sides. Meanwhile you will have prepared a cup of Rice Greek Style as follows:

RICE GREEK STYLE

Melt 2 scant tablespoons of butter and in it cook 2 tablespoons of onions, finely minced, for 1 long minute. Do not brown. To this, add 1 cup of glazed rice, unwashed, that is, leaving all the starch on it, and cook, stirring constantly, until the rice takes on a milky color; then pour over gradually, while stirring gently and constantly, 3 cups of veal stock. Cover tightly and set in a moderate oven (325°) for 20 long minutes, without stirring or disturbing. Remove from the oven and transfer the rice to another casserole or pan, adding then 2 tablespoons of butter divided into small bits, and placed here and there. Then add carefully, stirring very gently so as not to break the grains, 2 generous tablespoons of pork sausage meat, loosened, and cooked with 2 or 3 tablespoons of finely shredded green lettuce, add also 3 generous tablespoons of cooked peas (peas cooked with shredded lettuce), and 1 generous tablespoon of pimentos, chopped finely.

Arrange this rice over a hot platter, making 6 little nests into which place a small braised lettuce, and on top of each braised lettuce a bird. (The original recipe calls for a stew of kidneys of rooster, but the author has eliminated this and substituted or rather left the original sauce.) Pour over the bird, 2 tablespoons of Demiglacé sauce, to which has been added a teaspoon of "Fumet" (*see* recipe, How To Prepare Game Stock, page 45, and Sauces for Demiglacé sauce).

POACHED QUAIL FIGARO

Introduce a small piece of truffle into the cavity of each quail, previously cleaned, singed, and rubbed with lemon juice, then with salt and pepper. Place each quail in a piece of pork gut and before tying, add the size of a small walnut of "Fumet" (*see* recipe, How To Prepare Game Stock, page 45), leaving about 2 inches at each end to prevent bursting of the gut, which naturally shrinks during the cooking process. Boil the quail thus prepared in good veal stock. Drain. Serve as is with one of your favorite sauces, besides the traditional bread-crumb sauce, and the currant jelly.

QUAIL AU GRATIN

Take 6 quail. Clean and singe. Place in a casserole containing 5 generous tablespoons of butter, heated, and add 6 sprigs of parsley tied with 1 large bay leaf, ½ small clove of garlic, 2 cloves, a small pinch thyme leaves, and one of basilic (dried), ½ lb. fresh mushrooms, peeled, stems removed and sliced, caps cut in two or three pieces. Sprinkle over this, 1 tablespoon of flour, season to taste with salt and black pepper, and pour over enough chicken broth barely to cover to half. Cook slowly over a gentle fire for 15 minutes, then add 1 sweetbread, blanched, then cubed small. Continue cooking 20 minutes longer or until the sauce is reduced to half and is of the consistency of a thin cream sauce. Remove from the fire. Then remove the excess of fat. Transfer then the contents of the casserole to an earthenware dish, rather shallow and cover with the following:

Mince the quail livers very fine (if you have 2 or 3 extra livers so much the better, if not add 2 or 3 chicken livers), add 1 scant teaspoon of parsley (minced), 1 scant teaspoon of chives (minced), and 1 generous cup of freshly made bread crumbs, 1 generous tablespoon of butter, 3 egg yolks, salt and coarsely ground black pepper to taste. Mix thoroughly to a paste. Spread this stuffing over the mixture in the earthenware casserole, and brown slowly under the flame of the broiling oven.

You may spread this stuffing over the platter on which the quail will be served, brown carefully and slowly and serve the quail over if desired.

QUAIL AU LAURIER

(Quail in Bay Leaves)

Clean, singe 6 quail, remove the livers and mince them with 1 scant teaspoon each of parsley, chives, and shallot, minced fine. Season to taste with salt and coarsely ground black pepper, and add 2 generous tablespoons of butter. Mix thoroughly and fill the cavity of each bird with part of this stuffing. Sew and truss. Roast in a moderate oven (350°) for 25 long minutes, basting often with melted butter. (It is advisable to envelop the birds thus trussed, in a buttered paper, secured with string, to prevent the flavor from escaping, before setting the birds in the oven, but this is optional.) Meanwhile boil 4 to 5 bay leaves (small) in ¼ cup of chicken broth for 6 or 7 minutes. Strain this and use it with rich veal stock to make a cream sauce, rather thick. Dress the birds on a hot platter, and pour over the sauce, which will give a delicate flavor, remembering the flavor of the sage grouse. Garnish the border of the platter with small triangles of bread fried in butter, interspersed with thin slices of lemon.

HOT WINE PUNCH À LA FRANÇAISE

3 bottles of good red wine
⅓ ounce stick cinnamon

2 or 3 leaves (no powder) of mace
6 small bay leaves
1 pound sugar
Peel (thin) of 2 lemons

Boil the wine in an enameled pot with the sugar, and when sugar is melted, add all the other ingredients. Boil once more. Remove from the fire and light it with a burning paper. Let it burn for 3 long minutes, strain, and serve in glasses.

QUAIL À LA TURQUE
(*Turkish Method*)

First prepare a RICE PILAW, proceeding as indicated in recipe for PANNED QUAIL GREEK METHOD, page 105, and cooking the rice as indicated, but substituting ¼ of its weight of cooked eggplant, chopped fine (after having added the butter bit by bit), for pork sausage meat, cooked shredded green lettuce, peas, and pimentos. Dress the rice thus prepared on a hot platter, pyramid-like, and surround with 6 quail, cooked in butter over a gentle fire for 25 long minutes, turning often to brown on all sides. Surround the quails with a thin layer of Salmis sauce (*see* SAUCES) to which has been added a generous teaspoon of "Fumet" (*see* recipe, How To PREPARE GAME STOCK, page 45).

RISOTTO OF QUAIL
(*Or Quail on Gilded Rice*)

First prepare a risotto as follows: Wash 1 cup of rice in several waters, rubbing the grains between the hands as the Chinese do, then drain it in a colander. In an *iron skillet*, put 4 tablespoons of olive oil, if you have been initiated—otherwise use butter; and when it is hot, put in the well-drained rice. *Do Not Fry It,* but let it heat up slowly, and stir it lightly, but constantly, with a wooden spoon.

Presently the snow-white rice will begin to show a yellow tinge, and as it absorbs the oil (or butter), you must add more to keep it moist, lest it fry and harden. Little by little, the grains take on a peculiar gloss, they begin to glisten like jewels, and you are startled at the sight. Don't let them scorch, but stir them about until *each grain* is a separate gilded oval, the color of ripe field corn. Then it is time to set about the completion of the risotto (meaning gilded rice, in Italian). You will have prepared, previously, 2 cups of rich soup stock (game stock if possible) in which is steeped a chapon (piece) of dry bread rubbed with garlic, and you will add to the well-strained stock, 1 tablespoon of minced onion, well browned in 1 tablespoon of oil or butter. Pour the heated stock slowly upon the rice and it will drink it thirstily. You will be amazed to see how swiftly the liquid is absorbed. Keep pouring till the dish is well moistened, and the grains covered by the stock. Then season with salt and pepper to taste. You may add a generous tablespoon of tomato paste to the stock before pouring it in, if desired. This will add zest. This is done in some parts of Piedmont, Italy, where this delicious recipe was created, hence its name. Add now a generous ¼ cup grated Parmesan cheese and stir, also a small pinch of sweet basil, dry or fresh. The Spanish use saffron, pinch by pinch, but with respectful care. Lastly transfer the risotto to a shallow mold, copiously oiled, or buttered, and put the ring mold in a moderate oven for ½ short hour or until the rice is soft, but still firm, with the grains separate and distinct, although not too liquid, so as to allow it to keep in shape when unmolding on a very hot round platter.

Meanwhile clean 6 plump quail, singe, rub inside and out with good brandy. Fill the cavity of each bird with a small piece of bacon and the liver of the bird. Sew and truss. Cook in a casserole in which 4 or 5 tablespoons of olive oil, or butter, have been heated for 30 minutes, turning the birds often to brown on all sides. Unmold the risotto over a very hot round platter, dress the birds over neatly and pour the butter from the casserole over them, leaving about 2 tablespoons in the casserole, to which add ½ scant cup of meat stock, and stirring from the bottom of the casserole to deglaze. Finally, add 1 generous teaspoon of "Fumet" (*see* recipe, How To Prepare Game Stock, page 45), heat well and pour over the birds. Serve at once without any other kind of accompaniment or garnishing.

QUAIL À LA NOËL

(Recipe from the Hotel Gleneagles, Perthshire, Scotland)

Clean as many quail as required, singe, using the flame of burning brandy, split open from the back, but do not separate entirely, flatten, fry in plenty of sweet butter, over a very gentle fire for 15 long minutes. Let cool. Coat with smooth forcemeat to which has been added a little chopped black truffles (coating the inside only). Reshape and secure with string, and place in a moderate oven (325°), barely covered with port-wine sauce. Allow to *"Poach"* (as you would an egg) for 10 short minutes, turning the birds once during the cooking process. Dress on a hot platter, over a piece of toast, buttered, then spread with the liver of the birds, previously mashed with a few drops of brandy, salt, pepper, and a few drops of onion juice uncooked (the heat of the bird will cook the mixture sufficiently). Pour over the sauce. Garnish with Scotch Potato Buns made as follows:

Scotch Potato Buns (this should be prepared previously)

½ cup mashed potatoes	1 whole egg, unseparated, and
½ cup milk, scalded	well beaten
1 cake compressed yeast	2 tablespoons sugar
¼ cup lukewarm water	1 scant teaspoon salt
4 cups sifted flour (about)	3 tablespoons melted butter

Combine potatoes and scalded milk. Cool to lukewarm. Soften yeast cake in water and add to potatoes. Add enough flour to make a batter, beating well. Cover and let rise in a warm place until light. Add the well-beaten whole egg, sugar, salt, melted butter, and remaining flour to make a soft dough. Knead lightly and gently until smooth. Place in a well-greased mixing bowl, cover with a clean towel, and let rise again until double in bulk. Roll out on lightly floured board ½ inch thick. Cut with small floured, biscuit cutter. Place on greased baking sheet. Let rise again until double in bulk. Bake in a hot oven (400°) for 15 long minutes (more or less according to size of biscuits) or until done. This will make about 1½ dozen potato buns. You may brush them with melted butter, or with egg yolk, beaten with 1 teaspoon of milk, if desired, just before putting in the oven to bake.

BZURAT

(Indian Beverage)

Dry seeds of pumpkin, grind them fine—
One cup to glass of water; then consign
The mixture to a bag of linen; strain,
Then add the sugar, make the drink divine!

The orange blossom and the rose—these twain,
In liquid essence, add; then entertain
Your bachelor friend; and if he will not drink—
Why, let him go and drown him—in Champagne!

Mrs. A. Ayres

SALMIS OF QUAIL

(Southern Method) (Serves Two)

Cut neatly into joints a pair of underdone quail and divide the breasts into two pieces each. Put a cupful of good stock or consommé in a saucepan, season well with salt and black coarse pepper, add a minced medium-sized onion, a small carrot, chopped, and a stalk of celery, minced, with a little parsley. Cook slowly for 40 long minutes. Then rub through a colander, stirring in a tablespoon of brown roux (browned flour and butter). Add this to the cut birds.

Stir gently, keeping hot, but do not allow to boil, set in a saucepan of boiling water just where it will keep at the scalding point for 20 long minutes. Lastly put in half a cupful of small mushrooms (button mushrooms will do), heated in their own liquor, and serve with the following:

GAME GIBLET SPREAD

Cook the giblets and liver of the birds. Drain. Mince them fine, work them to a paste with equal amount of butter, seasoning to taste with salt and black pepper, and spread them on buttered toast upon the dish intended for the salmis. The toast will absorb the gravy and be delicious.

SAUTÉED QUAIL ROMAN STYLE

(Serves Two)

Clean 2 plump quail, singe, rub inside and out with a damp cloth, then with salt and black pepper. Truss, after filling the cavity with the bird's liver, and blanketing first with a vine leaf, then with a square of fat larding pork over the breast. Cook slowly in 5 table-spoons of olive oil (butter may be substituted if desired), turning the bird often to brown on all sides, for 20 short minutes. Meanwhile, slightly brown for 3 short minutes a small onion, finely chopped with 2 scant tablespoons of olive oil, stirring frequently. To this, add 1½ cups of fresh June peas; cover hermetically and cook over a gentle fire without any liquid. The peas will be done at the same time as the quail if put on the fire at the same time. Dress the birds on a hot platter over a piece of toast, profusely buttered. Serve the peas, either around the birds or separately. In Italy, the peas are served separately. The traditional fried bread-crumb sauce and the currant jelly, of course, will not be amiss.

SNIPE

(See WOODCOCK)

TEAL DUCK AND OTHER WILD DUCKS

The different methods of preparation of all the wild ducks including mallard, canvasback, and ruddy ducks, may be applied to the teal duck. Without exception, wild ducks should be cooked and served rare. The usual garnishing or side dishes served with wild ducks are currant jelly, fried hominy, wild rice. Wild ducks may be broiled, roasted, braised (when old), sautéed, stuffed, according to directions.

Usually the Supreme (sometimes called breasts, or fillets) are sautéed or poached with wine or a mixture of wine. Ducks should always be cleaned thoroughly, rubbed with a damp cloth or with lemon, brandy, or other spirits according to directions. In addition to their special methods of preparation, wild duck may also be prepared in all the different methods applied to the domestic duck, taking into consideration, of course, the different ingredients used sometimes only for wild ducks.

Wild ducks are seldom, if ever, blanketed with thin slices of fat pork. They should be cooked at a high degree of temperature (400–450°) unless otherwise indicated. The average time of cooking is about twenty minutes for an ordinary duck. Fat from a roasted wild duck should be poured off as soon as it collects. It *should not be used* in basting, unless otherwise indicated. Instead, a basting made of water, game stock, or meat stock, to which a little butter has been added, should be applied.

CANARD SAUVAGE AUX NAVETS
(*Variation*)

Although this method of preparation was made for the domestic duck, the wild duck may be cooked in the same way. It has been tried very often and has always brought good results. While the duck is first cooked in a casserole over a gentle fire, halfway, the completion of the cooking process is made in a hot oven (400°).

Clean, singe thoroughly, rub the inside and out with lemon juice, then with salt and pepper and fill the cavity of the bird with a few strips of celery which has been blanched for 10 short minutes, well drained then rolled in melted butter, and the liver of the duck, cut into small pieces, seasoned with salt, pepper, and a few drops of good brandy (lemon juice may be substituted). Sew and truss. Place the bird in a casserole containing 3 tablespoons of melted butter and cook over a hot fire, turning the bird often to brown on all sides for 15 long minutes. Lift out the bird and transfer to a kettle having a tight-fitting cover. Add then 1½ cups of good chicken stock, and the deglazing of the casserole in which the bird was seared, to which has been added ¼ cup of good white wine, stirring from the bottom of the casserole to loosen all the particles of gelatinous matter which may adhere; then add ½ cup of good Sauce Espagnole (*see* SAUCES), 6 sprigs of parsley tied with a bay leaf and return the duck to this sauce, adding 1 teaspoon of "Fumet" (*see* recipe, How To PREPARE GAME STOCK, page 45). Meanwhile, heat 4 tablespoons of butter and cook, or rather glaze, 2 dozen small white onions, peeled and parboiled; in another saucepan, brown 2 dozen small turnips (using white ones only), previously peeled, then turned into the shape of a large green olive, and parboiled 10 minutes, adding a little powdered sugar to glaze as you would for small white onions and over a hot fire. When the duck is done (about 40 minutes for a young one and 50 to 55 minutes for an older one), lift out. Place in another casserole, preferably an earthenware one, in which it will be served. Arrange the glazed onions and glazed turnips. Remove the excess of fat from the liquid in the first kettle and strain through a fine sieve over the duck and vegetables. Set over the fire a few minutes, to mellow and heat up, but do not boil. Serve in the casserole with a side dish of applesauce.

BRAISED WILD DUCK WITH OLIVES

Cook a cleaned, singed wild duck as indicated in recipe for CA-NARD SAUVAGE AUX NAVETS, above, first searing it, then braising as directed, for 40 minutes. Then add 2 dozen large green olives, stoned, and blanched 5 short minutes in butter. Cook 10 minutes longer. Lift out the bird. Dress on a hot platter with the olives. To the sauce left in the braising kettle, add 1 generous teaspoon of "Fumet" (*see* recipe, How To PREPARE GAME STOCK, page 45), stir well and pour over the bird and olives. Garnish the platter with triangles of fried hominy, interspersed with small triangles of bread fried in butter.

BRAISED WILD DUCK WITH ORANGES

Clean, singe, fill the cavity of the bird with its own liver, mashed with a fork, adding an equal weight of tart apples, peeled, cored, then chopped finely, mixing well and seasoning to taste with salt and black pepper. Sew and truss. Place the bird in a braising kettle with a cupful of celery, cut in small strips (julienne-like), 1 green pepper, seeds removed and also cut into small strips, and 1 dozen small mushroom caps, raw, peeled, stems sliced. Pour over 1½ cups of game stock made with the trimmings, and well strained, and ½ scant cup of white wine; then add 6 sprigs parsley tied with a small bay leaf and 1 small sprig of thyme (thyme leaves may be used if thyme in sprig is not available). Season to taste with salt and pepper, and cover hermetically. Set in a moderately hot oven (350°) and braise 35 minutes. Lift off the cover and add 2 large oranges, peeled (white stringy part removed) and sectioned. Adjust the cover and continue cooking 10 long minutes more. Serve in the braising kettle, which should be ornamental enough to be presented at table. No other accompaniment is necessary.

BRAISED WILD DUCK WITH ORANGE JUICE
(*French Method*)

Clean a young wild duck, singe, truss without adding any filling or stuffing. Place in an earthenware casserole with 4 tablespoons of heated butter and brown on all sides for 15 minutes, over a hot fire; reduce the heat and cook slowly, for 25 minutes longer, after adding 1 generous cup of Sauce Espagnole (*see* SAUCES) and ½ generous cup of brown sauce, mixed together with 1 generous teaspoon of "Fumet" (*see* recipe, HOW TO PREPARE GAME STOCK, page 45), turning the bird often into the sauce during the cooking process. Lift out the duck. Remove the excess of fat from the casserole, then reduce the sauce remaining in the casserole to half. Strain through a fine sieve, then add the juice of 2 large oranges, and the juice of half a small lemon. Add also the rind of half an orange and the rind of ½ small lemon, cut into very small strips. Do not boil any more, but keep at the scalding point. Brush the bird with melted "Fumet." Dress the bird on a hot platter, pour over the platter 3 or 4 tablespoons of sauce with the orange and lemon strips; correct the seasoning. Garnish with sections of oranges, seeded and skin removed. Serve with the remainder of the sauce aside.

SUMMER PUNCH

(*Serves 18–20*)

2 cups strained orange juice
2 cups canned grapefruit juice
1 cup grenadine
3 to 4 dashes orange bitters
4 to 5 dashes aromatic bitters
1 bottle of gin
1 large piece of ice
1 large orange, sliced
1 large banana, sliced
2 dozen green or red cherries

Mix orange and grapefruit juices, grenadine and both bitters in a pitcher. Add the gin and stir well. Place a large piece of ice in a punch bowl. Pour over the punch; add the fruit, stir gently. Serve in punch glasses.

BRAISED WILD DUCK WITH CHERRIES

Clean, singe, place in the cavity of the bird, its own liver mashed with a fork, nerves removed, seasoned to taste with salt and black pepper and sprinkled with a few drops of good brandy. Sew and truss. Place the bird in a braising kettle with the usual vegetables for a braise. Pour over 1 cup of good game stock, made from the trimmings and 1 teaspoon of "Fumet" (*see* recipe, How To PREPARE GAME STOCK, page 45). Cover and braise in a hot oven (400°) for 45 minutes, turning the bird once during the cooking process. Lift out the bird. Dress on a hot platter and keep hot. To the remaining sauce in the braising kettle, add ½ cup of Demiglacé sauce (*see* SAUCES). Bring to a boil, stirring from the bottom of the kettle. Strain the sauce over the bird, pressing a little so as to obtain all the liquid from the vegetables. Garnish the platter with small triangles of bread fried in butter alternated with fried hominy squares and serve a side dish of red or white cherries, prepared as follows: Pour into a saucepan a generous wineglass of good port wine with a blade of mace, a blade of powdered allspice, and a very small blade of powdered thyme leaves, the juice of a large orange and a scant ¾ teaspoon of grated rind of the orange used for the juice. To this, add 4 generous tablespoons of currant jelly. Stir well until thoroughly mixed and hot, then add 1 small can of well-drained cherries (red or white), stoned. You may also add to the syrup a tiny blade of nutmeg; this adds flavor and enhances the flavor of the fruit.

BRAISED WILD DUCK GRAND MÈRE
(*Very Old Recipe*)

In the bottom of an earthenware casserole, arrange a bunch of cleaned leeks, using the white parts only. Sprinkle over the leeks one sliced carrot, 6 sprigs parsley tied with a bay leaf, 1 minced celery stalk, 1 small sprig of thyme, or its equivalent in thyme leaves, 1 dozen very small white onions, 1 dozen small mushroom caps, peeled, the stems sliced, and pour over 1 cup of game stock, to which has been added 1 generous teaspoon of "Fumet" (*see* recipe, How To Prepare Game Stock, page 45). Over this arrange neatly, as in a nest, a cleaned, singed wild duck from the day's bag, the cavity of which has been filled with its own liver and half calf's sweetbread (previously blanched, then cubed small, liver and sweetbread seasoned to taste and sprinkled with a few drops of good sherry wine) before being sewed and trussed in the usual way. Season to taste with salt, black pepper, 1 whole clove, and 1 tiny blade of powdered mace. Pour over the duck 1 pony glass of good brandy. Cover hermetically and set in a hot oven for 35 minutes without disturbing. Serve in the casserole as is without removing the excess of fat or thickening the sauce.

BRAISED WILD DUCK NIEDERWALD

(*German Recipe*)

Arrange in the bottom of an earthenware casserole, first a layer of very thin slices of raw, lean ham. Over this place a layer of sauerkraut, well drained. In this nest, put a cleaned, singed wild duck, after filling the cavity with a little sauerkraut, mixed with loose meat sausage, taking care not to fill too much and to leave room for expansion. Then add 1 raw carrot, sliced thin, 1 medium raw onion, sliced thin, 1 bay leaf, 2 cloves, and 8 whole peppercorns, gently bruised. Finally sprinkle over a juniper berry, mashed. Pour then 1 wineglass of Moselle wine, and ½ cup of game stock, to which has been added 1 generous teaspoon of "Fumet" (*see* recipe, How To Prepare Game Stock, page 45). Cover hermetically and set in a hot oven (400–425°) for 35 minutes without disturbing at all. Serve in the casserole with small apple pancakes served aside.

MAMMY'S ROAST WILD DUCK

(*An Old Southern Recipe*)

Prepare a fine stuffing of 1 cooked sweetbread, diced very small, ½ generous cup of lean salt pork, chopped fine, 2 tablespoons (altogether) of parsley, chives, mushrooms, shallots, in equal parts and chopped fine, seasoning to taste with salt, pepper, a few thyme leaves, and a blade of mace. Fill the cavity of a cleaned, singed, wild duck, then sew and truss. Roast in the usual way in a hot oven (400°), basting profusely, with a wineglass of port wine, removing the fat as it comes down the dripping pan, and using Virginia port wine, which is generally recognized as one of the best port wines in America. It is of a deep-garnet, almost black, color, very heavy and heady, astringent and of a strong, aromatic flavor. Serve the duck dressed on a hot platter, the gravy aside, and the dish garnished with Sweet Potato-Orange Puffs made as follows:

Sweet Potato-Orange Puffs, Southern Method

2 cups mashed boiled sweet potatoes	¼ cup milk
	1 scant teaspoon salt
2 egg yolks, slightly beaten	2 egg whites, well beaten
2 tablespoons melted butter	1 small pinch pepper to taste

Orange shells

Into the mashed sweet potato, mix the egg yolks, butter, salt, pepper, and milk; then fold in the white of one egg, stiffly beaten. Fill the halves of orange skins with this mixture and top off with a bit of the remaining egg white, beaten to a froth. The flavor which comes from the orange rind gives the sweet potato a most exotic and piquant taste. You may substitute a bit of marshmallow for beaten egg white, if desired, for topping each puff. If you like the flavor of rum or brandy, the sweet potatoes might be given a little dose of these.

MARINATED WILD DUCK IN PORT WINE

Clean a wild duck, singe, rub with lemon juice, then with salt and coarse black pepper. Place in an earthenware casserole and cover entirely with port wine, adding 1 large bay leaf, 2 cloves, 1 small carrot, thinly sliced, and a small onion, also thinly sliced.

Allow to marinate for 24 hours. Next day, lift out the bird and roast in a hot oven (400°) in the usual way, basting exclusively with some of the port wine used for the marinade. Dress the bird on a hot platter. Garnish with small lozenges of fried hominy, interspersed with small mounds (molded if desired, or scooped with a spoon) of cooked wild rice. Serve with a port sauce made with the remainder of the port wine from the marinade.

MARINATED WILD DUCK À LA MANTOUANE

(Italian Recipe)

In an enameled deep dish, having a close-fitting cover, marinate in port wine 2 dozen fresh figs, carefully washed, stems removed, for 36 hours. Half an hour before serving, clean, singe, and truss a wild duck. Place in an earthenware casserole with 5 tablespoons of good butter and cook for 15 long minutes, turning often to brown on all sides; then and only then begin to baste (the cooking process should be done over the stove, and above a medium flame) with the port wine in which the figs have been marinated, keeping on basting until all the wine is used (about 1¾ cups). Transfer the bird to a braising kettle, surround with the marinated fresh figs; cover (barely) with a rich veal stock (using about 1½ cups); cover hermetically, and set in a moderately hot oven (350°) for 30 long minutes. Dress the bird on a hot platter. Surround with the figs; remove the excess of fat from the sauce, and pour over the bird. Serve at once, simply garnished with a large bunch of watercress.

ROAST WILD DUCK

(English Method)

IMPORTANT. As already said, wild ducks are seldom blanketed with fat larding pork, but it may be blanketed with very thin slices of ham just to protect the breasts from being overdone, the ham being removed after 10 minutes of cooking.

Clean a wild duck, singe, rub with lemon juice, then with salt and pepper. Blanket the breasts with very thin slices of raw ham. Truss. Place in a dripping pan and roast in the usual way, removing the ham slices after 10 minutes of cooking. Serve with a side dish of applesauce, and garnish the platter with triangles of fried hominy.

ROAST WILD DUCK BIGARADE

Clean a wild duck, singe, rub with lemon juice, then with salt and pepper, inside and out, then roast in the usual way, basting often either with hot water, to which may be added a little butter, game stock, or meat stock. Cook very rare (about 20–25 minutes, according to size, but do not attempt to roast an old bird; the result would be disastrous, and the only method for such a bird is the *"braise"*). Dress onto a hot platter; surround with sections of oranges, skin entirely removed, thin slices of lemon and a large bunch of crisp young watercress. Serve with a side dish of Bigarade sauce (*see* SAUCES).

ROAST WILD DUCK PORT WINE SAUCE

Proceed as indicated in recipe for ROAST WILD DUCK BIGARADE, above, substituting Port wine sauce for Bigarade sauce, and garnishing as directed. You may also serve a side dish of cranberry sauce, or still better a side dish of cranberries made as follows:

CANDIED CRANBERRIES

Select sufficient large, firm cranberries to make 3 cups (the remainder will not be amiss). Make 3 slits in each berry. Boil 3 cups of granulated sugar with 2 cups of cold water until very clear. Allow this syrup to cool, then add the berries and bring very slowly to the boiling point. If the berries are heated too quickly, the skin will burst before the syrup soaks into the pulp. As soon as the syrup boils, remove from the fire and let stand as is overnight, to mellow. Next day, drain the syrup from the berries and reduce to about half its original volume by boiling rapidly. Cool the syrup, place the berries in it, heat again very slowly, very gently and let simmer for 3 or 4 minutes. Remove from the fire and let stand for 2 hours in a cool place (not the refrigerator). Boil gently a third time for five minutes. Allow the berries to stand in the thick syrup overnight. Warm once more so that the syrup will be thin enough to pour easily and drain the berries. Spread them on oiled paper to dry. When dry, the berries should be bright, firm, plump, and semi-transparent. In this way, cranberries may be served with any kind of game, fresh meat, desserts, and even candies, and will keep more than 3 months.

HOW TO MAKE FALERNUM

For home consumption, this fine preparation will be found very handy for cups, punches, hot drinks, etc. The following recipe, which comes from an old-established wine and spirits merchant in Barbados, British West Indies, is for 25 gallons, you may add or diminish the ingredients, if more or less is desired.

10 gallons good, strong rum as clear as you can get it
1½ gallons lime juice
80 lbs. granulated sugar
¼ ounce essence of almond
1 ounce essence of clove
4 ounces isinglass, soaked in cold water, melted with hot water
12 egg whites

Melt sugar in as much water as will make up the quantity to make 25 gallons. Mix well and stir properly. Pound the shells of the 12 eggs very fine, and after stirring well, sprinkle the egg shells on top. Cover the container tightly, let it stand for 21 days or more, the longer the better; pour off carefully without shaking and strain through fine muslin, and bottle. Place the container on a level place to avoid shaking.

SALMIS OF WILD DUCK À LA MOSCOVITE

Clean, singe, truss and roast a wild duck for 15 minutes, in a hot oven (400°). Remove from the oven and disjoint, cutting the breasts in two pieces, crosswise. Place in an earthenware casserole and pour over a pony glass of good vodka (brandy may be substituted). Strike a match and touch the vodka, allowing the flame to burn out, shaking the casserole occasionally; then add 6 small white onions (peeled), ¼ cup of raw ham (cubed small), 1 dozen of fresh mushrooms (peeled, caps separated, stems sliced), 1 small truffle (peeled, then chopped coarsely), half of a calf's sweetbread (previously blanched, after being cleaned, then diced small). Pour over, 1 cup of good chicken stock or veal stock. Cover and allow to simmer gently in a moderate oven (350°) for 30 minutes. Remove from the oven. Take out the excess of fat, add the juice of half a small lemon; correct the seasoning. Dress on a hot platter, as hot as possible, and garnish with thin slices of oranges, alternated with small triangles of bread fried in butter. A side dish of stewed apples should accompany this really good dish.

SALMIS OF WILD DUCK À LA ROYALE

Clean a wild duck, singe, and rub with brandy, inside and out, then with salt and black pepper. Truss and roast in the usual way, for 15 minutes. Remove from the oven, and after cooling a little, remove the skin entirely from the bird. Disjoint the bird, cutting the breasts into two pieces. Arrange the pieces in a casserole with ½ cup of good chicken consommé. Keep hot on the side of the stove. Chop 6 shallots as finely as possible and place in a saucepan; add ½ teaspoon of grated rind of a small green lemon, ½ generous cup of champagne and bring to a rapid boil. Meanwhile you will have pounded the trimmings of the bird, bones and all. Add this to the champagne mixture with 1 tablespoon of "Fumet" (*see* recipe, How

To Prepare Game Stock, page 45), 1 bay leaf tied with 4 sprigs parsley and a small sprig of thyme and allow this to reduce to half. Strain this through a fine sieve and add to the bird pieces in the casserole. Cover and allow to simmer very gently for 30 minutes. When ready to serve, add a few drops of lemon juice. Dress on a hot platter; garnish with small triangles of bread fried in butter, interspersed with thin slices of lemon, each slice topped with a small piece of black truffle.

SALMIS OF WILD DUCK BOURGEOISE

This recipe calls for a blanket of thin fat larding pork, to prevent the bird from overcooking too much.

Prepare a wild duck as for roasting, blanketing the bird with a thin slice of larding pork, before trussing, and roast for 20 short minutes. Remove the legs, cutting off the ends, which set aside, then the breasts, cutting them into two pieces (each side). Place in an earthenware casserole. Cover and keep hot. Mash the liver, and pound the bones and trimmings with ¾ cup of fresh bread crumbs. Place in a saucepan and add ½ cup of good game stock, stir and bring to a boil. Rub this mixture, while hot, through a fine sieve. Return to the saucepan and add ½ cup of very good veal stock, 3 shallots, chopped fine, salt, coarse black pepper to taste, and 1 wineglass of good red wine. Bring to the boiling point, stirring occasionally. Remove from the fire and add 1 generous tablespoon of butter, mixing it with a wire whisk, alternating with the juice of a small lemon. Dress the duck on a hot platter, and pour this fine sauce over the duck pieces. Garnish with small triangles of bread fried in butter and serve with a side dish of currant jelly.

WILD DUCK SOLOGNOTE
(*Also Called "Canard Sauvage au Père François"*)

Father (*père* in French) François—François the Wise, as his neighbors used to call him—is dead today, dead of old age. He used to live in Sologne. The old lordly spruces and seemingly endless stretches of apple and beeches surround his large well-kept farm —The Farm of the Wise—as it is still known today. During the long summer days, the brave old man used to rest in the shade of these trees where the song of the wagtails and other birds mingled with that of the tree leaves lulled him asleep. He was a gentleman farmer in every sense of the word. He was also a gourmet, a connoisseur of fine food, and his succulent table was known miles around, while his cook, Rosa, a past master in culinary, was just as popular. She was reluctant and seldom willing to give away her culinary secrets. However, one day, I succeeded in getting her famous recipe for Wild Duck Solognote, and here it is:

Clean, singe, fill the cavity of a wild duck with its own liver, mashed, mixed with 1 teaspoon of chives, 1 scant teaspoon of shallot, both chopped fine and the whole thoroughly mixed and seasoned to taste with salt, pepper, a tiny blade of thyme leaves and a another of mace, sew, then truss. Place the swelled, perfumed bird in a casserole, just large enough to hold it, and add a large bay leaf tied with 6 sprigs of parsley, 2 whole cloves, 1 small onion, thinly sliced, and ½ cup of celery leaves, minced. Pour over this, 1 cup of good veal stock, to which is added 1 tablespoon of "Fumet" (*see* recipe, How To PREPARE GAME STOCK, page 45) and ½ cup of good cider. Cover and over a low flame bring this slowly, very slowly, to a boil. Reduce the heat and allow to simmer gently for 1 long hour. Lift out the bird carefully and keep hot. Strain the sauce through a fine sieve, pressing a little so as to extract all the best parts from the solid ingredients. Return the strained sauce to the fire. Remove the excess of fat and allow to reduce to half over a hot fire; then remove from the fire and beat in 2 egg yolks, one at a time, beating rapidly after each addition, then bit by bit, add 3 tablespoons of butter, beating violently after each addition. Finish with 1 teaspoon of Madeira wine, added slowly, off the fire, beating constantly meanwhile. Pour half of this sauce over the duck, and serve the remainder aside. Garnish with small triangles of bread fried in butter, and a large bunch of crisp watercress. Serve also a side dish of quince jelly.

WILD DUCK AU SANG

(*Wild Duck in His Own Blood*)

Like the domestic duck, wild duck may be prepared in this delicious way. I have no apostolic vocation, but if I had been a missionary
instead of a chef, it would have been most certainly my irresistible
duty to convert the culinary barbarism, the vandals, who under the
pretense of enjoying a roast duck, be it wild or domestic, begin to
bleed completely this delicious bird. They most certainly do not
know that the duck, above all its excellent gifts in cookery, is a
philosopher and as such never worries, never frets, and never loses
its presence of mind, having a sort of knowledge that it was born
to end in a pot for the enjoyment of the human species. Then why
throw away what is best, what is most precious in it—its blood?

Never bleed a duck whenever possible. Choose another method of
murdering it for your feast. Smother it and after it has been bled and
its blood saved, roast it "nature," plain, that is, with no stuffing at
all, to the desired point, about 20–25 minutes, according to size, so
that, when pricked with a fork, ruby-like pearls of blood will come
out of its epiderm. Serve as follows:

Slice the breast in thin fillets, learnedly, and dress the slices on a
hot platter. Keep hot. With great care, collect all the blood which
may run out and add to whatever you have saved previously. In it,
crush its liver, using a fork (liver should be raw) so as to obtain a
kind of paste, removing all the nerves. To this paste, rapidly add a
few drops of lemon juice to prevent the blood from curdling. Dust
with freshly crushed peppercorns. Don't be niggardly. The duck,
wild or domestic, loves it. A little salt, using good judgment, and a
few grains of nutmeg. Moisten this mixture with a small glass of
Zinfandel, this truly American wine, possessing body, a fine dark-
ruby color, a generosity and vigor that compares with the French
Saint-Émilion wine. Pour this sauce of the gods of gastronomy in
a small saucepan or still better in a double boiler (a chafing dish will
do). Do not worry if you see the sauce changing its color. The one

who is worried with cookery cannot relish and will not appreciate any culinary accomplishment. Stir very gently, until it is a brown, soft, unctuous, and a tempting mixture, a brown cream, the sight of which will make you leap for joy and impatience, and wake up your gourmand instincts. This result obtained, you reach the end of your tantalizing sufferings. Roll each piece of hot fillet of wild (or domestic) duck in this sauce, and methodically, religiously, slowly, eat this *summum* of epicurean art, simple, but how good. It is a culinary epic which you may prepare right on your dining table, using a chafing dish for the sauce preparation. Make the pleasure last as long as possible and this wild duck will seem a feather to you.

Canvasback, redhead, black duck, and mallards are, according to gourmets and connoisseurs, the best tasting of the wild ducks as they are broad-billed, grass-eating birds. With the exception of canvasback, who is a great fish eater, they live almost solely on wild celery and natural grasses. For one desiring a more gamy taste, hanging the duck in a cold place for a day or two, more if desired, but never more than three days, will make it a little more tender, especially if the bird be old. As a general rule, when a duck, or even a wild bird is not going to be stuffed, it is advisable to place an onion, or slices of apples, or chopped celery, or a small peeled carrot in the cavity, removing it when serving. This absorbs some of the wild flavor for those who do not care for it. Having wild game to serve is an event to many of us. Therefore, when one is fortunate enough to have some given to him, or have a husband who hunts, one should not clutter one's menu—let your ducks, pheasant, grouse, and the like hold the center of the stage. To make it the center of attraction, serve it daintily, in all its glory. Place your bird on the most handsome platter, or, if served in casserole, the best-looking casserole you may have. Surround it neatly and daintily with whatever be the garnishing. Decorate the setting with slices of orange, placed on the rice or any other cereal indicated, or between the rice, hominy, or polenta indicated and the duck. Watercress is the best ornament to a game dish. Parsley is out of date. Indicated or not, a jelly, according to taste, may be served with any kind of game, feathered or haired.

HUNTER'S PUNCH
(Very Old Austrian Recipe)

8 bottles Pilsen beer	A piece of ginger
1 lb. granulated sugar	(nut size)
1 small stick cinnamon	12 egg yolks
(about 2-inch)	1 cup of rum
Zest of a small lemon	1 cup Madeira wine

½ lb. sweet butter

Bring the beer almost to the boiling point, to which is added sugar, cinnamon, lemon zest, and ginger, stirring once in a while, but do not allow to boil. Meanwhile mix egg yolks in a dish and beat until very smooth; add to them the rum, alternating with Madeira wine, and beating rapidly and constantly all the while to prevent the curdling of the eggs. Add the sweet butter, a small piece at a time, beating rapidly after each addition. When all the butter is added, strain through a fine sieve into a crystal bowl. Serve in glass cups.

GEESE

Swans, geese, and ducks are awkward on land and harsh of voice; they fly over us closer to the clouds than to the earth, and their wild, impetuous ways are made wilder by the changing conditions of their life on this continent. But who now sees a wild swan, or hears its proud trumpet blast as it booms southward, elegant in white and black against the slaty background of advancing storm? Who, indeed, sees any water fowl except the hardiest hunters.

In addition to the following recipes, the different methods of preparation of the domestic geese, may be adapted to the wild geese.

BRAISED WILD GOOSE
(*Flemish Method*)

Have an old goose, clean, singe, reserving the liver for stuffing. Prepare a stuffing as follows:

WILD-GOOSE STUFFING

1 cup of soft bread crumbs	1 tiny blade of marjoram
Salt and black pepper to taste	2 tablespoons butter
1 blade of sage	½ cup celery, parboiled and
1 blade of thyme leaves	chopped fine

The goose liver

Mash the goose liver with a fork, removing all nerves. Combine all the remaining ingredients, and add to the liver. Mix thoroughly, moistening with a little white wine so as to obtain the consistency of an ordinary stuffing. Fill the cavity of the bird with the mixture. Sew and truss. Place in a braising kettle, the bottom of which is lined with a cupful of chopped raw ham. Add the ingredients for an ordinary "braise." Place the trussed, stuffed bird over this; pour over 1 cup of good game stock or chicken stock, add 1 scant half teaspoon of good gin. Cover and set the kettle in a hot oven (400°) for 1½ hours, without disturbing. Lift out the bird. Place in a dripping pan, carefully, brush it with melted "Fumet" (*see* recipe, How To PREPARE GAME STOCK, page 45). Dress on a hot platter. Keep hot. Remove the excess of fat from the braising kettle; place over a hot fire, sprinkle 1 scant tablespoon of flour over the mixture and bring to a rapid boil, stirring from the bottom of the kettle; then add ½ cup of white wine, boil once and strain through a fine sieve, pressing a little to extract all the liquid from the vegetables. Correct the seasoning if necessary. Serve aside with a dish of plain boiled rice; garnish the platter with Apple Rings, made as indicated under GARNISHINGS. Serve at once.

BRAISED WILD GOOSE WITH TURNIPS

Proceed as indicated in recipe for CANARD SAUVAGE AUX NAVETS, page 113, substituting goose for duck. Cook and serve as directed.

BRAISED WILD GOOSE

(*Bavarian Method*)

Clean, singe, place in the cavity of the bird 1 large apple, peeled, cored, and sliced as for an apple pie, and mixed with the goose liver, seasoning to taste with salt, pepper, and a little nutmeg. Sew and truss. Braise the bird in the usual way. Dress the bird on a hot platter and garnish all around with homemade Noodles, made as follows:

HOMEMADE EGG NOODLES

1 egg

½ eggshell cold water

1 cup of flour, or enough to make a stiff dough

½ teaspoon salt

Break the egg into a cup and add the half shell of cold water and salt and mix slightly. Sift ⅔ of the flour into a small mixing bowl, making a hollow in center; pour the egg and water mixture into the hollow and with the handle of a knife stir in one direction until the dough is so stiff that stirring is difficult. Add remaining flour or more if needed. Turn the dough out upon a floured board and knead until stiff; then roll out as thin as possible, turning the dough to prevent its sticking to the board. Lift the dough; lightly flour the board and allow to stand half an hour to dry. Fold the dough in two, three, or four folds, and with a pair of scissors, cut as narrow as possible, or larger if desiring large noodles and shake the noodle lengths apart to loosen. Let the noodles dry a few minutes. To cook the noodles, drop them into boiling meat stock. Drain the noodles thoroughly and sprinkle with a couple of tablespoons of the sauce left in the braising kettle. Serve with a side dish of buttered bread-crumb sauce, to which has been added a generous tablespoon of prepared horseradish, and another side dish of stewed prunes.

CONFIT OF WILD GOOSE
(*Cold*)

As already said at the beginning of this section, domestic and wild goose may be prepared identically if desired, so for this really fine preserve, as it keeps many months in a cool place, use a plump, fat wild goose, or several if desired. For one goose, proceed as follows: Clean, singe, and cut a goose into 4 pieces if small, or 6 pieces if large: the legs, the breasts, cut into two pieces, and two pieces of the carcass or bones. Rub each piece with coarse salt, mixed with a little allspice to taste, a pinch of thyme leaves, and a small piece of bay leaf, chopped very fine. Dress the pieces in a deep, cold platter and cover then with salt to marinate in this brine for at least 6 days, covered with a small board with a heavy weight over. After this period, sponge every piece with a damp cloth. Melt all the fat reserved from the bird in an enameled casserole. Arrange the pieces of goose in the melted goose fat and cook until nearly done (in some parts of Europe, such as Germany, Austria, Hungary, and in fact in almost all the countries of Central Europe, the entrails are added to the cooking, after being thoroughly cleaned and washed, but the writer recommends their omission), that is, about 2½ hours, over a very low flame. Then turn the pieces of goose into a scalded earthenware jar or crock and over them the fat from the cooking process. Cool. When thoroughly cold, pour over a little layer of melted lard (1-inch thick) and allow to solidify before placing in a cold, dry place for future use, after covering the jar or crock with a piece of paper, secured with string. You may strain and clarify the goose fat before pouring over the pieces of goose if desired.

This method of preserving wild or domestic goose has a very great advantage, in that one may enjoy goose at any time of the year. Also this kind of conserve may be very useful for impromptu luncheons, as the goose pieces may be heated and served either on rice, noodles, purée of cabbage, red cabbage, spinach, etc., and even when cubed small, served in patty shells, with cream sauce, to which may be added mushrooms.

DAUBED WILD GOOSE MOTHER HENRICH PULLIG

Select an old bird for this fine preparation. Clean, singe, skin entirely, and fill the cavity as follows: Have one dozen good chestnuts, cooked in milk, first and second skin removed, then slightly glazed in butter and sprinkled with granulated sugar. Sew and truss. Now lard through and through with narrow strips of bacon, rolled in a mixture made of: parsley, chives, shallots, a very tiny piece of garlic, sage, thyme leaves, basilic, the whole very finely chopped, seasoned with salt, pepper, and a little nutmeg. Place the bird thus prepared in a kettle large enough to hold the bird, after blanketing all around with thin slices of fat larding pork. Cover with half cup of good chicken stock, and ½ cup of good Moselle wine; then add 1 small veal knuckle, cut into 3 or 4 pieces, 4 small carrots, grated or scraped, 6 small white onions (peeled), 2 of which should be stuck with a whole clove, 1 small piece of parsnip (the size of a small egg), cut into two pieces, 6 sprigs parsley, tied up with 1 small bay leaf, salt, pepper, and allspice to taste. Cover hermetically, sealing the cover with a little flour diluted with a little water and set in a moderate oven (325°) for 3 hours, without disturbing, forgetting all about it during that time. Remove the kettle and lift out the bird carefully, remove the blanketing, then the excess of fat, and rub the sauce through a fine sieve. Return to the fire and add ½ cup of good chicken stock. Let this reduce to half over a hot fire. Cool. Clarify the jelly with an unbeaten egg white and its shell, in the usual way. Dress the bird on a cold platter, and pour the jelly over when it begins to set. Cool thoroughly, and, when ready to serve, garnish the platter with small Apple Surprise (*see* GARNISHINGS).

A fine German dish, practical too, for a large family gathering.

PEACH PUNCH

   1 dozen ripe peaches, peeled, stoned and sliced in a bowl
   Granulated sugar
   1 bottle of red wine
   1 bottle of dry white wine
   A large piece of ice
   1 quart bottle champagne (optional)

Place the sliced peaches in a bowl and sprinkle generously with granulated sugar, using good judgment. Let mellow for 2 hours. In another punch bowl, place a large piece of ice, and over it pour slowly the red and white wine, simultaneously. Then add the mellowed peaches, fruit, sugar, and juice. Let stand a few minutes, and, when ready to serve, pour over (optional) the bottle of champagne.

JUGGED WILD GOOSE IN RED WINE

Select an old bird, which has been hanging for 2 or 3 days. Cook 1½ dozen very small white onions in 3 tablespoons of butter, adding also ¼ lb. of salted pork, diced small, until onions and pork are golden browned. Lift out onions and pork, and keep hot. Into the fat left in the skillet, add an old wild goose, cleaned, singed, rubbed with a little lemon juice, then salt, pepper, and allspice mixed together. Cut the bird as for a fricassee, and brown (sear) on all sides, turning the pieces often. When the bird pieces are nicely browned, return the onions and pork to them, and add 1½ dozen small fresh mushrooms, peeled, stems separated, also peeled, then sliced thin, 6 sprigs of parsley tied with 1 large bay leaf, 1 small clove of garlic gently bruised, to help extract the essential oil. Stir very gently and cook slowly for 20 minutes, covered. Then pour over 2 cups of good claret, cover and bring to a steady boiling, rather gentle, for 25 minutes or until the sauce is reduced to half. Remove from the fire, add the blood of the bird, which should be set aside, and if any is available, use the blood of a chicken, stirring gently. Do not allow to boil any more. Dress the pieces and vegetables on a hot platter, and add to the sauce 1 generous teaspoon of "Fumet" (*see* recipe, How To Prepare Stock, page 45) and let heat, gently, but not enough to reach the boiling point. Pour the sauce over the goose and vegetables. Garnish with small triangles of bread fried in butter, interspersed with thin slices of oranges. Serve at once with a side dish of applesauce.

Pleasure is the reward of moderation.

Voltaire

PANNED WILD GOOSE WITH SAUERKRAUT

Clean a young wild goose, singe, fill the cavity after rubbing with lemon juice, then with salt and pepper, with ¼ lb. of pork sausage, highly seasoned and blended with a few drops of meat stock, then sew and truss. Heat 5 tablespoons of butter in an earthenware casserole, deep enough to hold the young bird, and cook it very slowly over a gentle fire, turning the bird often on all sides, for 35–40 minutes. Dress the goose on a hot platter, covered with a thick layer of sauerkraut, braised with goose fat. Garnish the edges of the sauerkraut with thin slices of lean pork, cooked with the sauerkraut. Serve with a side dish of Salmis sauce (*see* SAUCES) and a side dish of glazed cranberry apples (*see* GARNISHINGS).

POTTED WILD GOOSE
(*English Method*)

Another good recipe to use an old wild goose. Take a cleaned old wild goose, singe, rub with a damp cloth and boil for 2 long hours. Bone, being unmindful if you cut the bird, as it is to be ground. Weigh, and add the same weight of cooked lean ham, alternately, while putting the meat of the bird through food chopper, with ¼ lb. of melted butter (lukewarm) clarified, a generous blade of ground sage, as much thyme leaves, and allspice, salt, and cayenne pepper to taste. When the mixture is ground, rub through a fine sieve, adding 1 generous tablespoon of "Fumet" (*see* recipe, How To PREPARE GAME STOCK, page 45). Pack the mixture into clean, sterilized, heated earthenware jars as solidly as possible, leaving enough space at the top to seal with melted lard, or still better, with melted goose fat. Cover with a ring of paper dipped in melted fat, then cover with paper and secure with string. This will keep for months in a dry, cool place, and will be very useful for impromptu luncheons, to serve with salad, or spread on bread as for sandwiches.

ROAST STUFFED WILD GOOSE
(*English Method*)

Clean a wild goose, singe and rub with a damp cloth, then with salt and pepper, inside and out. Fill the cavity with the following stuffing: Cook in a hot oven (rather bake) 1 lb. of medium-sized onions without peeling, until done and soft. Cool and peel, then mince and add to them the same weight of fresh bread crumbs, soaked in milk, then pressed through a clean towel, and tossed to loosen, 1 teaspoon (scant) of ground sage, salt, pepper, and nutmeg to taste. Mix thoroughly. Sew and truss. Roast the bird in the usual way, basting very often. Dress the bird on a hot platter. Remove the excess fat from the roasting pan, leaving a little, as the gravy must be rather fat; to this sauce, add 1 generous teaspoon of "Fumet" (*see* recipe, How To Prepare Game Stock, page 45) and pour part of the sauce over the bird, serving the remainder in a sauceboat, with a side dish of applesauce slightly sweetened. You may garnish the edge of the platter with small triangles of bread, fried in butter if desired.

ROAST WILD GOOSE MÉNAGÈRE

Select a very young wild goose, preferably recently killed, clean, singe, rub the inside with a little brandy, then with salt and black pepper; then fill the cavity with tart apples, peeled, cored, and quartered, leaving enough space for expansion during the cooking process, the quartered apples, sautéed in butter for 3 minutes, then sprinkled with brown sugar (1 tablespoon), and a little nutmeg to taste, mixed with ½ cup of freshly made bread crumbs, stirring well but gently. Sew and truss. Roast in the usual way, dress on a hot platter, covered with wild rice, greased with the excess of fat removed from the roasting pan. Serve with the gravy from the pan and a side dish of Sultane sauce (*see* Sauces).

STUFFED WILD GOOSENECK IN BRANDY

(*French Recipe*)

Rocamadour, in France, known for its delicious and world-famed cheese, is also famous for its regional cookery. Those who have visited this picturesque little town of France, built on one of those numerous steep cliffs, typical of the Massif Central, and sheltered from the north winds by three churches, one overtowering another, may have lunched or dined at the Hotel Sainte Marie and eaten stuffed goosenecks, a sensational regional dish that may be prepared at home in the following manner.

Ingredients for the Marinade

6 goosenecks   1 pony glass of brandy
1 scant cup of vinegar   1 glass of dry white wine
   Spices: 2 whole cloves, 2 small bay leaves, 1 tiny pinch of thyme
   leaves, 1 small onion (minced fine), 1 small carrot (sliced fine),
   8 to 10 whole peppercorns (bruised gently), and 1 small clove of
   garlic (smashed).

Place all the above ingredients in a large bowl and add the goosenecks, from which the skin has been removed, carefully stripped to
avoid tearing, and the bones removed. Let stand overnight. Clean
the skins and leave in separate dish, alone. The next day have ready:

1 lb. pork-meat sausage   A little of the strained mari-
2 duck livers, finely chopped   nade
1 small truffle, finely chopped   The strained meat of the goose-
   Salt, white pepper, and allspice   necks, finely chopped

Put meat sausage, livers, truffle, and strained meat of the goosenecks through food chopper with the spices, moistening occasionally
with a little of the strained marinade. Stuff the cleaned skins with
this dressing; tie the ends and cook in boiling goose fat, until thoroughly golden browned all over, turning often. Dress on a hot platter, covered with homemade noodles, prepared as indicated in recipe
for Braised Wild Goose (Bavarian Method). Serve with a side dish
of Madeira wine sauce (*see* Sauces).

WILD GOOSE LIVER WITH TRUFFLES

A good wild and domestic goose liver should be of a blondish-
pinkish color and firm when pressing it with the fingers. Remove
the gall carefully (the green part found under the liver). Lard each
liver through and through with small sticks of black truffles; then
blanket the liver with a thin slice of fat larding pork, secured with a
string. Place in a small (if only one liver is cooked) earthenware

baking dish having a tight-fitting cover, with a little "braise," a few drops of good Madeira wine, and ¼ cup of good chicken stock. Cover, and set the baking dish in a hot oven (400°) for 35 minutes without disturbing. Lift out the liver and dress on a hot platter. Place the baking dish over the fire, after removing the excess of fat, and add 1 teaspoon of tomato purée, stirring from the bottom of the baking dish until mixture boils. Strain through a very fine sieve. Boil once more, skim, and pour over the liver, placed on a piece of fresh toast. Garnish the platter with small squares of wine jelly (*see* GARNISHINGS) alternated with small triangles of bread fried in goose fat.

Goose liver may be prepared in more than a hundred different methods, one more delicious than another, and all the different methods of preparation of calf, lamb, and pork livers may be adapted to goose and duck livers.

WILD GOOSE À LA MOUTARDE
(*Wild Goose Mustard Sauce*)

Select a very young and plump wild goose, clean, singe, reserving the liver, which you mince after removing the gall, and mix with 2 shallots, minced, 1 very small piece of garlic, minced fine, 1 scant teaspoon each of parsley, chives, finely minced, salt, pepper, and a few grains each of basilic, thyme leaves, and sage to taste, 1 generous tablespoon of butter and mix thoroughly. Fill the cavity of the bird with this mixture, sew and truss. Roast in the usual way, basting often with butter. When the bird is nearly done, add to the butter in the pan with which the bird has been basted, 1 teaspoon of prepared mustard, and baste the bird with this mixture, sprinkling meanwhile some fine bread crumbs over the bird, until it is entirely covered with the bread crumbs, flavored with butter and mustard. Finish to roast until the bird is delicately browned (the bread). Dress the bird on a hot platter; garnish with rings of apples (*see* GARNISHINGS) and serve with the following sauce:

MUSTARD SAUCE FOR DUCK AND GOOSE

Place in a saucepan, 2 tablespoons of butter kneaded with 1 scant tablespoon of flour, and 1 teaspoon (scant) of prepared mustard, 1 scant teaspoon of tarragon vinegar, and ½ cup of good game stock, salt and pepper to taste. Cook, stirring constantly until mixture is thick and creamy. Pour part of this sauce around the bird on the platter and serve the remainder aside, with another side dish of shredded cabbage cooked in goose fat. A side dish of applesauce may also be served aside if desired.

SANDRINGHAM PUNCH

    1 cup granulated sugar
    2 cups freshly made strong tea
    1 small glass port wine
      Peel of a whole lemon, thinly pared
    1 bottle of very good whisky
    1 generous pony glass of brandy

Brew the tea, strain and sweeten with the sugar, adding more sugar if necessary. Add port wine and lemon peel. Stir well and pour over the whisky and brandy (brandy may be omitted). Serve at once while hot in glass cups.

WILD GOOSE À LA MODE DE VISE

Clean, singe, and braise a young plump wild goose in the usual way with 2 small carrots, sliced, ½ cup celery, chopped fine, using green and white parts, 5 sprigs parsley tied with 1 large bay leaf, 1 small leek, thoroughly washed and minced fine, for 40 minutes in a moderately hot oven (375°). Lift out the bird, and cut into serving pieces. Bread each piece, English method, that is, first dipped in beaten egg, then in freshly made bread crumbs. In a separate saucepan, blend 1 tablespoon of butter and 1 of flour, and moisten with ¾ cup of very good game stock, or chicken stock, seasoning with salt, pepper, half clove of garlic, and a pinch of allspice to taste. Allow this sauce to simmer for 15 minutes, then skim well, and add ½ cup of good fresh sweet cream. Heat to the boiling point, and allow to simmer gently while sautéing the breaded pieces of goose in plenty of butter, turning often to brown delicately on both sides. Dress the goose pieces on a hot platter over a fancy folded napkin. Garnish with thin slices of oranges and lemons, interspersed, and a generous bunch of watercress. Serve the sauce aside, with a side dish of stewed apples.

WILD TURKEY

An old wild turkey, as in fact a domestic one (tom turkey), should be boiled or braised. However, the different methods of preparation of domestic turkey, domestic hen, wild goose, may be adapted to the wild turkey when not above 10 to 12 lbs. In young turkey the skin is soft, fine grained, and velvety, with a layer of fat forming beneath it. Where the fat has not yet formed, the skin is transparent and the flesh may have a bluish cast. Another characteristic of young wild turkeys is a flexible breast bone. The young hen turkey is more rounded in contour than the young tom. The tom has a deeper breast bone.

How To Prepare a Wild Turkey for Roasting

Have turkey drawn, slit skin down the back of neck from shoulder to head, disjoint the neck at the shoulders and remove it, saving it for giblet sauce with the giblets to give a rich stock gravy. Singe turkey, remove pinfeathers, wash thoroughly, and wipe dry. Sprinkle the inside with either lemon juice, brandy, or whatever liquid indicated, then rub with salt and black pepper, then fill the inside from the rear. Stuffing packed too tightly will burst the skin in cooking. This applies to all wild and domestic birds. Truss as directed on page 141, to hold bird in shape, folding the wings back on skin of neck and tying legs and tail together, then brush with melted fat.

How To Roast a Wild or Domestic Turkey

There is no difference in roasting a wild or domestic turkey. Place the trussed, stuffed turkey, breast side up, on rack in open roasting pan. Do not add any liquid unless so directed. Roast in moderate oven—this is very important, as domestic turkey should be placed in a very hot oven (450–500°) to sear, while a wild turkey should not be seared under any circumstances, but should cook very slowly, the bird turned occasionally to allow slow browning on all sides. The turkey will then be very tender and juicy, and I advise the roasting of a young domestic turkey in the same way. Do not baste before the bird has been in the oven for 20 minutes; then baste either with the liquid indicated or use melted butter mixed with ¾ parts of hot water. Then baste with the liquid from the pan. Allow 15 long minutes per pound for a young bird, and 12 to 15 minutes per lb. for an older bird, that is above 12 lbs. Do not salt the bird before it has been in the oven for half an hour.

To Carve a Wild Turkey (or a domestic one)
1. Use a very sharp, long-bladed carving knife and a large platter.
2. Place the bird on its back with its breast at your left. Insert carving fork at point of breast bone, tines straddling the ridge, and hold bird firmly.
3. Carve the breast meat in thin slices, cutting down.
4. Cut through skin separating the legs from the body. Pull back the leg, disjoint, and remove it.
5. Separate drumstick from the thigh by cutting through at the joint.
6. Slice the meat from the leg (the leg bone is never served).
7. Remove the wing by cutting down through the joint close to the body.

Never attempt to serve an old bird unless prepared in the boiling method, and served boiled, and never attempt to roast a boiled old bird. Another important point. *Do Not Prod a Roasting Turkey with a Fork* to test its tenderness, because the juices will gush forth like water before the rod of Moses. There is a time for juice to flow when slices of breast are laid off with a keen knife and poured dripping upon hot plates, but behind the scenes one does not bite or stab the defenseless creature to test its quality. The modern range will do the cooking almost unaided if given time and polite attention.

STUFFING

The stuffing is not the least of the day's concern and in drab moments we recall some sage-and-bread *poultices* that we have *tasted but not eaten*. In that mere handful of stuffing is a cook's chance for applause and a reputation, and they are not won by stirring up some soaked bread with some herbs. The great masters of the culinary art taste *As They Go* (this applies to any ingredient which is cooked, be it a soup, a sauce, and so forth), and the second- or third-rate amateur cook should know before the stuffing goes into the bird that it will emerge as a rich, moist, crumbly composition delicately and suggestively—not violently—seasoned with thyme and parsley and with sage and marjoram, too, if one likes them all. Some piquant dressings are of nothing more than bread, butter, chives or shallots, parsley and thyme, with the juices of the bird; and it's a matter of fancy whether one shall add mashed chestnuts, sliced fresh mushrooms, or minced bacon.

> *The stomach is a slave that must accept every-*
> *thing that is given to it, but which avenges*
> *wrong as slyly as the slave does.*
>
> ÉMILE SOUVESTRE

THREE IN ONE GAME
(*Roast Stuffed Wild Turkey*)

One universal habit of those devoted to the culinary art has been to wrap up choice morsels in leaves, dough, or puff paste, to be popped into hungry and gourmand mouths without loss of juice, flavor, or aroma.

Much latitude is enjoyed in the stuffing of a bird, especially turkey. Hundreds of varieties of stuffing, one more delicious than another, have been created by ingenious chefs, and even amateur cooks. Full many a golden-browned turkey has appeared on our tables, especially during the holidays, the hunting season, and special feasts, for turkey, wild or domestic, is distinctly a ceremonial American dish. The ruddy farmer's wife's dressing of New England has been well advertised, it is known throughout the continent, from north to south and east to west, but the following stuffing has kept the intimate tone of few households, and even first-class hotel restaurants, if any, and is known only where there are gourmets and gastronomes. Stuffing of a bird is a problem at home. The cook's repertory is soon exhausted. Following is an unusual experiment for the hostess and chef to try; one which may have many variations if one is a real epicure, coupled with some creative imagination.

Clean and pick a grouse, a quail, or a small young duck, and after singeing it, bone carefully. Place a small black truffle in center, roll and tie securely with a string. You may substitute a little seedless raisins, a few sections of oranges, skin carefully removed and sprinkled with a few drops of sherry, Madeira wine, or brandy, or fine champagne—there is no limit as to choice. Now brush with butter and insert the bird thus prepared in a well-cleaned, picked, singed, prairie hen, also boned and trussed carefully. Next place the prairie hen thus prepared into the cavity of a well-cleaned, singed, rubbed wild young turkey of about 10–12 lbs. Fill the cavity, that is the space between the prairie hen and the walls of the turkey, with the liver of the quail, or grouse, or whatever bird is first used, the liver of the prairie hen and the liver of the wild turkey, both livers mashed, seasoned to taste with salt, pepper, and allspice to enhance the flavor, mixing this paste with parsley, chives, and shallots, finely chopped. Do not stuff too full, lest the bird burst.

Now roast as you would an ordinary turkey, in a moderate oven (350°), basting often, first with melted butter and water, then with the drippings from the roasting pan, following the directions indicated at the beginning of this paragraph, adding after 30 minutes of roasting, 3 tablespoons of good Madeira wine to the drippings. If any part is likely to brown more rapidly, wrap the bird in a buttered paper. Do not forget to baste often, even over the buttered paper to keep a constant moisture. Remove the paper 15–20 minutes before the bird is done to allow browning.

What happens during the cooking process? The flavor and juices of the turkey mingle with that of the prairie hen, which in turn mingle with that of the quail or grouse, thus developing a tempting aroma. To serve: Remove the prairie hen from its perfumed (flavored) jail, then the quail or grouse from the prairie-hen jail, and place this appetizing trinity: the turkey, the prairie hen, and the quail or grouse on a hot platter or on two platters. The three will be carved by the host or hostess, who will serve a bit of this and a bit of that to each guest, passing aside a dish of traditional giblet sauce, another of cranberries, either jellied or candied (*see* GARNISHINGS), without omitting the bread-crumb sauce for the prairie hen and quail or grouse. The contrast of texture between the crisp exterior and the moist interior of the turkey and the delightful variation in the high flavor of the three different birds, plus the bland savor of the livers, make this dish score success. Besides, the leftovers will—if there are any—afford an excellent ready-made dish of originality for the next day, when served with a green salad.

ROAST WILD TURKEY CHASSEUR

Clean a young, plump wild turkey, singe, and rub inside and out with lemon juice, then with salt, pepper, and allspice to taste. Fill the cavity of the bird with a small pork tenderloin (smoked), found on the market already boned and smoked. Sew and truss. Roast in the usual way, basting very often. Dress the bird on a hot platter, and the smoked-pork tenderloin, removed from his jail, on another. Serve at once with a side dish of applesauce, a side dish of boiled wild rice, and a side dish of cranberry jelly.

ROAST WILD TURKEY WITH PRUNES

Clean, singe a young, plump turkey, which has been hanging for 2 days, before plucking. Rub the inside and out with a little sherry wine, and fill the cavity of the bird as follows: Brown a small onion, minced in a scant tablespoon of butter, and 1 cupful of freshly made bread crumbs, ¼ lb. meat sausage, and break a fresh egg over the mixture. Mix thoroughly over a low fire, stirring constantly for 5 short minutes. Meanwhile you will have pitted 2 dozen small plump prunes soaked overnight in hot chicken stock (veal stock is much better if available), drain and add to the bread-sausage mixture, then add 1 teaspoon of chives (minced), 1 teaspoon of shallot (minced), and 2 tablespoons of butter. Stir, heat well, but do not boil. Fill the cavity of the bird with this mixture, sew, then truss securely. Rub the bird first with good olive oil, then with a little mace—oh, very little—just to give a little flavor. Place the bird in a moderate oven (350°) and roast in the usual way, basting often. Remove from the oven, dress on a hot platter and serve with the traditional giblet sauce, made from the liver and giblets, flavored with a few drops of Madeira wine, and a side dish of cranberry jelly.

POPE'S PUNCH

2 large oranges stuck with whole cloves and roasted in
    a warm oven
1 pound of granulated sugar
1 pint boiling water
2 bottles of red Burgundy wine

When the oranges have acquired a good dark-brown color, cut them into quarters, removing the seeds, and leaving the cloves. Place in a saucepan, add the sugar and water, press the oranges, stirring meanwhile. Bring to a boil; strain. Replace the strained syrup in a saucepan, add the red Burgundy wine, and let simmer over a gentle fire until a white foam appears on the surface (do not boil). Remove from the fire and serve in glass cups.

WILD TURKEY EN DAUBE

Select an old, but not too old, wild turkey for this preparation. Clean, singe, and rub inside and out with good brandy, then with salt, pepper, and allspice. Do not stuff, but sew and truss, after blanketing the bird with thin slices of fat larding pork, rubbed with a mixture of chives (minced), a small piece of garlic (minced), 3 shallots (minced), salt and pepper to taste, a few thyme leaves, a tiny blade of mace, and a tiny blade of allspice, the whole thoroughly mixed and finely chopped. Place the bird in a deep earthenware casserole, pour over 2 scant cups of white wine, 1 cup of good chicken stock. Cover and cook very slowly, very slowly for 2½ hours or longer, according to size of the bird. Lift out the bird. Cool. Reduce the cooking liquor over a hot fire, strain through a fine sieve, and when beginning to set, pour over the cold bird. Serve cold, garnished with small dice of wine jelly (*see* GARNISHINGS) and a green salad.

WILD TURKEY RUSSIAN STYLE

Select a very young bird, clean, singe, and split open from the back. Then bone entirely. Lay the two sides of the bird flat and rub the inside with a little vodka, then with salt and allspice and coarsely ground black pepper to taste. Over the seasoning spread with a very smooth stuffing, made as follows:

½ lb. of cooked veal (lean), ground
¼ lb. cooked ham, ground
2 egg yolks
Salt, pepper, and a blade of mace to taste

2 tart apples, peeled, cored, then chopped fine
2 tablespoons butter
1 teaspoon of chopped truffles and enough thick brown sauce to blend smooth

After spreading this mixture over each side and evenly, roll each side separately, as tightly as possible, as you would a jelly roll, and secure with strings. Place both rolls in a braising kettle, with 1 cupful of cut-up vegetables, as indicated for "braise." Pour over ¾ cup of good chicken stock, 1 cup of good dry white wine, and add 6 sprigs parsley tied up with a large bay leaf, 2 whole cloves, 12 whole peppercorns, slightly bruised, and 1 blade of mace. Adjust the cover tightly and set the kettle in a hot oven (400°) for 1¾ hours without disturbing at all. Lift out the turkey rolls. Dress on a hot platter covered with sauerkraut, cooked as indicated in recipe for PAN FRIED PHEASANT WITH SAUERKRAUT, page 68. Remove the excess of fat from the braising kettle. Strain over another saucepan, pressing a little, bring to a rapid boil, and allow to reduce to half; then add 1 cup of good game stock made from the trimmings of the turkey (bones, giblets, etc.), and 1 generous teaspoon of "Fumet" (*see* recipe, How To PREPARE GAME STOCK, page 45). Serve with a side dish of apple rings, and garnish the edge of the platter with thin slices of oranges, alternated with small triangles of bread fried in butter.

WOODCOCK
also
SNIPE

According to connoisseurs and gourmets these two birds, when slightly "high" (mortified), are really fine, and both may be prepared in the same ways. Brillat Savarin recommends that the woodcock ". . . should be conserved several days with feathers on and must be *bien fait*" that is, well mortified. The woodcock, as well as the snipe, should never be cleaned; only the giblets are removed to be used according to directions. The best method for trussing a woodcock, or a snipe is to pass the string through and through, to keep the legs crossed. Woodcock and snipe should always be blanketed with a thin slice of fat larding pork. The woodcock, when roasted, requires an average of 15 to 18 minutes of cooking, in a hot oven (400°), while the snipe demands only 9 to 10 minutes, also in a hot oven (400°). Besides the following recipes, the woodcock and the snipe may be prepared, cooked, and dressed in all the different methods of preparations used for the partridge, the quail, and the grouse, as well as the different wild hens.

The woodcock and the snipe require a rather high seasoning, and the preferred wines seem to be Burgundy and champagne. Unless otherwise indicated, both wild birds are always dressed on a piece of toast just before being served, so that the liquid which runs out from these birds may be absorbed by the bread, giving it an exquisite flavor.

In the following recipes a woodcock is considered sufficient for two persons, while a snipe is for one only.

If there were no grouse, the woodcock would be the first game bird as regards its flavor. But the woodcock has on the grouse that which cannot be appreciated but in the countries where found, the advantage that its flavor is less fleeting, and that it may stand mortification, while the grouse, a very fine game bird, indeed, does not stand mortification and should be eaten in the fresh state, although a little *staling* may be allowed, but no longer than two days, while the *Woodcock and the Snipe* are really in full flavor when mortified, although not as long as required for the pheasant.

The snipe is the reduced form of the woodcock, but is distinguished from it, by its flavor. The snipe abides constantly in marshy, boggy, and swampy land, while the woodcock is always found in wooded land provided with clear pools.

Although several varieties of snipe are known, the following recipes apply to both woodcock and snipe.

WOODCOCK À LA SOUVAROFF

Cook for 5 short minutes, 4 small black truffles in a half wineglass of Madeira wine and 1 generous teaspoon of "Fumet" (*see* recipe, How To Prepare Game Stock, page 45), in an earthenware casserole; then add 3 generous tablespoons of raw goose liver (duck liver may be substituted), cubed small. Cook 2 short minutes longer and with the truffles and liver cubes, fill the cavity of a plucked woodcock, singed, rubbed inside and out with a damp cloth, or with lemon juice if preferred. Sew and truss, after blanketing the bird with a thin slice of fat larding pork. Heat 2 tablespoons of butter in the casserole in which the truffles and liver have been cooked and golden brown the bird on all sides for 5 long minutes, turning it often; then add ½ wineglass of good Madeira wine, as much of game stock, season to taste with salt and black pepper; cover hermetically and set the casserole in a hot oven (400°) for 15 short minutes. Serve in the casserole with a side dish of freshly made toast, another of currant jelly and, if desired (optional), another of wild rice.

CASSEROLE OF WOODCOCK À LA
FINE CHAMPAGNE

When the woodcock has been mortified, pluck carefully and truss in the usual way without any stuffing. Pan fry it in plenty of butter, turning often so as to brown on all sides, until the bird is cooked to the desired point, which should be very rare if one wants to enjoy its full flavor. Remove the cooked bird and cut neatly into 6 pieces. Arrange the pieces in a deep casserole, which should be of earthenware, placing the head, which should be in its entirety, on top. Keep hot. Deglaze with a scant pony glass of fine champagne, to which a match has been touched; add the entrails, chopped and diluted with a little game stock made from the trimmings, a teaspoon of "Fumet" (*see* recipe, How To PREPARE GAME STOCK, page 45), a few drops of lemon juice, and a dash of cayenne pepper, stirring from the bottom of the skillet. Pour this coulis or sauce over the pieces of woodcock; heat, but do not boil, and serve as is.

CASSEROLE OF WOODCOCK VALENCIA

Let a plump woodcock mortify for 6 long days, then pick, singe, and rub with good brandy, inside and out, but do not season. Cut into pieces as you would for a chicken fricassee, and roll in salted and black peppered flour (dredging). Heat 3 tablespoons of good goose fat until it smokes and brown in a *cazuela* or Spanish casserole of earthenware composition, adding 6 very small onions, peeled, a tiny clove of garlic, crushed, turning the pieces of woodcock often to color on all sides. Now add a pinch of saffron. Do not use this herb sparingly, as saffron is the life, the spirit, the leitmotif of this delectable dish. When the pieces of woodcock are delicately browned, add 1 large green pepper, seeds removed, and minced fine, 1 wineglass of good sherry wine, 3 slices of red pimento, also chopped fine. Now pour over the whole, 1 scant ¾ cup of good game stock made from the trimmings (neck, and so forth), correct the seasoning, and cover as tightly as possible. Set the casserole in a very hot oven (450 to 500°) for 15 long minutes, and serve piping hot with a side dish of plain boiled wild rice.

CUTLET OF WOODCOCK SARAH BERNHARDT
(*Modernized Recipe*) (*Cold*)

Roast 2 mortified woodcock, in the usual way. Cool and bone.

Cube small the supremes of one woodcock, and add the same amount of cooked beef tongue, also cubed very small, reserving about 2 tablespoons of this mixture for later use. Now with the liver of one of the woodcock, also cut into small cubes, and the reserved 2 tablespoons of the mixture, make a stuffing, blending with a little jelly or fumet of game. Fill 6 small black truffles, scooped very carefully, with this stuffing. Pound the trimmings in a mortar and the remaining liver, and to this add the scooped part of the black truffles. Rub the pounding through a very fine sieve, being careful to do this work in a cool place, and bind with enough "thick fumet" so as to obtain a mixture similar to the one used for croquettes. Shape into croquettes, then flatten in cutlet shape. Place the cutlet thus made in individual mold, and pour over a slightly melted "Fumet" (*see* recipe, How To PREPARE GAME STOCK, page 45), alternating with a little amount of the first mixture, that is, the supremes and the tongue. Cover with more "Fumet," and set in a refrigerator. When ready to serve, arrange the cutlets in a circle on a cold round platter and garnish the center with a crisp bunch of watercress.

BOSTON VIOLET PUNCH

½ cup freshly made strong tea
Juice of three large lemons
Juice of three large oranges
1 cup of grape juice
Syrup made with 2 cups of sugar and 2 cups of water
1 cup grated fresh pineapple
1 bottle of rum (optional)
1 small bunch of fresh violets

Cook the pineapple in 2 cups of water for 15 short minutes. Strain through a fine cloth, and add the remaining ingredients, but the violets, with 1½ quarts of water. Place a large piece of ice in a large punch bowl and slowly pour over the mixture, which has been slightly cooled. When ready to serve, that is, when the punch has cooled to the desired point, strew a loose bunch of fresh violets over, and serve with a single violet added to each glass cup.

ROAST WOODCOCK À LA MONACO

Let a plump woodcock mortify for 5 long days; pick, singe, remove the gizzard and giblets as well as the entrails, which save. Rub the bird with fine champagne, and set aside, after rubbing it slightly with salt and plenty of coarse black pepper. Try 1 generous tablespoon of grated fresh pork in a casserole, add the entrails and 3 chicken livers. Stir and let cook very slowly over a gentle fire; then strew ½ cup of fine fresh bread crumbs over the mixture, mixed with a blade of allspice, a blade (scant) of nutmeg, and a blade of thyme leaves, stir and moisten with 2 tablespoons of rich Sauce Espagnole (*see* SAUCES) or 2 tablespoons of rich, spicy tomato sauce, and 1 scant teaspoon of "Fumet" (*see* recipe, HOW TO PREPARE GAME STOCK, page 45). Cook this 2 short minutes, stirring all the while and rub over a fine sieve (a hair sieve if possible). Then to this mixture, add 1 generous tablespoon of white (black may be substituted if white truffles are not available) truffles, finely chopped. Spread this mixture over freshly made toast, and dress on each piece of toast, half a freshly roasted woodcock. Pour over a generous tablespoon of Spanish sauce, enriched with a little melted "Fumet," serve at once with a side dish containing the remaining rich Spanish sauce.

ROAST WOODCOCK BONAVENTURE DAVID

Roast a plump woodcock in the usual way which has been mortified 5 long days, seeing to it that the bird is underdone (15 minutes being quite sufficient for roasting), in a hot oven (425°). Cut into serving portions, that is the wings, the legs, and the breast, and keep hot on a hot platter. On a plate, mash the liver and the entrails, squeezing over this mixture a small lemon, and adding ½ generous teaspoon of grated lemon rind to it. Dress the carved roasted woodcock on a very hot platter, sprinkling with a little salt. Pour over the following sauce or, rather, dressing: 1 teaspoon of prepared French mustard, 1 scant wineglass of sweet white wine (Sauternes wine is advised), coarsely ground black pepper, each piece of woodcock receiving an equal share. Now place the platter on a gentle fire, and turn the pieces of bird into this mixture, so that each piece is penetrated by this seasoning. Do not allow to boil, and if the mixture seems to dry up, add a few drops of olive oil. Serve at once with a side dish of freshly made toast, and a side dish of shoestring potatoes, not omitting the traditional side dish of currant or quince jelly.

SALMIS OF WOODCOCK I

Operate exactly as indicated in recipe for SALMIS OF QUAIL SOUTHERN METHOD, page 111, seeing to it that the bird should be very rare. Cook, dress, and serve as directed with the usual accompaniment.

SALMIS OF WOODCOCK II

Roast a mortified woodcock very underdone, leaving the entrails inside during the roasting process. Then cut the bird into 6 pieces removing the skin as you go along. Trim each piece very carefully and place in an earthenware casserole, sprinkling over a generous teaspoon of good brandy to which a match has been touched, and letting the flames die out. Cover with a profusedly buttered paper. Keep warm, but not too hot, lest the meat toughen.

Now pound the bones and trimmings with the intestines, liver, and the gizzard as finely as possible, and place in a saucepan, with ½ generous cup of dry white wine, previously reduced to half, 3 small shallots, chopped fine, coarse black pepper and a few grains of salt to taste. Heat this to the boiling point, then let reduce to nearly nothing, as far as the liquid is concerned. Add 1 cup of good Spanish sauce, to which has been added 1 teaspoon of good "Fumet" (*see* recipe, How To Prepare Game Stock, page 45). Allow this mixture to simmer gently for 15 minutes, then rub through a hair sieve, pressing as much as possible to extract all the essences from the solid parts. Return the sieved mixture to the fire, and allow to heat to the scalding point, then strain anew through a fine sieve. Add 1 scant tablespoon of good sweet butter, stir and pour over the pieces of woodcock set aside. Sprinkle over 2 dozen fresh button mushrooms, cooked in butter, 1 tablespoon of chopped black truffle, or the equivalent in thin slices. Dress on a very hot platter; garnish with small triangles of bread fried in butter, alternating with thin slices of oranges (cut in two), and serve with the traditional bread-crumb sauce, and a side dish of currant jelly, or any other kind of jelly to taste.

Prepared in this way, a salmis of woodcock is a real culinary triumph, the full flavor of the game remains, and the mixture is not too dry, nor too saucy.

SUPREME OF WOODCOCK

The supremes of woodcock may be prepared in all the different methods used for the pheasant, the partridges, the grouse, and in fact all the medium-sized wild birds. *See* Supreme of Pheasant, page 89, as to the meaning of the word "Supreme," and the recipe for Supremes of Pheasant with Divers Sauces, page 90.

HOT WINE AND ORANGE PUNCH

Over ¾ lb. of sugar in lump, pour 1 generous cup of boiling water, then add the grated rind of 2 small oranges, and allow to infuse for 15 long minutes; then pour over a bottle of good red Burgundy wine, heated for 30 minutes in a pan of boiling water.

Serve in glass cups, with a slice of seeded, but not peeled orange in each cup. The addition of ¼ cup of good brandy will not be amiss.

TIMBALE OF WOODCOCK NESSELRODE

This excellent recipe requires at least 2 mortified, plump wood-cocks; but the mortification should not exceed 4 days. Pluck, clean, saving the intestines, liver, and giblets; rub the inside first with lemon juice, then with salt and coarse black pepper. Truss and rub the outside with lemon juice, then with butter, highly seasoned with salt and black pepper. Blanket both birds with a thin slice of fat larding pork, and truss. Heat in an earthenware casserole, 6 table-spoons of butter, and pan cook the birds for 15 short minutes, turn-ing them often to brown on all sides. The bird should be very under-done. Lift out of the casserole, cool a little, and with a sharp knife, lift out the fillets, also called, as already said elsewhere, su-premes, or breasts (which in poultry and game are synonymous). Set these supremes or fillets aside. Bone the rest of the bird, and pound the meat, separated from the bones, with ¼ of their weight of raw goose liver. Strain this mixture, or rather rub it through a fine hair sieve, then add to the mixture thus obtained, the same weight of fine, smooth stuffing made with soaked bread, the liver of the two woodcocks, and seasonings such as allspice, nutmeg, sage, etc., to taste, using good judgment. Turn the bones and trimmings into the butter left in the casserole, and pour over 1 pony glass of fine champagne. Let this simmer for 10 minutes, then strain and re-turn the sauce thus obtained to a saucepan, adding 6 small black truffles, turned in olive shape by means of a sharp knife.

Now line a charlotte mold with rich pastry crust or, still better, with puff paste which has been generously buttered. On the bottom of the mold, arrange a thin layer of the stuffing, also on the sides; then place over, the fillets of the birds, sliced thin, leaving the center with a space large enough to place the small truffles. Cover with 3 tablespoons of Spanish sauce, rather thick, and to which has been added 1 teaspoon of "Fumet" (*see* recipe, How To PREPARE GAME STOCK, page 45); then another layer of stuffing; and cover with a crust of puff paste (or rich piecrust, if you have begun with this kind of crust). Set the mold in a moderate oven (350°), for 45 minutes, the mold placed in the center of the oven. Unmold on a hot platter; surround the timbale with 4 tablespoons of Demiglacé sauce (*see* SAUCES), to which has been added the remaining game stock, if any, or some game stock from another bird. Serve with the traditional bread-crumb sauce, and red currant jelly.

Quail, pheasant, grouse, as well as prairie hen, may be prepared in the same way.

TIMBALE OF WOODCOCK SAINT MARTIN
(*Modernized*)

Roast 2 woodcocks which have been mortified at least 5 long days, and after removing the insides, blanketed with the usual fat larding pork slices, in the usual way, keeping the two birds rather underdone. Meantime, line a shallow timbale mold, greater in width than in height and generously buttered, with a rich piecrust or puff paste. Lift out the supremes of the two birds, and arrange in alternate layers of slices of supremes and raw goose liver, also sliced but not too thin (the liver may be placed in hot butter for 1 or 2 minutes if desired), layer of black truffles, sliced thinly, and layer of fresh large mushrooms, cut in julienne-shape, that is in small strips after being peeled, using only the caps.

Remove the meat from the legs, and pound with the bones, trimmings, intestines, and giblets in a mortar, adding a scant ¾ teaspoon of essence of truffle. Rub this pounding through a fine hair sieve, pressing a little so as to obtain all the soft parts of the mixture, then strain anew through a fine sieve. Heat this sauce, but do not allow to boil. When heated to the scalding point, add the juice of half a lemon, and a generous pony glass of fine champagne. Pour this delicious coulis over the slices of ingredients contained in the mold, cover with a crust, slash the center to let the steam escape, and bake in a moderate oven (350°) for 45 minutes. Unmold on a hot platter; surround (optional) with rich tomato sauce, to which has been added a teaspoon of "Fumet" (*see* recipe, How To PREPARE GAME

STOCK, page 45), and garnish the edge of the platter alternately with slices of oranges and small cubes of wine jelly (*see* GARNISHINGS). Serve immediately with a side dish of bread-crumb sauce and a jar of currant jelly, mixed in equal parts with sweet butter and thoroughly blended.

> *In cookery . . . as in all arts, a connoisseur mistrusts a giant. Would not you give away a roast beef or a roast stuffed domestic turkey, for an ortolan or a woodcock prepared in one of these different methods? Or a quail à la Châteaubriand? Does the Rhodes' Colossus with all the large steamers passing between its brass legs, reach even the knees of the Venus de Milo? Well, a bird, such as woodcock prepared as indicated above, is worth to a real gourmet, a real connoisseur, ten roast beefs, or ten roast stuffed turkeys.*
>
> *According to François Rabelais, a timbale of woodcock or snipe is considered as a broom to the stomach, as it acts in the same way spinach does. This has been confirmed by medical authorities.*

SALMIS OF WOODCOCK À LA RABELAIS

The following dish, when made according to directions, is not merely a dish, but a revelation.

Remove the legs and wings and breast carefully from a raw plump woodcock mortified for 5 long days, then plucked, singed, the head removed and thrown away, as well as the gall and gizzard. Pound the remainder of the raw bird to an unctuous and firm paste of the consistency of a rather thick cream, adding occasionally, while pounding, enough stock or clear, rich consommé, preferably of game, if available, to facilitate the pounding. Rub this paste through a hair sieve. For each woodcock thus prepared, add the size of a large walnut of kneaded butter (equal parts of flour and butter kneaded together to a smooth paste) and ½ wineglass of good red claret, 2 small whole shallots, peeled, 3 sprigs of parsley tied with a small piece of bay leaf, 1 crushed whole clove, 4 bruised whole peppercorns, and a thin slice of a small garlic clove, pounded or rather mashed. Bring this indescribable delicacy of the god of gastronomy to the scalding point over a very, very low flame, let simmer, rather smile imperceptibly, for 15 minutes. Now lift out the shallots and the parsley and bay leaf tied together, squeezing them carefully, so as not to let a particle of the fine sauce go to waste, and discard; then, and only then, add 1 tablespoon of good olive oil, a single squeeze of half small lemon and salt to taste, using good judgment. In this soft and smooth sauce place the 4 limbs of the woodcock, and allow to heat, but not to boil. Dress the pieces on a fried square of bread and pour the nectar of a sauce over all. That's all.

You may use a snipe, a quail, a grouse, a pheasant, and in fact any kind of small game bird if desired instead of a woodcock, taking into consideration the size of the bird, when adding the other ingredients.

WOODCOCK À LA FAVART
(A Soufflé)

For this super-delicious recipe, the woodcock should be mortified for at least 6 days. Pluck, clean, reserving the liver, intestines, and giblets, but the gizzard and the head, rub inside and out with lemon juice, then slightly with salt and coarse black pepper. Blanket the bird with a thin slice of fat larding pork, and truss. Heat 3 generous tablespoons of butter in a skillet and when hot, cook, rather pan fry, the bird for 15 long minutes, turning it on all sides to brown evenly. Lift out the supremes while the bird is still well underdone and keep hot. With a pair of strong scissors or a long, large sharp knife, trim the carcass of the bird in the shape of a case. With the liver, the raw meat removed from the legs, the trimmings, the raw meat from another woodcock, 1 egg white, the intestines of the two birds, and ¼ lb. of raw goose liver, prepare a very smooth stuffing in the usual way, seasoning highly and to taste with salt, pepper, allspice, nutmeg, and sage and thyme leaves. Mix thoroughly, then rub through a fine hair sieve. Fill the trimmed carcass with this fine, smooth stuffing, so as to reshape (approximately and as nearly as possible to the original shape of the bird), surrounding it with a strong buttered paper to prevent any deformation, securing the paper with string. With a little of the stuffing set aside for this purpose, and to which has been added an equal weight of goose liver, mashed raw, garnish small tartlets, or elongated pieces of rich piecrust, unless one prefers puff paste, with this last mixture, and set in a moderate oven (325–350°), after placing over each one a slice of the breast of the woodcock, placing the soufflé of woodcock in the oven at the same time, placed in the reshaped bird. Bake 25–30 minutes. Serve with a side dish of Demiglacé sauce (*see* SAUCES), to which has been added a teaspoon (scant) of "Fumet" (*see* recipe, How To PREPARE GAME STOCK, page 45). You may, instead of placing the reserved stuffing on rich crust or puff paste, omit the crust and arrange the sliced breast of the woodcock symmetrically over the soufflé, if desired.

WOODCOCK SOUFFLÉ À LA CZARINA

Let a plump woodcock mortify for 3 long days only. Pluck, singe, clean, rub the inside and outside with vodka, then with allspice, to which has been added a small juniper berry, ground fine, salt and black pepper to taste. Now cut the bird into small dices, reserving the intestines, liver, giblets, except the gizzard and the head, which discard.

Place in a mortar the trimmings, all the bones, the liver and the intestines, with 1 generous tablespoon of good sweet butter. Off the fire, pound as fine as possible. Turn the poundings into a saucepan and add 1 generous cup of rich dry white wine, 4 sprigs of parsley tied with 1 sage leaf, and 1 small sprig of thyme. Set over a gentle fire and allow this to come slowly to a boil; then turn on the full flame and allow to reduce to nearly nothing, that is the liquid; then pour over 1 cup of good chicken stock and allow to simmer for 1 long hour. With the liquid, strained through a fine sieve, make a cream sauce, omitting the milk, using the liquid only; then add the diced woodcock. Bring to a boil, and rub the mixture through a fine hair sieve. Transfer the strained mixture, which should be a fine succulent paste, into a saucepan and add 1 generous tablespoon of butter, and work this with a spoon or a spatula, gradually incorporating 5 egg yolks, one at a time, continuing working the mixture rapidly after each addition of an egg yolk. Lastly, after correcting the seasoning, fold in the whites of 5 eggs, beaten to a stiff froth. Turn the mixture into a soufflé dish, slightly buttered and set in a hot oven (400°) for 30 minutes. Remove from the oven and serve at once with a side dish of Malaga wine jelly (*see* GARNISH-INGS) and a side dish of Moscovite sauce (*see* SAUCES). Snipe, pheasant, grouse and quail, may be prepared in the same method.

WOODCOCK À LA MODE D'ALCANTARA

Operate exactly as indicated in recipe for PHEASANT À LA MODE D'ALCÁNTARA, page 69, substituting woodcock for pheasant. Cook, dress, and serve as directed.

WOODCOCK À LA NAGORNOFF
(*Modernized*)

Bone 2 woodcocks thoroughly, which have been mortified for 4 long days, reserving the supremes, attached to the wings intact. Pound the bones and remaining parts together with a cupful of stuffing made of 1 cup of soaked bread, well dried, and the two livers of the woodcocks, as well as the entrails, seasoning highly with salt, pepper from the mill, allspice, sage, thyme leaves, and a few grains of nutmeg, using good judgment, adding, when pounding, a whole unbeaten egg white. Rub this mixture through a fine hair sieve. To the paste thus obtained, add gradually and slowly, while stirring constantly, 1 cup of thick rich cream, alternating with 2 egg whites, beaten to a froth, little by little at a time. Fill a profusely buttered mold with this mixture, and bake 45 minutes, in a moderately hot oven (350°), the mold placed in a pan containing hot water. Meanwhile, prepare a game stock as follows: To the pounded bones already used, add 1 generous cup of good meat stock, and ½ cup of lean veal (raw) ground, 3 slices of onion, 1 tablespoon of finely chopped celery leaves, 4 slices of carrot, a bit of bay leaf, 1 clove, 4 whole peppercorns, a few thyme leaves, salt and cayenne to taste. Let this come slowly to a boil, then reduce the heat and allow to simmer gently for 25 minutes (you may add the peelings of 2 or 3 mushrooms if desired). Then bring anew to a rapid boil, reducing the liquid to nearly nothing. Pour over a cupful of good Spanish sauce, and 1 pony glass of good sherry wine. Strain and correct the seasonings. When this custard-like substance is ready, unmold over a hot round platter, garnish around with small pieces of goose liver, cooked slowly in butter and seasoned to taste with salt and pepper, alternating with thin slices of truffles, the supremes of woodcock, poached in butter, and pour the strained sauce over the whole. Serve at once. For effect, you may unmold the custard of woodcock over a base made of cooked hominy, using it as a socle, if desired.

No bread sauce should be served, but a small glass of white currant jelly, mixed with half quantity of sweet butter, and thoroughly blended, should be passed around with small pieces of fried toast.

KALTCHALE

(A German Punch)

Peel and slice 1 lb. of fresh juicy peaches; do likewise with a small fresh pineapple, also with a large well-ripened cantaloupe. There should be half as much cantaloupe as there are peaches; add 1 quart of equal parts of raspberries, and white and red currants. Place all these fruits in a large punch bowl, and keep on ice for 2 long hours. Meanwhile make an infusion with a 2-inch piece of nutmeg with ½ bottle of dry white wine brought to the boiling point, and boiled until a white foam comes to the surface, adding 2 generous cups of sugar (more or less, according to taste), the grated rind of a small lemon, and allow to cool, stirring occasionally. To this infusion of white wine, add 1 quart of fresh strawberries, mashed and strained after being hulled, and as much red and white currants, in equal parts, also mashed and strained. Strain this through a fine cloth over the prepared fruits, after placing a large piece of ice in the punch bowl, and finish with a quart of good champagne, poured over the ice. Let stand 10 long minutes before serving in glass cups, adding to each cup a few pieces of fruit.

WOODCOCK IN ASPIC

AUTHOR'S NOTE

Aspic probably was used a century or two before Gallic pigs rooted up the first truffle for appreciative epicures; and every patron of the more formal hotels and restaurants has seen it glittering on plates and platters; yet the word scarcely occurs in the working vocabulary of the average man, and the average housewife has never dreamed of bothering with such a frivolous bit of culinary affectation.

Aspic, after all these years and centuries, actually is being advertised—is being introduced to the classes and the masses; and deadly peril lurks in the certain menace to its charm of mystery and elegance. For aspic—tender, fragile, delicate aspic—comes now in packages and is talked about on the air waves with that familiarity that fairly courts contempt. Yes, in packages, with directions printed on the cover, and the housewife and the June bride fetch measuring cups and spoons, and in a jiffy there is aspic sparkling in the kitchenette and in the dinette alcove. All this, mind you, while chefs still puzzle over formulas and work frantically with the crucibles and mortars, pounding herbs and essences to liquid paste, adding a dash of this elixir and a spot of that—and savoring the brew on sensitive tongues and under quivering nostrils for bouquet and aroma and the elusive charm of piquancy and pep.

But why should not the masses have their aspic, after all, and why should it have been for so long like caviar to the general public? For aspic certainly is good, and worthy to be loved, else how could it have survived the long, long march of time and the searching tests of age and custom?

Try it yourself, not in the restaurant, but in the kitchenette, and out of the package, if you like—for you may not have the skill or patience to make a topaz consommé and clarify it till not a cloud or flaw remains in the crystal. It casts the aura of class about a salad for a party. It makes the children cry out, "Oh, boy!" when the platter of cold boiled chicken, or roasted woodcock, or quail, or grouse, or is it a partridge, or Virginia ham is brought in. Molded in graceful forms about choice tidbits of game or chicken, it elevates you, the creator, to the rôle of an artist.

For aspic is nothing more or less than jellied soup. Yet it has to have flavor and piquancy as well as crystal clarity and sparkle.

If I do insist upon the proper way of preparing aspic, it is because, to my humble opinion, as well as that of all those who appreciate good food, aspic is nourishing, healthy, and often seen on the home table. Here is the way to prepare the foundation of a real, clear as crystal aspic. The ingredients are inexpensive, the results amply repay the little trouble taken. From the following recipe you will have a very excellent hot or cold soup, according to season and occasion, and the remainder will be the foundation of a very good dish, which may be prepared several days ahead, in prevision either of a party, or a Sunday supper.

Essentially, a jellied soup is just a combination of either strong, clear soup of poultry or game or meat. The French "Pot au Feu," meaning "pot on the fire," is a piece of beef put into cold water, with a little salt, condiments and spices, and vegetables of several varieties.

For good bouillon, the water must be heated gently so that the albumen will not coagulate within the meat before being extracted; it must only simmer or "smile," to permit the various soluble parts to mix thoroughly and naturally. Vegetables or roots are added to the stock, to improve the flavor, and impart their mineral salts. For each quart of water, take 1 lb. of beef. For each lb. of meat, add 1 lb. of bones (beef bones). Salt to taste. Place the stock pot on the fire. Add the meat, well sponged, and the bones, well washed. Then pour in the cold water—no hot water at all. Let simmer slowly, until the scum rises to the surface, which should be skimmed entirely and very carefully if a clear, crystal-like consommé or bouillon is desired. When this scum has all disappeared, then add: 2 rather large carrots, quartered after peeling; 1 white turnip, quartered—not a yellow turnip, but a white one; 1 large onion, stuck with 3 whole cloves, the heads removed, 1 large bay leaf, 1 large stick of celery, cut into pieces about 3 or 4 inches; a little chervil, if available, or else use parsley which may be tied up with the bay leaf, 8 peppercorns (whole), 1 sprig of thyme, if available, or else use a pinch of thyme leaves, using good judgment. Salt to taste.

Cover tightly and allow to simmer very gently for 3 or even 4 hours, the longer the better the bouillon will be, and the jelly solid. Remove from the fire; with a spoon, remove the fat which floats on the surface, correct the seasoning, and the Pot au Feu, often called beef soup, is ready. Following these directions the next day you will have a consommé in jelly without the addition of any gelatine. As a variation you may flavor with wine, Madeira, sherry, white wine, etc.

Now for the WOODCOCK IN ASPIC.

Prepare your jelly, a day or two before; clean, singe, remove the insides of a plump woodcock mortified for 3 or 4 days. Truss, and roast in the usual way, basting very often so as to obtain a juicy bird. Allow to cool; then lift up the fillets, also called supremes, or breasts, and slice them in three parts, lengthwise. Pound, then strain, the trimmings, the meat from the legs, the entrails and make a rather firm stuffing from the result, moistening with a little brandy and a little jelly from the prepared consommé, and with this stuffing fill each slice of the breast, after making a slash large enough to place at least the size of a small walnut between the opening. Roll these stuffed pieces of breast into a little thick cream sauce, to which has been added a little jelly, using soup jelly (no gelatine at all). Place a little layer of slightly melted jelly on the bottom of a small round or square mold, first dipped in cold water. When this first layer is set, place two or three pieces of the fillet, over. Repeat with the jelly, then with the pieces of breast, until all is used up and the mold is full. You may add here and there, slices of green or black olives, small pieces of egg white (hard-cooked) cut in fancy shapes with the small French cutters, small pieces of raw white celery, parsley leaves, etc., according to taste and availability. Set in the refrigerator and let congeal for at least 3 hours. When ready to serve, unmold over a cold platter covered with finely shredded lettuce, or any other salad, and garnish with whatever you desire, for decoration. Serve with a side dish of mayonnaise, remoulade, or any other sauce desired (cold).

WOODCOCK EN SALMIS À LA NAVARIN

Operate exactly as indicated in recipe for SALMIS OF WOODCOCK II, page 154, substituting the garnishing of triangles of bread fried in butter and the slices of oranges for 4 fried eggs, fried separately, and neatly trimmed, so as to leave only an inch of white on each egg, placed on a round of toast, profusely buttered, and interspersed with small tomato slices fried in garlic butter. Serve a side dish of Italian sauce, besides the traditional bread-crumb sauce, and the red currant jelly.

> *Human reason has so little confidence in itself that it always looks for a precedent to justify its decrees.*
>
> DE FINOT

WOODCOCK ALEXANDRE DUMAS METHOD

AUTHOR's NOTE

It is a well-known fact that Alexandre Dumas was a gourmet, a fine cook, and the author of a cook book which still today has authority. Speaking of this recipe he said, ". . . *Vous comprendrez bien qu'il n'y a même pas à discuter la supériorité d'une pareille méthode de la préparation."*

Take a plump woodcock which has been mortified for 5 long days. Pick, singe, and clean thoroughly, reserving the intestines and the liver for later use. The head should be cut just at the base of it, leaving a long neck, which twist and turn between the two clavicles, so that the neck will penetrate into the cavity of the stomach (Belgian method). Sew the skin of the neck so as to close the wounds of the breast hermetically. Into the other cavity, put the bird's own liver, after removing the green part, the size of a large walnut of butter kneaded with salt and pepper to taste. Use black pepper, game birds love that kind. Place the bird in a dripping pan, over a broiler so as to leave some space between the bottom of the dripping pan and the bird, and roast in the usual way, starting in a hot oven (400°) for the first 10 minutes, then reducing to moderate (350–375°) for the last 15 short minutes. After the first 10 minutes of roasting, pour into the bottom of the dripping pan the size of a small egg of fresh butter, and 1 scant cup of good thick cream, and with this delicious mixture, baste often. Dress on a hot platter. Garnish the edges of the platter simply with small triangles of bread fried in sweet butter, then sprinkled with black pepper to taste, and strain part of the sauce over the bird and the remainder in a sauceboat. That's all, but how good! Try! The original method calls for roasting the bird, hanging by the feet over a fire, then basting it constantly so as to introduce cream and butter into the back cavity.

WOODCOCK AU PORTO BLANC

Pick a mortified woodcock, singe, clean thoroughly, rub the inside and out with fresh orange peels, then with salt and black pepper to taste. Fill the cavity with its own liver, two rings of onion, 1 small piece of bay leaf, a few grains of thyme leaves, a tablespoon of green celery leaves, and a juniper berry, bruised rather hard, still better mashed, and add the size of a large walnut of good sweet butter, kneaded with a little allspice. Sew, and truss without blanketing with larding pork. Place in a braising kettle, the bottom of which is spread with a scant cupful of "braise," or mirepoix, made as indicated in recipe for GROUSE IN AUSBRUCHE, page 29, and pour over half cup of good veal stock and ¼ cup of good white port wine; season highly with salt and a few grains of cayenne pepper, and a few grains of curry powder, 1 bay leaf tied with 6 sprigs of parsley and 6 green celery leaves (small ones). Cover and set in a hot oven (400°) for 30 long minutes without disturbing. Lift out the bird. Dress on a hot platter. Keep hot. Strain the sauce from the braising kettle into a saucepan, using a fine sieve and pressing the solid ingredients a little so as to extract all the liquid; place the saucepan over a medium flame and pour in, when the sauce is boiling, gradually and slowly, ½ cup of heavy cream, beating vigorously while pouring. Lastly, add 1 tablespoon of good "Fumet" (*see* recipe, How To PREPARE GAME STOCK, page 45), stir and strain part of the sauce over the bird, and the remainder into a sauceboat. Garnish the border of the platter with small tomatoes, sliced, broiled, then brushed with melted "Fumet," interspersed with small mounds of asparagus tips, also brushed with "Fumet." No other sauce should be served with this recipe, nor any jelly, but it is advisable to serve a side dish of broiled peaches (*see* GARNISHINGS).

BISCHOFF PUNCH

Pour into a large punch bowl, 1 bottle of champagne, 1 Madeira glass of linden tea, 1 large orange and 1 large lemon, sliced thin, skin on, and enough sugar to taste. Allow this to mellow for an hour, in a cool place (the refrigerator may be used). Strain through a very fine sieve and turn the mixture into a hand freezer, turning until the mixture is snowlike. Then add 4 pony glasses of fine champagne. Serve in glass cups.

WOODCOCK COMTESSE DU PORTZIC

Pluck and singe a woodcock mortified for 5 long days. Rub the inside and out with good cider, then with salt and black pepper. Fill the cavity of the bird with the following mixture: Mash the intestines, after removing the gall, with the liver of the bird, and 3 chicken livers, 1 tablespoon of grated fat pork, 2 tablespoons of good pork-meat sausage, 1 teaspoon of chives, minced, 1 scant teaspoon of shallots, minced, salt and pepper and allspice to taste; lastly, add 1 juniper berry, pounded, and mix thoroughly. Place this mixture in a casserole, rubbed with garlic, and containing 1 tablespoon of sweet butter, to which has been added a few thyme leaves, and powdered bay leaf. The butter should be smoking before adding the stuffing mixture. Cook only 2 short minutes, stirring constantly. Remove aside and cool. Then fill the cavity with it. Now blanket the bird, first, with a thin layer of good meat sausage, then over this arrange a blanket of a thin slice of fat larding pork. Truss and sew the opening. Place the bird in a braising kettle, the bottom of which is spread with a scant cup of "braise," or mirepoix, made as indicated in recipe for GROUSE IN AUSBRUCHE, page 29). Then pour over ¾ cup of good Madeira sauce (*see* SAUCES). Adjust the cover tightly and set in a hot oven (450°) for 30 long minutes without disturbing. Serve as is, in the braising kettle, which should be decorative enough to be brought to the table, with a side dish of bread-crumb sauce, and another side dish of apple rings (*see* GARNISHINGS).

WOODCOCK À LA HENRI BAILLY

Stuff a mortified woodcock (4 days only) first plucked, singed, and rubbed with lemon juice, then with salt, black pepper, and a little sage, mixed together and to taste, with the following mixture: 2 generous tablespoons of grated fat fresh pork (larding pork), the bird's liver, and the size of a large egg of duck liver mashed together with a fork, 1 scant teaspoon of shallot and 1 tablespoon of green celery leaves, chopped very fine, seasoning to taste with salt and black pepper, the whole mixed thoroughly. Sew, then brush the bird with olive oil, and over this sprinkle a teaspoon of finely chopped chives. Blanket the bird with a thin slice of fat larding pork. Truss. Roast the bird in the usual way but only 15 long minutes in a hot oven (425°), basting often with melted butter, mixed with a teaspoon of "Fumet" (*see* recipe, How To PREPARE GAME STOCK, page 45). Dress the bird on a hot platter, covered with cooked string beans, rubbed through a sieve and greased with part of the basting, taken from the roasting pan. Serve with a sauce made as follows:

Chop 2 peeled shallots with the size of a large egg of duck liver and place in a casserole containing 1 tablespoon of butter, adding a pinch of thyme leaves, 1 bay leaf (small piece), and 1 scant ¾ cup of good red wine. Cook, allowing to reduce to half, then add, ¼ generous cup of veal stock (heated), and 1 scant teaspoon of "Fumet." Boil once and remove from the range and beat in 2 tablespoons of good butter, added piece by piece. This sauce should be fluffy, and highly seasoned with salt and pepper as well as a few grains of cayenne pepper. Garnish the platter simply with a large bunch of green, crisp watercress.

WOODCOCK PRINCE RUPRECKT

The following recipe requires 2 mortified woodcock, and will serve easily 6 persons.

Pluck the birds, singe over the flame of burning brandy, place in the cavity of the birds (in each one) 2 thin slices of lemon, 2 thin slices of white onion, 4 sprigs of parsley tied with 1 small piece of bay leaf, and 4 thin slices of tart apple. Do not mash, but stuff as prepared. Sew, blanket first with a very thin slice of cooked ham and over this a blanket of thin slice of fat larding pork. Truss and roast rather underdone, in the usual way. You will have set aside the entrails and the livers of the two birds. Remove the gall from the liver and place intestines and livers, mashed with a fork, in a saucepan with 2 tablespoons of good lard, a pinch each of allspice, thyme, powdered bay leaves, and mace to taste, using good judgment, 5 or 6 chicken livers also mashed with a fork, and 3 tablespoons of calf's liver, mashed with a fork, tubes and nerves removed. Cook over a medium flame. Allow this to cool. Pound and rub through a fine hair sieve. To this add, 3 tablespoons of brown gravy, made from game stock, if available, or ordinary brown sauce, rather thick, and to which has been added 1 scant teaspoon of "Fumet" (*see* recipe, How To PREPARE GAME STOCK, page 45), a generous teaspoon of Madeira wine, and mix thoroughly. Now add 4 egg yolks (raw) and a few grains of nutmeg. With this mixture, spread generously, thickly, 6 pieces of bread fried in butter on one side only, spreading the mixture on the fried side. Return the toast to a large skillet containing 3 tablespoons of butter, well heated, and set in a moderately hot oven (375°) until the toast is toasted underneath, and the top, that is, the spread, well heated (about 5 short minutes). Serve this with the birds, simply garnished with a large bunch of crisp watercress and a few thin slices of lemon. The traditional bread sauce and the red currant jelly also should be served as a side dish.

WOODCOCK PIE

Proceed as indicated in recipe for GROUSE PIE (*cold*), page 28, English Recipe, substituting woodcock for grouse, unless you prefer the RUSSIAN METHOD (*hot*) which is prepared as follows:

Clean and joint; wipe dry; season the woodcock with salt and pepper to taste and sauté them in hot drippings (bacon drippings are advisable) in which a medium-sized onion, sliced, has been fried. Butter a deep dish and lay in the meat alternately with layers of fat salt pork, chopped fine, hard-cooked eggs, chopped fine, and the giblets of the birds boiled and minced fine. Dredge flour over the woodcock pieces as they go in. When the dish is full, pour in a cupful of rich veal stock, or a cupful of the water in which the giblets were cooked (in the North of Russia, sour cream or Smitane is used). Season each layer with salt, pepper, and a tiny leaf of tarragon. Cover the pie with a rich piecrust, cut several slits in the middle, and bake an hour in a moderate oven (350°).

FURRED GAME RECIPES

". . . Come, for the loons are laughing
Shrill through the moon-white silence . . .
Listen—among the rushes
Yonder a moose treads splashing. . . ."

HAROLD WILLARD GLEASON

FURRED GAME RECIPES

Every country has its own ways of cooking game, the result of years of practice, so the author, who is convinced that the American gourmet is much interested in good game cookery, has searched for recipes, in short the best recipes to be had the world over. They are all here, that is, as many as the leaves of this book can hold. However, several ingredients, either too expensive or difficult to obtain, have been eliminated or substituted by other similar ones, endeavoring to follow as closly as possible the original recipe or formula, modernized to the American taste.

The American standard measures in the recipes have been adapted to serve an average family of six persons, unless otherwise indicated. These recipes and formulas may be increased or modified by varying the measures and quantities of ingredients in exact proportions to meet any given condition. These recipes and formulas represent a small part of the cooking lore of the world and are widely varied under each kind of game. The directions are accurately detailed but are sufficiently elastic so that one may express his individuality and suit the tastes of the guests or family, according to one's means, availability and conditions, ever bearing in mind that the cheapest foods or cooking ingredients are always the most expensive in the end. And . . .

> *Now these are the laws of good cooking*
> *And many and mighty are they.*
> *But the cup and the spoon of the law,*
> *And the sifter and bowl is . . . obey . . .*
> *Your recipe!*

With apologies for paraphrasing Kipling,

L. P. De Gouy

BEAR

The most appreciated parts of the bear, in cookery, those which are most sought for by connoisseurs, are: (1) The round bottom of the forelegs, (2) the bottom part of the forelegs, (3) the loin, which is to the bear what the same part is to the beef, (4) the fillet, of course, (5) the plate, for stew, (6) the flank and shank, for braising, and (7) the liver. The hind parts and the neck are usually tough, because the beast uses these parts constantly; the kidneys could be used, but require a thorough scalding, and the covering skin carefully removed.

All the above parts may be adapted, when slightly mortified then marinated, to all the different methods of preparation of the beef. A bear cub need not be long mortified, but should be marinated. One of the best methods of preparation is the barbecue, this age-old method which goes back to the ice ages, according to Dr. Frank H. H. Roberts, Jr., of the Smithsonian Institution, who lately (1935) uncovered two large sites littered thickly with the split and charred bones of an extinct variety of bison, which can be explained most plausibly as the remains of gluttonous feasts of Folsom men, the earliest inhabitants of North America of whom authenticated archeological traces have been found. The ancient barbecue remains were uncovered on the Lindenmeier site in northeastern Colorado, a place which appears to have been a semipermanent hunting camp of the Folsom men who were following on the heels of bison herds that browsed in the meadows just behind the retreating ice sheets.

The flesh of the bear, as in fact all or almost all the meat of the furred game, young or old, does not demand a too high seasoning and one should be niggardly with black pepper and cayenne pepper; while the sauces add the final touch to the furred game, spices are used with the utmost discrimination in their preparation, so as not to destroy the natural piquancy of the meat. However, in certain recipes or formulas, it will be seen that high seasoning is indicated for certain preparations.

Larding is highly recommended, because, as a rule, furred-game flesh, being dark, is usually lean, and needs "nourishment." The larding operation should be thorough, that is, the small sticks of fat larding pork should pass entirely through the piece of meat, and not superficially. If rice is the usual accompaniment of the wild birds, in general, the furred game, especially the large ones, are usually served with a side dish of corn, especially the green fresh corn, simply cooked American style, that is the ears of corn are boiled, scraped, then rolled in good butter.

Furred game love acid sauces, especially the bear, and the basting during the roasting process is usually made with part of the marinade, alternating with fat, be it lard, butter, or oil. Like game birds, furred game should be served piping hot and simply garnished. Crisp young watercress, and small triangles of bread fried in lard or butter, are the usual garnishings.

Another point of great importance is that any part of bear used in cookery, except the liver, should be thoroughly denerved, that is, all the large nerves removed.

SACK POSSET

(By Sir Fleetwood Fletcher)

From famed Barbados on the Western main
Fetch sugar half a pound; fetch SACK from Spain,
A pint, and from the Eastern Coast
Nutmeg, the glory of our Northern Toast.
Over flaming coals together let them heat,
'Till the all-conquering SACK dissolves the sweet.

Over such another fire set eggs twice ten,
New born from foot of cock and rump of hen;
Stir them with steady hand and conscience pricking
To see th' untimely fate of twenty chicken,

From shining shelf take down your brazen skillet,
A quart from gentle cow will fill it,

When boil'd and cool'd put gentle SACK to Egg,
Unite them formly like the Triple League,
Then covered close together let them dwell
Till Miss twice sings, "You must not kiss and tell"!
Each lad and lass snatch up their murdering spoon
And fall on fiercely like a starved Dragoon.

Grapes and grain and fruits of the earth,
The good God made them all,
'Tis little fools that drink too much
And great fools not at all.
OLD JINGLE.

MARINADE FOR BEAR, No. I

For a 5- to 6-lb. piece, whatever the part, prepare a marinade as
follows:

½ quart of good wine vinegar
1 bottle of good claret
1 teaspoon thyme leaves
12 sprigs parsley, tied with
2 large bay leaves
4 shallots, bruised
2 medium-sized carrots, sliced
   thin

4 sprigs of wild thyme called
   "serpolet" in drug stores
1 extra large onion, sliced very
   fine, the rings separated
2 small cloves of garlic, bruised
   gently
1 piece of parsnip, outside part
   only, the size of an egg

Salt, 1 tablespoon, and 16 peppercorns, bruised

Place the piece of venison (bear) in a large bowl (earthenware)
in which all the above ingredients have been added and thoroughly
mixed and let stand for at least 4 days.

MARINADE FOR BEAR, No. II

6 small carrots, grated and
  sliced thinly
12 small white onions, peeled
  and quartered
4 small cloves of garlic, mashed
6 whole cloves, bruised gently
20 whole peppercorns, bruised

2 large green peppers, minced
3 juniper berries, bruised
4 sprigs thyme tied with
18 sprigs parsley, and
4 large bay leaves
6 leaves of sage, or ½ generous
  teaspoon of ground sage

½ cup salt

Place all the above ingredients in a saucepan (large) with ½ cup of good lard or oil, heated to the boiling point, and cook for 5 long minutes, stirring constantly. Then pour over 1 quart of vinegar, 4 cups of good beef stock, and cook, uncovered, until the mixture has boiled 3 or 4 times. Remove from the fire and allow to cool in the saucepan. Take a piece of bear venison of 5 to 6 lbs., sponge with a damp cloth, lard through and through with narrow, long pieces of fat larding pork or whatever additional larding the recipe may call for, and pour over the marinade. Let stand for 5 to 6 days, turning the meat once in a while, but at least twice a day, and adding more vinegar and meat stock, in equal parts, which have been boiled previously, then cooled, if the liquid evaporates too rapidly. Keep in a cool place, but not in refrigerator. The above two marinades, if poured into bottles, carefully corked, then place in refrigerator, may be kept several months.

MARINADE FOR BEAR, No. III

2 onions, sliced (medium-sized)
2 medium-sized carrots, sliced
1 celery stock, coarsely chopped
1 quart of good white dry wine
1 tablespoon salt

½ pint vinegar
6 shallots, mashed
1 large clove of garlic, mashed
2 large bay leaves
16 whole peppercorns, bruised

2 leaves of tarragon herbs

· 179 ·

Combine all the above ingredients in a large saucepan and bring to a rapid boil, then let boil 3 or 4 times and allow to cool. Place a 5- to 6-lb. piece of venison bear in a large earthenware or stone jar, and pour over the cold mixture. Let stand for 4 to 5 days, turning the meat occasionally.

BEAR AU GRAND VENEUR

Have a piece of bear loin weighing 6 lbs., sponge, then lard with narrow, long strips of fat larding pork, through and through, using a good ¼ lb. of larding pork. Place in MARINADE No. III, above, let stand for 4 long days. Place the meat in a pan on top of the vegetables strained from the marinade and roast for 1½ hours, allowing 15 minutes of roasting per lb., in a hot oven the first 15 minutes (450°), then in a moderate oven (375°) for the remainder of the time, basting often with the drippings from the meat. Lift out, keep hot, and place the roasting pan containing the vegetables and drippings over a hot fire, adding 4 ladles of the liquid of the marinade. Bring to a rapid boil, and allow the mixture to reduce to a generous cup, stirring occasionally from the bottom of the pan to loosen all the particles of gelatinous matter which may adhere; then add 1 cup of fresh heavy cream, scalded and hot. Boil once, and strain through a fine sieve, pressing a little so as to obtain as much as possible of the pulp of the vegetables. Then add 2 tablespoons of red currant jelly, stir well, and finish with (optional) 1 scant teaspoon of "Fumet" (*see* recipe, How To PREPARE GAME STOCK, page 45). Stir and pour half this fine sauce over the meat and serve the remainder aside. Garnish both ends of the platter with watercress, and slices of lemon, cut in half, interspersed with small triangles of bread fried in butter.

Burgundy wine is the usual wine served with venison of bear. However, another good red wine may be substituted if desired.

BEAR STEAK ALEXANDRE I
(*Russian Method*)

Take a thick slice of the loin of the bear, as thick as your conscience will allow. For 6 persons there should be 4½ generous lbs. Marinate for at least 24 hours in Marinade No. I (*see* MARINADE recipe No. I, page 178). Lift out, sponge and sear on both sides under a high flame. Then reduce the flame and broil it to that particular stage which you call "just done," basting often with butter. Lightly dust with salt and pepper. Keep hot while preparing the following succulent sauce, which may be prepared before placing the steak under the broiler. Take one of your most beautiful platters, and the largest one, please, and, on this, mash a small clove of garlic, and rub it all over the platter, which should be very hot, so as to enhance the essential oils of this blessing in disguise. Next dot the platter with butter, about 3 tablespoons, kneaded with finely minced chives, then dot with prepared French mustard or something similar if French mustard is not available, using one generous teaspoon, no less! Add then 1½ generous tablespoons of tomato paste for zest; for zip a few drops of Worcestershire sauce; don't be niggardly with this important seasoning. Now over this, place a thick layer of smothered onions, real smothered onions, in long threads, light golden colored, shining with butter. Over this pleasing little turmoil, shake a half teaspoon of salt, a flourish of pepper, and a crimson halo of real paprika. Arrange the steak over this soft and delicious bed, and, over the steak, arrange 2 lines of fresh mushrooms, caps only, sautéed in brown butter. Dust with finely chopped parsley and serve as hot as possible. Not a particle will come back, be sure of that.

FILLET OF BEAR PIQUÉ À LA BROCHE

Take the whole fillet of a bear. Remove all the nerves and trim neatly. Place the fillet in MARINADE No. III, page 179, using only half the ingredients, after larding it through and through at both ends with long, narrow strips of fat larding pork, and in the middle, lard it through and through with strips of green pepper, choosing a large green pepper for this purpose. Allow to stand in the marinade for 3 long days, and, as the broche or spit is out of the question today, roast it in a hot oven (450°) for 15 minutes, turning it once, then reduce the temperature to moderate (350°) and allow 12 short minutes to the pound, counting the time only when reducing the temperature. The bear fillet should be eaten as rare as possible, if one wishes to enjoy its full flavor and tenderness, basting often with melted butter. Place the roasted fillet on a hot platter, the bottom of which is covered with a thin layer of Poivrade sauce (*see* SAUCES). Garnish with small cubes of wine jelly, alternated with thin slices of lemon cut in two, and topped with a large black olive, cooked a few minutes in butter, after being stoned, and a generous bunch of watercress at either end of the platter, a sprig or two being served to each guest. Serve with a side dish of the same sauce.

FILLET OF BEAR LUMBERJACK
(*Canadian Recipe*)

Marinate a bear fillet prepared as indicated in recipe for FILLET OF BEAR PIQUÉ À LA BROCHE, above, for 3 days only. Lift out, sponge, and cut into small slices as you would for Swiss steak. Place in a saucepan containing the following sauce:

LUMBERJACK SAUCE

2 tablespoons butter	A bit of garlic, minced
2 tablespoons flour	1 teaspoon paprika
1½ generous cups of the strained marinade	1 tablespoon of capers
2 tablespoons of fresh mushrooms, chopped fine after peeling	1 tablespoon parsley, chopped fine
	1 tablespoon chives, chopped fine

Salt and pepper to taste

Blend the butter and flour thoroughly, then gradually add the strained marinade, stirring meanwhile. Bring to a boil, then add all the remaining ingredients. Allow to cook slowly for 5 long minutes, stirring occasionally with a wooden spoon from the bottom of the saucepan. Serve at once without any other accompaniment, but a side dish of plain boiled potatoes.

BEAR FILLET
(*Transylvanian Method*)

Marinate a bear fillet in MARINADE No. I, page 178, for 3 long days. Lift out and braise as a Beef à la Mode, that is, as follows:

After marinating the fillet as indicated above, sponge and lard it through and through with one dozen long strips of fat larding pork, previously marinated with brandy, and sprinkled with chopped parsley. Rub the bear fillet with salt, freshly ground pepper and a little nutmeg to taste, mixed together. Place the meat in a deep skillet with 2 or 3 tablespoons of lard, and sear the fillet all over, until nicely browned. Remove from the fat and transfer to a braising kettle, adding then 6 small white onions, peeled, 3 small carrots, grated, then sliced thin, and 2 calves' feet, boned and blanched. Cover and let simmer 10 long minutes; then add a pony glass of good brandy and the marinade, cover again and let simmer 5 minutes, then pour over 2 cups of good red wine, add 7 or 8 sprigs of parsley, tied with 6 or 7 green celery leaves, and a large bay leaf, tied together, 1 large clove of garlic, bruised. Adjust the cover hermetically and set the braising kettle in a moderate oven (325–350°) for 2 hours; then add 3 tablespoons of dry sherry wine. Let cook 15 minutes longer. Lift out the meat fillet and calves' feet, place on a hot platter. Keep hot. Correct the seasoning of the sauce in the braising kettle. Boil once over a hot fire, remove the excess of fat, let reduce ⅓, and pour over the bear fillet. Serve at once with Potato Dumplings made as follows:

POTATO DUMPLINGS

6 large potatoes, cooked in their skins, and cooled	3 egg yolks
1½ teaspoons salt	4 tablespoons of flour
	3 pieces of freshly made toast
2 generous tablespoons of butter	

Peel the cooked, cold potatoes and grate. Add flour and salt, then egg yolks and toast, diced very small and fried in butter. Shape in circles, 1½ inches in diameter. Have a kettle with 2 generous quarts of boiling stock (water may be used) and carefully drop the dumplings, one at a time, boil 5 long minutes. Do not cover the kettle.

BEER PUNCH
(Transylvanian Recipe)

3 bottles of good beer   ¾ cup sugar (more if
2 cups milk   desired)
         6 egg yolks

Heat the beer and milk in separate saucepans; meanwhile, beat the egg yolks until very light, with the sugar; gradually add the hot milk to the beaten egg yolks, stirring vigorously and constantly, lest the egg cook; then add the hot beer, stirring constantly. Serve very hot in glass cups.

BRAISED BEAR LEG IN RED WINE

Marinate the top part of a hind leg (the ham part) for 5 long days in MARINADE No. II, page 179, turning occasionally. Then lard through and through with long, narrow strips of fat larding pork. Place the meat in a braising kettle with all the strained vegetables of the marinade and 1 cupful of the liquid and 2 cups of red wine; add then ½ cup of good goose fat. Cover hermetically and braise, that is, set in a moderately hot oven (375°) for 3 long hours. After the first hour of cooking, add 2 calves' feet, boned. Adjust the cover again and continue cooking without disturbing. Lift out the meat. Place on a platter and cover with a paste made of rolled bread crumbs mixed with a generous teaspoon of dry mustard, 1 generous teaspoon of brown sugar, one egg and one egg white beaten together, and enough sauce from the braising kettle to moisten the paste. Spread this all over the bear meat. Into this paste, press 2 dozen whole cloves, and put in the oven to brown. Meanwhile, place the contents of the braising kettle in a casserole, after removing the calves' feet, and the excess of fat. Bring to a boil, add 1 tablespoon of flour and cook for 10 minutes, stirring occasionally. Strain through a fine sieve, pressing a little so as to obtain all the liquid from the solid parts. Correct the seasonings, and serve aside with the meat, simply garnished with a large bunch of watercress at either end of the platter. Another side dish of sauerkraut may be served if desired.

BREAST OF BEAR SOUR CREAM

Marinate a breast of bear in MARINADE No. III, page 179, for 5 long days. Lift out, sponge, and lard through and through with narrow, long strips of fat larding pork, using 1 dozen, interspersed with long strips of celery, also through and through. Place in a large kettle and sear on all sides in 3 tablespoons of lard. The meat should not be too seared, and 10 long minutes over a hot fire will be quite sufficient. Pour over, after removing the melted lard, or, still better, transferring the meat to another large kettle, 4 cups of sour cream, add 3 whole cloves, 12 whole peppercorns, unbruised, and 1 cup of white wine. Cover hermetically and set in a moderate oven (375°) for 3 long hours, taking care to turn the meat occasionally. Remove the cover and allow the top of the meat to brown (about 15 minutes), basting frequently. Remove the excess of fat, add 1 scant tablespoon of extract of beef, the juice of a medium-sized lemon, and a small pinch of coarsely ground black pepper. Lift out the meat. Dress on a hot platter. Keep hot, while reducing the sauce a little over a hot fire. Strain the sauce through a fine sieve, pour part of it on the meat, and serve the remainder aside.

BRAISED BEAR LIVER
(*Russian Method*)

Scald and remove the tubes and skin of a 3½- to 4-lb. piece of bear liver. Lard through and through with strips of larding pork. Marinate in 2½ cups of white wine for at least 3 long hours, turning the meat occasionally. Wipe dry. Sear on all sides in 3 tablespoons of lard. Then envelop the liver in thin slices of pork fat spread with the following mixture:

1 tablespoon of finely chopped onion

1 tablespoon shallots, chopped fine

1 scant tablespoon parsley, minced

½ cup meat sausage

½ cup raw mushrooms, minced fine

1 pinch thyme leaves

1 generous tablespoon of paprika

1 blade of powdered sage

2 leaves tarragon herbs, chopped fine

Salt, pepper, cayenne and nutmeg to taste

Put this thoroughly blended mixture through food chopper twice to ensure smoothness, adding as you go along for the last time 1 egg white. Tie securely. Place in a buttered casserole having a tight-fitting cover. Pour over the wine used for the marinade, and add:

8 whole peppercorns, bruised

2 whole cloves, bruised

8 sprigs parsley tied with

1 large bay leaf

2 slices of lemon

Adjust the cover and set the casserole in a moderate oven (350°) for 2½ hours without disturbing but once, after one hour of cooking, to turn the liver. Dress the liver on a hot platter. Keep hot. Strain the gravy after removing the excess of fat, through a fine sieve, then add 1 cup of sour cream, scalded, and 1 generous *tablespoon* of real paprika. Boil once. Pour part of this sauce over the liver, and serve the remainder aside. Surround the liver with 12 large mushrooms, peeled, and sautéed in butter.

FISH HOUSE PUNCH

(Fish House Punch as Brewed by the State in Schuylkill Since 1732)

Slack ¾ pound of loaf sugar (you may use lump sugar) in a large punch bowl. When entirely dissolved, add 1 quart lemon juice; then 2 quarts Jamaica rum, 1 bottle brandy, 2 quarts water, 1 wineglass of peach brandy. Put in a large piece of solid ice in the punch bowl and allow the mixture to brew for about 2 hours, stirring occasionally.

In the winter when the ice melts slowly, more water may be used; in summer, less, as the melting dilutes the mixture sufficiently.

FILLET OF BEAR À LA ZINOFF

Marinate for 4 short days, a whole fillet of bear, in MARINADE No. III, page 179. Lift out, sponge, and cut into small individual serving slices. Place these slices in a large kettle and add the strained marinade, 3 juniper berries, powdered, ½ teaspoon of mustard seeds, 8 or 10 sprigs parsley tied with the same amount of top leaves of wild celery, and 2 large bay leaves. Set the kettle over a hot fire and at the first boil reduce to moderate and allow to simmer gently for 2 hours, covered. Lift out the slices of fillet and place on a hot platter covered with freshly grated cooked green corn, generously buttered, and seasoned to taste with salt and black pepper. Strain the liquid left in the kettle, and keep only 2 generous cups. Place these 2 cups in a saucepan and set over a hot fire. When boiling, add 2 tablespoons of kneaded butter and 2 tablespoons of chopped green olives with equal parts of capers. Serve at once with the sauce partly poured over the meat, and the remainder served aside.

DEER

The flesh of the deer, especially the old, demands a slight mortification, to soften and enhance its full flavor; the very young deer may be cooked in the fresh state, this being optional. However, the marinating is almost compulsory for old deer, besides a few days of mortification. Old and young deer may be cooked in all the different methods of preparation adapted to lamb and mutton, respectively.

For CIVET or STEW use shoulder, neck, breast, and flank, using the blood of hare or even rabbit to bind at the last minute, lest the stew will be an ordinary stew. As for lamb or mutton, the meat is cut into serving portion and seared over a hot fire. The blood of the deer, young or old, cannot be served, as it does not keep fresh long enough, so hare or rabbit blood is usually used, as in hare or rabbit civet.

For CHOPS and DOUBLE CHOPS use the rack, the loin, exactly as you would the same parts of lamb or mutton. Good olive oil is the best shortening. Dress according to directions.

For ROAST use the leg, which should be stale, that is, mortified for a few days, then marinated for several hours or over night. The garnishing is made according to directions.

For STEAKS, MIGNONS use the loin, the fillet, tenderloin, flank, and rump. Garnishing and saucing according to directions.

For ROAST SADDLE, or CIMIER, or BUTTOCK, or HAUNCH: The saddle may include the rack and shoulders, or the rack and loin. The saddle is usually larded with narrow, long strips of fat larding pork, after the nerves have been removed, as in fact in all parts of the deer, young and old. Certain recipes omit the marinade. The round may also be prepared as the saddle, when the rack is attached to it.

GARNISHINGS

In the following recipes, the garnishing is indicated. The usual accompaniment of prepared deer, whatever be the part, is red currant jelly, red currant jelly mixed with horseradish, high seasonings, applesauce, mashed chestnuts, quince jelly, grape jelly, and kumquat preserves.

With the other parts of the animal, delicious chopped and ground meat preparations may be made. With the shoulder, appetizing loaves, or pâtés, also are made, among other preparations.

CIVET OF DEER

This delicious dish may be prepared exactly as a Hare Civet. However, as the deer has a certain pronounced gamy taste, the pieces should be rubbed with a damp cloth, dipped in lukewarm water, then wrung. The pieces are then sponged and the remainder of the recipe follows:

If the deer is young, use both shoulders and part of the neck, so as to obtain about 8 lbs. for 6 persons, not including ½ lb. of the liver of the animal, from which the gall is carefully removed. Use the blood of a rabbit, or hare, of which there should be a generous ½ cup. Cut the meat into serving portions, and place in a bowl with:

4 tablespoons brandy	½ scant teaspoon thyme leaves
4 tablespoons olive oil	1 tablespoon flour
2½ glasses of red wine	2 dozen small white onions,
4 sprigs parsley, and	peeled, sliced
4 tops of green celery, tied with	2 dozen of small fresh mush-
2 thyme leaves	rooms, peeled, stems re-
2 small cloves of garlic, gently	moved and sliced, caps quar-
bruised	tered

Salt, pepper, a few grains cayenne pepper to taste

Mix the above ingredients thoroughly and put over the pieces of deer. Cover and allow to marinate for 6 long hours, stirring occasionally.

When ready to prepare, fry ½ lb. of salt pork, previously parboiled and diced small in a little butter, and drain as soon as brown. In the very same pan and fat, add the pieces of deer, well drained and sponged thoroughly, and sear on all sides, turning the pieces now and then. Lift out the pieces, place on a hot platter and keep hot. To the fat remaining in the pan, sprinkle with a generous table-spoon of flour, cook, blending well until the mixture acquires a golden tinge. Rapidly put the pieces of fried pork and deer into the flour mixture and moisten with the marinade, solid and liquid parts. Cover and set in a moderate oven (350–375°) for 40 long min-utes. Remove from the oven and set over a very, very low flame. Gradually heat the rabbit blood (hare blood will be better) almost to the scalding point, over hot water, and stir in ½ teaspoon of flour or ¼ teaspoon of arrow root, diluted first in a little sauce, and strained over the blood. When ready to serve, and only then, add the piece of liver, raw and cubed small, then add the blood-flour mixture, stir, bring slowly to the scalding point, not the boiling point, and serve on a very hot platter, surrounded with small triangles or heart-shaped bread fried in butter at the last minute. No other garnishing is necessary. However, for effect and to add to the garnishing, you may (optional) fill half tomatoes (small ones), scooped carefully, with kumquat preserves, arranged between the triangles or heart-shaped fried bread.

CIVET OF DEER HUNTER STYLE

Select as much as possible of an old animal's breast and ½ lb. of its liver. Sponge with a hot damp cloth; cut into serving pieces, place the pieces in a large bowl, then add 1 medium-sized onion, peeled and sliced in rings, 1 tablespoon of pickling spices, 1 generous tea-spoon salt, a small bay leaf tied with 4 sprigs of parsley, and pour over enough wine vinegar to cover entirely. Let stand 24 hours. When ready to cook, transfer the entire mixture to a large kettle, and bring the mixture to a boil; then reduce the heat and allow to sim-mer for 3 long hours. Thicken the gravy with flour and butter, browned, using equal parts of each, so as to make a tablespoon. Boil once, set aside 5 short minutes to simmer and mellow and serve with Potato Dumplings, made as follows:

Potato Dumplings

2½ cups freshly made, hot ½ cup of flour
    potatoes ¼ teaspoon mace
4 whole eggs ¼ teaspoon of nutmeg
1 generous tablespoon butter A few grains white pepper to
1 cup cracker crumbs   taste
        1 teaspoon flour

Cream the butter, add salt, spices and the beaten egg yolks and stir vigorously and rapidly. Gradually combine with the mashed potatoes, which should be very smooth, not lumpy, and the cracker crumbs. Mix thoroughly. Sift the flour, and mix well. Finally, fold in the stiffly beaten egg whites. Shape into small balls, the size of an egg, with well-floured hands, and insert 3 small triangles of freshly made toast in the center of each dumpling. Place the dumplings on top of the simmering civet, cover tightly, bring to a rapid boil and let boil 10 long minutes. Fry the liver pieces, cubed small, 3 short minutes, adding to the civet. Dress the dumplings on a hot platter all around the civet, and dust generously with minced parsley.

KNICKERBEIN

(A German Punch) (Serves One)

This very old German recipe, Knickerbein, meaning cracking bones, and it does crack your bones, is a delectable concoction from which our Eggnog seems to have originated. This drink carries a potent punch, especially if more than one helping is taken. It is a dangerous beverage which may prove too much for the uninitiated, who would do well to avoid it. However, if this does not wake and warm you up, especially on a cold day, nothing else will. Yet, I repeat, stick to one helping lest you fall, your leg cracking, weakening under your own weight.

RECIPE

Keep a mixture of the following ready made on hand, thoroughly combined, in the proportion given:

⅓ each of Curaçao, Benedictine, and Maraschino.

When mixing a drink, fill a straw-stem port-wine glass ⅔ full of the above mixture, float the unbroken yolk of a newlaid egg on the surface of the liqueur, then build up a kind of pyramid with the stiffly beaten white of the same egg on the surface of the latter, a few drops of Angostura bitters, and drink as directed.

DIRECTIONS FOR TAKING THE KNICKERBEIN

The following directions for taking the Knickerbein should be religiously adhered to:

I. Pass the glass under the nostrils and inhale the flavor, as you would for a Fine Champagne Napoleon, usually served in a large tulip glass. Then pause a long minute. Then repeat twice.

II. Hold the glass perpendicularly, close under your mouth, open it wide, and suck the froth (beaten egg white), which sometimes is sprinkled with a little nutmeg (optional), by drawing a deep breath. Pause again one long minute.

III. Point the lips (as if you were pouting), and take ⅓ of the liquid contents remaining in the glass without touching the yolk. Pause once more a long minute.

IV. Straighten the body, throw the head backward, as if ready for the worst, and swallow the entire remaining contents in the glass all at once, at the same time breaking the egg yolk in your mouth.

Courtesy of the Chef of the Dom Hotel, Cologne, Germany.

OLD-FASHIONED DAUBED DEER

Marinate a 5-lb. piece of loin of deer (roebuck if available) for 24 short hours. Sponge, then lard through and through with long, narrow strips of fat larding pork, using about a good ¼ of a lb., interspersed with long strips of green pepper, also through and through. Place in a braising kettle and pour over enough MARINADE No. III, page 179, barely to cover, substituting red wine for white wine, and using the marinade liquid and solid parts altogether. Adjust the cover hermetically, set the kettle in a moderate oven (350–375°) and do not disturb for 5 long hours, but once, after 4 hours of cooking, add 2 dozen small white raw onions, peeled, and 2 dozen small mushrooms (fresh), caps separated and peeled, but whole, and stems peeled and sliced thin.

When ready to serve, dress the piece of deer on a hot platter, correct the seasoning and add, after removing the excess of fat, ½ cup of heavy cream. Bring the sauce to a boil, pour part of it, vegetables and liquid, over the meat and serve the remaining part in a sauceboat with a side dish of eggplant made as follows:

EGGPLANT FARCI À LA PARISIENNE (For 6 persons)

Select 3 large handsome eggplants of the same size, and cut them in halves lengthwise. With a sharp knife, score the cut sides deeply, then sauté them in good olive oil till they are delicately browned. With a large spoon, carefully scoop out the pulp, leaving the purple shell about ¼ inch thick, without damaging it. Cut the pulp of the eggplants into small cubes. Now sauté in plenty of butter one scant pound of fresh mushrooms, caps and stems, peeled and sliced. In another pan, brown thin slices of onion (using a large one) until delicately browned, and add 6 slices of freshly made toast, cubed very small or else crumbed coarsely; then pour the onion and bread mixture over the mushrooms, butter and all, add 2 tablespoons of parsley, minced fine, and 2 generous tablespoons of Chinese soy sauce (bought in grocery store), a generous sprinkling of black pepper, a dash of cayenne, and a teaspoon of brown sugar. With this stuffing, the eggplant shells are filled and heaped up, then very fine buttered crumbs are scattered over the tops. Butter a large pan to receive the six boats and put the pan and boats in a hot oven (400°) for 15 long minutes or until thoroughly, and appetizingly browned. Serve piping hot.

A dry white wine is *de rigueur* for such a delicious combination. A wine, as the Niersteiner Riesling, on which a connoisseur has made the following comment: ". . . It exhilarates without producing after heaviness and according to well-known medical authorities purifies the blood. A wine with a delicately scented bouquet, light and finely fruited."

BUTTOCK OF DEER
(*Royal Canadian Method*)

Lard the rack and attached shoulder of a young deer, after removing the first skin. Place in MARINADE No. II, page 179, adding a small pinch of dried basilic, and allow to stand for 4 long days, turning twice daily. Drain thoroughly. Sponge, and envelop (optional), if using a spit, with a profusely buttered paper. If roasting in an oven, omit the buttered paper. Roast in the usual way, first in a hot oven (450–500°) for 15 minutes, then reduce the temperature to 350°, for the remaining part of the roasting process, allowing 12 to 15 minutes to the pound for cooking. Serve with a Poivrade sauce (*see* SAUCES) and a side dish of applesauce.

FILLET OF ROEBUCK PURÉE OF CHESTNUTS

From a roebuck deer fillet, carefully denerved, cut thin slices of about ½-inch thickness, but do not flatten them. Lard each slice with 4 narrow strips of fat larding pork, trimming neatly and evenly with the meat. Place in a braising kettle or still better in an earthenware casserole having a close-fitting cover, 1¾ cups of "braise" or mirepoix (*see* GROUSE IN AUSBRUCHE, page 29). Place the fillet slices over. Pour over ½ cup of MARINADE No. III, page 179, well strained, and ¼ generous cup of red wine. Cover and cook over a hot flame until the liquid is nearly evaporated and the bottom of braise or mirepoix slightly browned. Then pour over the liquid, in which the trimmings have been cooked, barely reaching half the mixture. Place a round, generously buttered paper over and set the casserole in a moderately hot oven (375°) for 30 short minutes. Remove the paper, and baste constantly to glaze the top of the meat. Dress crownlike on a hot round platter. Remove the excess of fat from the gravy carefully; garnish the center of the meat platter with fresh green peas, generously buttered. Pour the sauce over the fillet slices and serve with a purée of chestnuts and another side dish of applesauce.

PURÉE OF CHESTNUTS

Split on the sides (flat sides) 2½ dozen good chestnuts. Throw them into rapidly boiling water, for 2 short minutes, so to be able to peel more easily. Cook the peeled chestnuts in good meat stock, or in milk if desired, adding a small bunch of celery (3 small white pieces) tied together. Drain and rub the chestnuts through a fine sieve, or put through a ricer as you would potatoes prepared for mashing. Season to taste with salt, and white pepper, then beat in vigorously a little of the milk used for cooking them, and 2 tablespoons of butter. Serve as you would mashed potatoes.

FILLET OF DEER

(*Italian Method*)

Prepare a dumpling mixture, following the directions as indicated in recipe for PARTRIDGE DUMPLINGS, page 54, substituting an equal amount of trimmings of the fillet for partridge. With a third of this preparation, line the bottom of a large service platter to ½ inch thickness or even thicker, in ring shape. Smooth well with a spatula dipped in hot water. Place the remainder of the dumpling mixture in a pastry bag and press around the ring small dumplings in the shape of a snail shell, that is, twisting the hand while pressing so as to finish the top of the dumpling pointed. Keep in a cool place. This preparation should be cooked at the door of a hot oven or still better under the flame of the broiler, 10 minutes before serving. Trim a half saddle of deer without removing the fillet, which should be attached to it. Lard the saddle and the attached fillet with long, narrow strips of fat larding pork, and roast in the usual way, that is, with half cup of the marinade in which the saddle has been marinated for at least 3 days, strained, and mixed with ¼ cup of good butter, basting often, and allowing 15 minutes for each pound of meat. Remove the meat from the oven, and slice the fillet in slices, and diagonally. The slices should be about 1 inch in thickness. Dress these slices over the ring of dumpling mixture which has been placed under the flame of the broiling oven to brown delicately, turning the platter constantly to obtain an even hue. The slices should be placed so as to form a crown, and each slice overlapping another. Garnish the center of the crown with small stoned olives, parboiled, then thoroughly drained. Cover the olives and the small dumplings in snail-shape with a fine Spanish sauce, reduced with good red wine and a scant tablespoon of "Fumet" of deer made as indicated in recipe How To Prepare Game Stock, page 45, but where deer meat has been substituted for game bird. Serve with the remainder of the sauce in a sauceboat. The saddle may also be served but separately.

This recipe was often served at the Court of Germany by Urbain Dubois who was the Chef of the Kaiser Wilhelm der Grosse.

JUGGED DEER FILLET REMOISE

This recipe has been found by the writer in the library of Rheims, in Champagne, France, and is dated 1429. It used to be the formula of the Hôtellerie de l'Asne Rayé (meaning the Zebra Hotel). Certain ingredients have been eliminated, however, and the writer has endeavored to present the recipe as accurately as possible, although modernized.

Take the entire fillet of a deer and marinate for at least 4 days in MARINADE No. III, page 179. Drain, sponge, and place in a kettle with the entire marinade, solid and liquid parts, adding the same weight of breast of salt pork, cut in serving portions, 3 juniper berries, crushed, and 1 generous tablespoon of flour mixed with ¼ teaspoon of good saffron. Cover and let simmer very gently over a small flame for 4 hours. Dress the fillet on a hot platter, sliced in portion size, the salt pork on each side, and the sauce strained, through a sieve, pressing a little so as to obtain as much as possible of the pulp of the different ingredients used for the marinade and the cooking process. Boil the sauce once. Correct the seasoning. Pour over a part of the sauce, or rather gravy, and serve the remainder aside with a side dish of candied pears (*see* GARNISHINGS).

DEER LIVER À LA GOMBERVAUX

AUTHOR'S NOTE

Deer liver may be prepared in all the different methods adapted for the beef, calf, lamb, and pork liver. However, it should be larded. Narrow strips of fillets of anchovies, may also be interspersed with the narrow strips of fat larding pork. All the different sauces used for the ordinary liver of domestic animals may be served with almost all the wild furred game, large or small. The wild game liver needs marinating.

RECIPE

Take the whole liver of a young deer. Marinate for 3 days in MARINADE No. I, page 178. Drain and lard through and through with narrow strips of lard and anchovies, interspersed. The anchovy fillets should be sponged thoroughly, and carefully trimmed. Place in a braising kettle, pour over 2 cups of strained marinade, and add

1 bouquet garni (6 sprigs of parsley tied with 1 large bay leaf), 1 pony glass of good Madeira wine, and a tablespoon of beef extract (bought in store). Set the kettle in a moderate oven, tightly covered, and do not disturb for 2 long hours (oven at 350°). Lift out the liver. Dress on a hot platter. Place the strained liquid in a saucepan. Reduce to half, over a hot fire, and add 1 cup of good, fresh heavy cream. Correct the seasoning. Pour part of the sauce over the liver and serve the remainder aside with another side dish of cooked noodles, the top of which may be strewn with 1 cupful of cooked, or rather stewed, prunes with very little juice of the prunes poured over. The noodles should be very hot and generously buttered.

HOT HOPPELPOPPEL

(*A German Punch*)

Place 1 quart of sweet cream, 2 generous tablespoons of sugar in an enameled saucepan, and bring to the scalding point, stirring occasionally. Into a little cold milk, beat 4 egg yolks until fluffy and creamy (you may add a small pinch of nutmeg if desired, as is done in Bavaria). Then stir into the beaten egg yolks, 2 cups of good rum. Beat well and gradually stir rapidly into the scalded cream. Serve in glass cups.

Instead of cream, you may use milk, or even water or tea, or linden tea, as is done in certain localities of Germany.

COLD HOPPELPOPPEL

(*Meaning Jumping Jack*)

The yolks of four eggs and a little grating of nutmeg are stirred into half a pint of cold fresh cream and beaten to a thick foam, 1 cup of good rum is added which may be mixed with 1 cup of linden tea, plain tea (both cold), and the mixture is sweetened to taste. In some parts of

Germany, a topping of whipped cream is added to each cup (glass cups) before serving, then a grating of nutmeg is made over each topping.

HUNCH OF DEER SWEET SOUR SAUCE

Place in a marinade a hunch of deer, there should be 7 or 8 pounds, using MARINADE No. II, page 179, for 3 long days. Lift out, sponge, and lard through and through with long, narrow strips of fat larding pork, using a good half pound. Place the neatly trimmed, that is, the larding strips cut even with the meat, into a large kettle and add all the vegetables as for a beef soup, adding 1 quart of good red wine mixed with enough cold water so as to cover the meat, but no more than covering. Cook exactly as for a beef soup for at least 3½ to 4 hours, skimming after the first boil, then covering and allowing gently to simmer constantly. After the third hour of simmering, remove the cover, so as to allow the liquid to reduce a little. Dress the meat on a hot platter. Boil down the stock left in the kettle to nearly 1½ cups (generous), over a very hot fire or flame. With the remainder of the stock, make a sauce as follows:

SWEET SOUR SAUCE

Chop as finely as possible 2 or 3 shallots (onion may be substituted, if shallots are not available, but the flavor will not be the same) and place in a saucepan with 2 tablespoons of wine vinegar. Let this reduce to half, over a hot fire, then add the reduced stock (which is wine and water, but with the entire fragrance and flavor of wine) over, gradually, while stirring frequently. Then add 1 tablespoon of tomato paste, 1 whole clove, and cook for 10 long minutes over a medium flame. In a saucer, mix 1 scant tablespoon of flour, a few grains of cayenne, 1 tablespoon of prepared mustard and 1½ tablespoons of capers. Heat well until the mixture reaches the boiling point. Let boil once. Skim, simmer a few minutes to remove the rancidness of the raw flour. Pour half of this sauce over the meat, serve the remainder aside with a side dish of stewed celery, and garnish the platter with apple rings (*see* GARNISHINGS) and at either end of the platter, place a nice bunch of crisp watercress. Serve at once.

JELLIED DEER IN PORT WINE

Rub a 6-lb. piece of hind leg of deer with a dry cloth, after removing the first skin, leaving the meat completely bare. Soak in salt water for an hour, then put on to boil with 1 medium-sized onion, stuck with 3 cloves, a few grains of cayenne pepper to taste, 10 whole peppercorns, bruised, salt to taste, 1 teaspoon of cinnamon, 10 sprigs parsley tied with 2 small bay leaves, a blade of mace, 3 juniper berries, a small clove of garlic, and enough water to cover entirely, for at least 2 hours, over a gentle fire, covered. Lift out the piece of deer. Place on a platter and allow to cool. To the stock left in the kettle, add a veal knuckle and continue cooking for 1 long hour, the knuckle cracked lengthwise, but not separated. Strain the broth and allow to reduce to one cup, over a hot fire, and uncovered. Cool this natural gelatine. Place the piece of cold deer in a large mold after trimming so it will fit a square mold pressing a little. To the reduced broth, add ½ generous cup of good, rich red port wine. Heat a little and pour over the meat in the square mold. Place in refrigerator to set and cool. Unmold over a platter covered with a thick bed of crisp watercress, and serve cold with your favorite green salad. Bear, reindeer, and in fact all the large furred game may be prepared in this way. The meat will keep all week in a refrigerator.

A fact to be remembered when marinating game, is that the longer the marinating, the stronger the gamy flavor, so this process is entirely left to individual taste. Twenty-four hours of marinade will leave the game in its natural flavor; forty-eight hours will bring out the high strength of the game, and above that limit the game will be stronger accordingly.

ROAST BACK OF DEER CHASSEUR

Remove the first skin from a piece of the back of a deer of about 6 lbs. Rub with salt and pepper, lard through and through with 4 rows of long, narrow strips of larding pork, rolled in very finely chopped onion, garlic, and parsley. There should be a generous tablespoon. Place then in MARINADE No. II, page 179, for 3 days. Lift out dripping and place in a roasting pan with 1 cup of the marinade and ¼ cup of lard. Set in a hot oven (450°) for 15 long minutes, then reduce the temperature to 350–375°, and roast in the usual way, basting often with the marinade and lard in the dripping pan, allowing 15 minutes to the pound of meat. Dress on a hot platter. Keep hot. Place the dripping pan over a hot fire and bring the mixture to a boil, after removing the excess of fat. Strew a tablespoon of flour over and stir from the bottom of the pan, for 3 short minutes. Allow then to boil, slowly, for 5 long minutes. Strain through a fine sieve, pressing a little so as to obtain all the pulp and liquid from the solid parts. Then add 1 teaspoon of prepared horseradish, well drained, and 1 tablespoon of good Madeira wine. Pour part of this sauce over the meat and serve the remainder aside.

ROAST LEG OF DEER

(*Hungarian Method*)

Prepare and marinate a 5½- to 6-lb. leg of deer as indicated in recipe for ROAST BACK OF DEER CHASSEUR, above. Lift out of the marinade, and cover the leg with a greased paper, using lard. Place in roasting pan with ½ cup of lard, or bacon drippings and a generous cup of the marinade, vegetables, and liquid. Set in a hot oven (475°) for 15 minutes, turning the leg once. Reduce the heat to 350° and continue roasting, basting often, allowing 15 long minutes to the pound. When done, pour over a pint (2 cups) of sour cream and continue roasting, basting often for 15 minutes longer. Cut enough slices of the leg to go around once. Place the remaining piece of leg on the very same platter, pour half the unstrained sauce over the slices, and serve the remainder aside after sprinkling both, sauce over the slices and sauce in the sauceboat, with 1 tablespoon of real paprika. Serve with a side dish of

STEAMED MUSHROOMS HUNGARIAN STYLE

Wash a pound of fresh mushrooms thoroughly, peel, remove the stems, using only the caps, whole. Place in plenty of butter, season to taste with salt and pepper, sprinkle with 2 tablespoons of flour mixed with a little cold meat stock, cover and let steam for 45 minutes.

ROAST LEG OF DEER RICHARDIN

Place a 5½- to 6-lb. leg of deer, after removing the first skin to leave the meat bare, and larding with long, narrow strips of larding pork rolled in allspice, in MARINADE No. III, page 179. Let stand 5 long days (the meat will be very gamy). Lift out. Sponge and roast in the usual way, allowing 15 long minutes for each pound of meat. Dress on a hot platter and garnish simply with a large bunch of watercress at either end of the platter. Serve with the following sauce:

SAUCE RICHARDIN

Blend 2 tablespoons of flour and 2 tablespoons of butter thoroughly, and let brown a little. Moisten with 1 generous cup of the strained marinade, stirring constantly, and pouring the liquid gradually, until mixture begins to thicken; then add 1 generous tablespoon of "Fumet" (*see* recipe, How To PREPARE GAME STOCK, page 45), substituting deer meat, trimmings of the deer, for game bird, 1 pony glass of fine champagne, salt, black pepper to taste, and allow to reduce ¼. Meanwhile, boil 4 shallots (of the same size) in 1 generous tablespoon of the strained marinade, the shallots finely minced, until the liquid is almost evaporated. Add this to the sauce. When ready to serve, add to the sauce the reduced gravy from the roasting pan, previously and thoroughly cleared of all the fat, and strained, using only ½ cup. Pour part of this sauce over enough slices of the leg of deer to go around, and serve the remainder aside.

DEER CHOPS OR CUTLETS OR MIGNONS

As already said at the beginning of this section, chops and cutlets, as well as mignons or noisettes (pope's eye) are trimmed as those of the lamb. Two pieces are usually served as a portion. The usual rule is to fry them rapidly in good olive oil, which adds to the flavor. They are always sponged before being dressed on the platter, and butter or any other mixture substituted for the oil, which is never served. All the different methods of preparation of lamb and mutton chops may be adapted to those of the deer. Chops, cutlets, and mignons may be larded, marinated or not, according to directions. They should be always underdone lest the meat be tough. The mignons, similar to the fillet mignons of beef, may also be prepared in all the different methods of preparation adapted to the fillet mignons of beef. However, as chops and cutlets, they should be very underdone.

Their ordinary garnishings are small cubes of jelly, small triangles of bread fried in butter. However, there are some differences to the above and certain recipes call for butter instead of olive oil, but this is always indicated in the directions. Whatever the method of preparation, deer chops, cutlets, or mignons should always be served with a side dish of either applesauce, or jelly, according to directions or taste.

DEER CHOP SAUTÉ WITH CHERRIES

Trim one dozen young deer chops, as you would for lamb chops. Sauté rapidly in very hot olive oil, keeping the chops underdone, and turning once during the cooking process to ensure browning on both sides. Sponge each chop with a kitchen towel. Dress crownlike on a hot platter, each chop separated with a small piece of gingerbread, cut triangle-shape and lightly colored in butter. Garnish the center of the crown with fresh cherries in compote (stewed) and cover each chop with a scant teaspoon of Venaison sauce (*see* SAUCES). Serve with a side dish of Pea Soufflé made as follows:

PEA SOUFFLÉ AMERICAN STYLE

Either fresh or canned peas may be used for this preparation. Heat the contents of a No. 2 can of peas (large) in a saucepan for ten long minutes with 1 tablespoon of granulated sugar, ½ teaspoon salt, a pinch of white pepper to taste, 2 or 3 slices (thin) of white onion, and a few grains of thyme leaves. Drain thoroughly and rub through a fine sieve. Beat in 2 generous tablespoons of butter, then gradually, and one at a time, beat in 3 egg yolks, beating rapidly after each addition. Now add 1 cup of dry bread crumbs, soaked in milk, then squeezed through a cloth and tossed a little. Mix thoroughly. Finally fold in 4 stiffly beaten egg whites with a few grains of salt. Turn mixture into a copiously buttered soufflé dish, and bake in a hot oven (400°) for 35 long minutes, without placing the soufflé dish in a pan of hot water.

CARDINAL'S PUNCH I

3 large oranges, sliced thin
3 whole cloves, heads removed
1 blade of mace
3 drops of essence of nutmeg
3 bruised cardamon seeds
4 oz. dissolved barley sugar
1 pint boiling water
1 bottle of good Rhine wine

Place in a saucepan the water, sliced oranges, and the condiments and spices. Cover and bring to the boiling point. Remove from the fire and let infuse near the flame, which should be very low, for 10 long minutes. Then strain with pressure into another saucepan. Add the Rhine wine, cover and let simmer gently (*do not boil*) until a white foam appears on the surface of the mixture. Remove from the fire and serve as hot as possible in glass cups.

DEER CHOPS AU GENIÈVRE FLAMBÉ

Sauté rapidly 2 dozen deer chops, prepared in the usual way, in very hot olive oil, until golden brown on both sides, but well underdone (4 to 5 minutes, according to size). Sponge. Dress each chop crownlike on a hot platter, separated with a small piece of bread, cut heart-shape and fried in butter on both sides. Remove the oil entirely from the pan in which the chops were sautéeing and pour in a pony glass of good gin, then touch with a match, add 2 small juniper berries, bruised, or, still better, pulverized, 1 scant cup of heavy cream, and let this reduce a little over a hot fire, stirring occasionally. Add then the juice of a half small lemon, 4 tablespoons of Poivrade sauce (*see* SAUCES), and pour this sauce over the chops. Serve at once with a side dish of applesauce, not too sweet, and hot.

DEER CUTLET LUMBERJACK

Cut 6 thin slices from the back of a young deer. Sprinkle with salt and pepper (black) and marinate in olive oil, using ½ cup, to which add the juice of a medium-sized lemon, 4 peppercorns (coarsely ground), salt to taste and 1 generous tablespoon of parsley (minced), 1 small piece of bay leaf, a small clove of garlic (crushed), and allow to stand 1 hour. Lift out. Drain and sponge. Place in a baking dish, generously oiled. Pour over 6 tablespoons of the marinade and 2 tablespoons of good sherry wine. Bake in a hot oven for 20 minutes (400°), basting every five minutes. Dress on a hot platter, crownlike, squeeze the juice of a small lime over (lemon may be used). Place in the center of the ring, 1 dozen fresh mushrooms freshly broiled. Serve with a side dish of cream sauce, to which has been added 1 teaspoon of good gin. Serve with a side dish of currant jelly, mixed with half amount of prepared horseradish, well drained.

CARDINAL'S PUNCH II

2 whole oranges each stuck with 1 dozen whole cloves,
   head removed and roasted before the broiler or in a
   warm oven
1 quart of good champagne—sugar to taste

When the oranges have acquired a good dark-brown
color, cut into quarters and remove the seeds. Place in a
saucepan and pour over the champagne. Sweeten to taste.
Let simmer (to the scalding point) over a gentle fire, but
do not boil, until a white foam appears on the surface.
Remove from fire at once and serve in glass cups with a
quarter of orange in each cup.

DEER CHOP NAPOLITAINE

AUTHOR'S NOTE

The following recipe may seem difficult, but it is not and the little
trouble taken in its making will amply reward a connoisseur, if the
directions are followed exactly.

Prepare 6 chops as indicated at the beginning of this section, that
is as for lamb chops, trimming neatly and removing the bone entirely. The chops must be rather thick and it is advisable to have
what is called in culinary terms a double chop. Marinate for 1 long
hour in olive oil, to which has been added the juice of a small
lemon, a bay leaf, 6 whole peppercorns, coarsely ground, 4 small
sprigs of fennel, salt to taste, turning the chops frequently in their
bath. Now lift out and sponge carefully. Place on a broiler, after
rolling each chop in pure olive oil, and broil under a hot flame, so
as to sear both sides, one long minute on each side being sufficient.
Remove the chops from the broiler. Pack on both sides a layer of
cooked, chopped macaroni, chopped fine and bound with a little
hot tomato paste. Wrap each chop in a piece of fell, the thin papery
substance which surrounds a leg of spring lamb, which by the way

should never be removed from lamb, but removed from an old mutton leg. Tie securely. Arrange the chops thus blanketed in a baking dish, generously oiled. Set the baking dish in a hot oven (450°) for 10 short minutes, brushing twice with lightly melted "Fumet" (*see* recipe, How To Prepare Game Stock, page 45), or extract of beef and turning once during the cooking process. Dress, crownlike on a hot round platter. Fill the center with macaroni prepared in the same style as the one used for stuffing the chops, garnish with green peppers (small) prepared as follows:

Stuffed Green Pepper Napolitaine

Slice the top from each small green pepper, all of the same size. There should be 6. Remove the seeds and rinse the green pepper then drain. Rub the inside with salt and black pepper mixed with a few grains of allspice. Now combine 3 apples, peeled and diced small, with ¼ cup of raisins, seedless, and plumped in hot water, then chopped after being sponged, 2 tablespoons of pignolia nuts, a few thyme leaves, olive oil, using ¼ cup, 4 generous tablespoons of grated fresh Parmesan cheese, 1 teaspoon of sugar, salt and black pepper to taste, in a bowl, previously rubbed with garlic. Mix very thoroughly and fill the green pepper cups with the mixture. Place a piece of anchovy fillet on the top of each pepper cup. Adjust the top, that is the slice removed so as to allow the cleaning of the inside of the pepper cups. Stand the peppers upright in a baking dish, and pour around them the following liquid: 4 generous tablespoons of good olive oil, as much good beef stock, 1 generous teaspoon of beef extract, salt, pepper, and allspice to taste, 1 tablespoon of very finely chopped onions. Set the baking dish in a moderate oven for about an hour, according to size of the green peppers, the oven set at 350°, basting frequently.

Sauce Napolitaine

To the sauce remaining in the baking dish, add 1 tablespoon of good Madeira wine. Bring to a boil over a hot fire. Remove aside and gradually add, bit by bit, 2 generous tablespoons of butter, beating vigorously after each addition. Pour part of this foamy sauce over the chops only and serve the remainder aside.

FILLET MIGNON OF DEER
(*Belgian Method*)

AUTHOR'S NOTE

Almost all the different methods of preparation of the fillet mignons of beef may be adapted to the fillet mignons of deer. However, and unless directed differently, the fillet mignons of deer should always be larded and marinated. All the garnishings of the fillet mignons of beef, as well as those of beefsteaks, whatever the cut, may be adapted to the deer mignons.

Prepare the fillet mignons as you would fillet mignons of beef. The weight of each mignon is usually 7 or 8 ounces. They should be thick, but small, rounded, and carefully trimmed. There should be 6 fillet mignons. Lard through and through with narrow strips of fat larding pork, rolled in crushed, or rather pulverized, juniper berries, using 3 berries for 6 mignons. Broil under the flame of a hot broiling oven, searing each side thoroughly. Reduce the flame and allow 5 long minutes of broiling for each of the mignons. Dress and serve with the sauce indicated in recipe for DEER CHOPS AU GENIÈVRE FLAMBÉ, page 205.

FILLET MIGNON VENAISON SAUCE
(*Master Recipe*)

From the following recipe, you may prepare and serve fillet mignons of deer with any kind of sauce selected from the Contents. You may broil or sauté the fillet mignons according to taste, and the garnishing may be one according to your fancy, selected from GARNISHINGS. As a rule, the mignons of deer, are served, besides the favorite vegetable dish, with either a side dish of mashed celery, mashed chestnuts, parsnips, or turnips. The sauce is always followed with a side dish of applesauce, currant jelly, or any other of your favorite jellies.

BREAST OF DEER IN RED WINE

Proceed as indicated in recipe for JUGGED SHOULDER OF WILD BOAR
IN RED WINE.

ROAST SADDLE OF DEER CHASSEUR

Marinate a saddle of deer for 24 hours in MARINADE No. III, longer
if a strong gamy taste is desired, but no more than 3 days, lest the
gamy flavor be too strong. Lift out. Sponge carefully, and lard
through with long, narrow strips of fat larding pork, rolled in pulverized juniper berries, mixed with very finely minced, dried parsley, salt and black pepper to taste. Strain the marinade and place
the vegetables in the bottom of a dripping pan. Over this, place the
sponged, and larded saddle. Roast in a very hot oven (500°) for 15
minutes, reduce the temperature and continue roasting at 350°, allowing 15 short minutes for each pound of meat and basting often
with lard. Dress on a hot platter and carve enough slices to go
around. Garnish with pears stewed in red wine, to which has been
added enough sugar to taste (the pears and wine should not be too
sweet) and a small stick of cinnamon, at either end of the platter.
Keep hot. Place the dripping pan over a hot fire, add 1 generous
cupful of game stock made from the trimmings, and allow to boil,
stirring from the bottom of the pan to loosen all the particles of
gelatinous matter which may adhere and sprinkle a tablespoon of
flour over. Strain through a fine sieve, pressing a little so as to obtain
all the pulp of the vegetables. Let stand one minute. Remove all the
fat from the top of the sauce, add 1 tablespoon of good sherry and
1 or 2 tablespoons of currant jelly, stir, boil once. Pour part of the
sauce over the sliced pieces, and serve the remainder aside with a
side dish of

CORN SCRAMBLE

To 1 can of condensed tomato soup, add 4 tablespoons of good
olive oil (other oil may be used if desired, but the olive oil gives a

nutty flavor), 1 generous tablespoon of finely minced onion, 1 generous tablespoon of finely minced green pepper, and 1 can of corn. Heat to the scalding point; then reduce the heat and add 4 beaten eggs, yolks and whites, ½ teaspoon salt, pinch of pepper to taste and a tablespoon of real paprika. Stir, and cook stirring rapidly and constantly until mixture is set but not firm. Serve at once, either in green pepper cups, tomato cups, or on generously buttered toast, topping with grated American cheese. An American delicacy dating from the pilgrims.

ARCHBISHOP'S PUNCH

1 large whole orange stuck with 12 cloves and roasted under the flame of the broiling oven or in a hot stove (400°) until of a good dark-brown color.
1 quart of white wine (claret may be substituted if desired) or sherry wine, or any other good wine, white or red. Sugar to taste.

When the orange has acquired a good dark-brown color and is delicately flavored with the cloves, cut it in half and remove the seeds. Place in a saucepan, pour over the selected wine and sweeten to taste. Let simmer over a gentle fire, but do not allow to boil, until a white foam appears at the surface. Remove from the fire and serve in glass cups.

STANDARD MEASUREMENT FOR BEVERAGES

A mixing glass holds 12 ounces, or 6 jiggers, or 24 level tablespoons.
A jigger holds 2 ounces, or 4 level tablespoons.
A pony glass holds 1 ounce, or half a jigger, or 2 level tablespoons.

A liqueur glass holds 1 ounce, or half a jigger, or 2 tablespoons.

A sherry or port glass holds 2 ounces, or 4 level tablespoons.

A cocktail glass holds 2 ounces, or 4 level tablespoons.

A Bordeaux or Burgundy glass holds 4 ounces, or 8 level
tablespoons.

A champagne glass holds 5 ounces, or 10 level tablespoons.

A tumbler holds from 8 to 9 ounces, or 16 or 18 level
tablespoons.

SADDLE OF DEER À LA CHERVILLE

The following recipe does not require marinating. However, the
saddle should hang at least 3 long days to mortify slightly. As usual,
remove the first skin of the piece of meat leaving the flesh exposed.
Just before roasting, rub the meat first with lemon juice, then with
salt and pepper, using black coarsely ground or crushed pepper liber-
ally. Roast in a dripping pan, the bottom of which contains 2 cups
of "braise" or mirepoix made as indicated in recipe for GROUSE IN
AUSBRUCHE, page 29. Pour over the braise or mirepoix a cup of good
cider, then ½ scant cup of good lard, melted. This will be used for
basting frequently. Roast in the usual way, allowing 15 minutes for
each pound of meat. Dress on a hot platter, enough slices to go
around for the first helping. Garnish the edge of the platter with
raw apples, scooped carefully, and of the same size, the pulp minced,
seasoned with a little cinnamon, returned to the scooped apples,
then baked as an ordinary baked apple, without being niggardly
with butter to top, before setting in the oven. At each end of the
platter, place a large bunch of crisp young watercress, which for
effect may be dipped in paprika, flour, or nutmeg (optional), then
shaken a little. Serve with a side dish of Gooseberry sauce (*see*
SAUCES), to which has been added, for each cup, a generous tablespoon of prepared horseradish, thoroughly drained.

SADDLE OF DEER À LA CRÈME

The following recipe requires a long marinating of at least 4 days. This long marinating will not influence the strength of the gamy flavor, because this will be attenuated by the sauce, which by the way is really a treat. The marinating should be in MARINADE No. III, page 179, and should not be used hot, but rather cold.

When the meat is marinated to the desired point, place in a dripping pan, on top of the vegetables (drained) from the marinade. Roast in the usual way, that is, allowing 15 long minutes for each pound of meat. Remove from the dripping pan as soon as to the point and place on a hot platter. Place the dripping pan over a hot flame, and pour over 1 scant cup of the strained marinade, allow to boil rapidly, stirring meanwhile from the bottom of the pan in every direction, until the liquid is almost entirely evaporated. Remove the excess of fat, or still better all the fat, and add 1½ cups of good, fresh heavy cream, stirring constantly in every direction, to loosen the particles of gelatinous matter which may adhere, after adding 2 juniper berries, pulverized. Allow this to boil so as to reduce the liquid ⅓ its volume. Then, and only then, add 1 scant teaspoon of extract of beef, or beef jelly. Strain through a very fine sieve. Pour part of this sauce, the seasoning being corrected, over enough slices of the saddle to go around for the first helping, and serve the remainder aside with a side dish of currant jelly, and another one made as follows:

CELERY ROOT (CELERIAC) AND CHESTNUT AUVERGNATE

Cut the tops from a bunch of celery knobs, also called celeriac, celery root, and so forth, according to locality—a bunch usually contains 3 or 4 knobs or roots. Wash thoroughly in cold water. Peel, slice rather thin, and cut each slice into quarters. Place in a saucepan with enough boiling water to cover generously, adding 1 scant teaspoon of lemon juice, cook uncovered for 15 short minutes, or until pierceable, but not breakable. Drain, reserving the liquid for other uses such as soup, sauces, etc. Shell ½ lb. of chestnuts as follows: cut a cross with a very sharp knife on the flat side of each chestnut. Put the chestnut in a saucepan with a teaspoon of lard; toss well. Then set over a low flame and heat until the shells open, shaking the saucepan often. Cool slightly. The shells and inner brown-furred skins can then be removed easily with a knife. Put the chestnuts thus shelled into a saucepan containing 2 cups of scalded milk (water may be used if desired, but the milk, besides enhancing the flavor, adds to nourishment). Season to taste with salt, using approximately ½ teaspoon; cover and cook until the chestnuts are pierceable but not broken, about 15 long minutes, according to size of chestnuts. Now drain; alternate layers of celery root, chestnuts, and medium cream sauce, using the milk which has been used for cooking the chestnuts, well strained through a fine sieve, for making the cream sauce, in a shallow generously buttered baking dish. Bestrew the top with profusely buttered bread crumbs, using ⅓ generous cup. Bake in a moderately hot oven (350–375°) until the sauce bubbles, or about 15 long minutes, and the crumbs delicately browned. Serve from the baking dish.

SADDLE OF DEER CREOLE METHOD I

Marinate a saddle of deer for 6 hours only in MARINADE No. II, page 179, after larding through and through with narrow, long strips of fat larding pork, rolled in a mixture of allspice, nutmeg, salt, pepper, and finely chopped parsley, after removing the first skin covering the meat right under the haired skin or pelt. Roast over a bed of the vegetables of the marinade, and 1 cup of the liquid of the marinade, basting often, and allowing 15 long minutes for each pound of meat. Dress on a hot platter. Garnish with bananas sautéed in butter, slice enough to go around for the first helping. Pour a few tablespoons of Poivrade sauce (*see* SAUCES) over the slices, serve with the remainder of the sauce aside, and a dish of corn fritters.

SADDLE OF DEER CREOLE METHOD II

Marinate a saddle of deer for 3 long days, in MARINADE No. III, page 179. Drain. Sponge and lard through and through with narrow strips of fat larding pork, trimming even on the surface of the meat. Place the saddle of deer in a braising kettle, the bottom of which contains 3 generous cups of Creole sauce, made as indicated below. Pour over a cup of the marinade liquid, and a cup of good red wine. Cover and set the braising kettle in a hot oven (400°), allowing 15 minutes for each pound of meat, plus 15 minutes to start the cooking process, without disturbing at all, the basting being made automatically. Lift out the meat, cut enough slices to go around for the first helping, and dress these slices over the Creole sauce.

CREOLE SAUCE (as it is made in Louisiana) (for game)

Cook in 5 tablespoons of butter, 5 tablespoons of sliced—not chopped—onions and 1 generous cup of sliced—not chopped—green peppers, seeds and white ribs removed, over a gentle fire, stirring gently frequently, but do not brown. Add to this ½ lb. of fresh mushrooms, peeled, caps and stems sliced—not chopped, 2 dozen small green olives, stoned and quartered. Cook 5 long minutes, stirring occasionally. Pour over, 2½ cups of very good meat stock, preferably beef stock. Season with salt, coarse ground black pepper, a few grains of cayenne pepper, ½ teaspoon of thyme leaves, 10 sprigs of parsley tied with 2 large bay leaves, 2 juniper berries (crushed), 1 small clove of garlic (crushed), 3 whole cloves, a blade of mace, and a blade of allspice. Let simmer very gently, covered, over a low flame and add 1 tablespoon of good gin. Stir, and serve. A side dish of stewed pears in red wine is *de rigueur*.

SADDLE OF DEER

(*Divers Sauces*)

Besides the above recipes with special sauces, the saddle of deer may be, when roasted, served with Diana, Grand Veneur, Italian, Hussarde, Hunter, Madeira, Moscovite, Oxford, Port wine, Roebuck,

Roman, Russian, Smitane, Saint Hubert, Salmis, Sultane, Tyrolian, Venison, and Yorkshire sauces if desired.

SADDLE OF DEER
(*Scotch Method*)

In Scotland, they have a delicious method of preparing and cooking the saddle of deer, especially, when the animal is young. The marinade is made of white dry wine, and all the other ingredients, except the liquid ones, used for MARINADE No. III, page 179, for a very short period, only 2 long hours. The saddle is marinated in this aromatized wine, then sponged, blanketed in large, thin layer of fat larding pork. Secure carefully then roast in the usual way, allowing 15 long minutes for each pound of meat, basting often with the marinade, the solid part of which is laid down in the bottom of the dripping pan, a cupful of the marinade added with 3 tablespoons of melted lard. Dress the saddle, from which enough slices have been cut for the first helping, on a large, sizzling hot platter, the bottom of which is covered with a cupful of Poivrade sauce which, when poured on the platter, bubbles from the heat. Garnish with small balls of potato prepared as for croquettes, but rounded, then fried to a delicate brown in hot fat, and a large bunch of crisp watercress. Serve with a side dish of Venaison sauce (*see* SAUCES), another side dish of chestnut purée (mashed chestnuts), and a side dish of fresh string beans, cooked in plain salt water and generously buttered, English method.

BISHOP'S PUNCH

This punch may be made the day before using it.

1 large, whole lemon stuck with a dozen whole cloves, the heads of which have been removed

½ lb. granulated sugar pounded in a mortar with the following spices and condiments: ¼ teaspoon freshly grated nutmeg—a pinch of ginger powder—

¼ teaspoon of cinnamon powder—a pinch of clove powder—¼ teaspoon of allspice powder—½ teaspoon of grated lemon peel
½ pint (2 cups) of boiling water
1 full bottle of red Bordeaux wine
1 cup of good port wine and ½ cup of cherry brandy

When the lemon has acquired a dark-brown color, remove aside and keep hot. Place in a large enameled saucepan the water and all the spices and condiments, pounded together and thoroughly mixed. Bring to a rapid boil; remove from the fire, let infuse a few minutes; strain through a fine cloth. Then add the red Bordeaux wine, the port wine and the cherry brandy. Place on a very low fire and add the roasted lemon, sliced and seeds removed. Let this simmer very gently over a very low flame until a white foam appears on the surface of this nectar. Remove and serve very hot in glass cups. If prepared in advance, the mixture should be heated, but not boiled. A slice of lemon should be served with each cup.

ELK or MOOSE DEER

The elk, also called moose deer, is one of the largest ruminants of the deer family or covides. This much-sought-after animal by the lover of big game sometimes reaches a fabulous size. This member of the deer family was known to the Romans, during the reign of Julius Caesar, and called "alce," an obvious corruption of the Celtic word "elk," and which in certain parts of northern Europe is still applied to this covides. In Canada and the United States it is known as moose deer, while the French call it "elan."

The flesh of the elk is very light, digestible, and nourishing. The Canadians hold it in great esteem, as well as those who know game and appreciate a roast buttock, or round of elk, simmered gently in red wine with onions (plentifully stuck with whole cloves), parsnips, turnips, and leeks, until the wine is almost reduced to nothing and served with a sweet-sour shallot sauce or a Smitane sauce; or an elk steak, from the round, pounded, marinated in white or red wine overnight and slowly broiled, then served with one of the favorite sauces to be found in the Contents.

The elk may be prepared in almost all the different methods applied to beef, as well as those recipes for deer. However, the elk meat requires a slow-cooking process, and the marinating should be of very short duration, not exceeding 24 hours, unless one likes the gamy flavor; in that case, the meat may be marinated according to taste.

REINDEER

The deer family is older than any other ruminant, dating back to the Lower Miocene Period, when they were very small and without antlers.

From the culinary viewpoint, the nutrient power of a member of the deer family is almost equal to that of beef, and almost all the various methods of preparation of beef, as well as those of the deer, may be adapted to reindeer, such as steaks, roasts, braising, stewing, boiling, and sautéing. However, the reindeer reaches its culinary apogee when, after being larded and then marinated several hours (using MARINADE Nos. I, II, or III, pages 178–179), the braising process is applied with parts of the marinade used, to which may be added a little red wine, according to directions. The haunch is the most appreciated part of the reindeer. In England the roast reindeer is usually served with small ham dumplings, and a side dish of blackberry jam. Prunes, that is stewed prunes, are the usual accompaniment of the reindeer.

HARE—RABBIT—MUSKRAT

The mere sight or suggestion of rabbit or hare conjures up mouth-watering pictures of hasenpfeffer, the German spiced hare, and its cognates, English jugged hare, French civet of hare, and Southern potted hare. Yet so universal and ubiquitous are the two animals that there must be hundreds of distinctive ways of cooking them. Old hare in the South, let the age be what it may. In the North and West it is rabbit, tame or wild.

The flesh of both, when over a year old, is dry and somewhat tough; the young ones, when nearly full-grown and fat, are tender and make a rather delicious dish. A young hare or rabbit has soft paws, which are not entirely opened, while the paws of an old hare are open and worn. The ears of a young hare are very soft, while those of an old one are stiff and comparatively rough. A hare or rabbit tastes better when a little "seasoned," aged, or when the flesh is "mortified"; but it must not be mortified too much. As long as the body is rather stiff it is good, but when too limber, and the flesh has a black-bluish appearance, it is necessary to examine it carefully.

Although it is common in America to hear different species of hares or rabbits designated by the name of rabbit, this is one of those extraordinary mistakes in nomenclature, in reference to the fauna of the American continent; in many places in the Middle West and South, especially, hare is called jack rabbit. However be it called, hare or rabbit, or otherwise, the culinary preparations are the same for either one and all.

As for the muskrat—marsh rabbit to you—the North American aquatic rodent, yielding a valuable fur (that's the way the dictionary defines this animal—down South on the Eastern Shore of Maryland it is called a marsh rabbit), "is an edible game." Some like hare, rabbit, or marsh rabbit mortified—another matter of taste—but, in good cookery, a day is quite sufficient to bring raciness, and as for marinating, overnight is enough.

Every part of a hare is edible—even the blood, which should be carefully set aside when preparing a hare. Except for making loaves, pâtés, and stew, old hares are seldom used for culinary preparations.

How To Skin a Hare or Rabbit or a Muskrat

The best way to skin a rabbit is to hang it, by its hind legs, on hooks. Cut the skin the full length of the belly. Now proceed to remove the skin on either side, first up to the first joint of the hind legs. Make incisions on the backs of the legs but do not remove the skin yet. Skin the tail the same way and then continue skinning the head and the back. Cut off the ears at the base and leave the skin on the forelegs. Cut the skin round the eyes and hips. In this way the skin comes off in one piece.

BARBECUED HARE

Skin the hare, wash off the blood, which save. Cut off the hind part, so as to leave the breast and two legs. Clean the blue skin off with a knife, scraping thoroughly. Then prepare a marinade as follows:

Pour 2 cups of cold water and 2 cups of good vinegar in a large, long earthenware crock, terrine, or bowl and add:

12 whole peppercorns, bruised	½ scant teaspoon thyme leaves
1 generous tablespoon salt	3 whole cloves, heads removed
1 large lemon rind	¼ teaspoon allspice
2 large bay leaves	1 blade sage
1 large onion, sliced in thin rings	¼ teaspoon celery seeds
1 medium-sized raw carrot, thinly sliced	12 sprigs parsley tied with the bay leaves

Mix all the above ingredients thoroughly, and transfer to a large saucepan. Bring to a rapid boil. Remove from the fire and allow to cool. When lukewarm, pour over the hare placed in the crock, terrine, or bowl used to mix the marinade. Cover and let stand for 48 hours, less if a not too gamy flavor is desired. Lift out. Sponge dry and rub with salt and pepper to taste, mixed. Envelop the hare with thin strips of bacon. Place in a copiously greased dripping pan, using ¼ cup of lard or still better bacon drippings, and pour over 1 cup of the strained marinade. Roast in a moderate oven (375°) for 40 minutes, basting often with the liquid of the dripping pan. Lift out. Dress on a hot platter. Keep hot, while preparing the barbecue sauce as follows:

MISSISSIPPI BARBECUE SAUCE (for rabbit and hare)

Place the dripping pan over a hot fire, after removing the parsley and bay leaves and the excess of fat, almost all. Boil once and add 2 small cloves of garlic, peeled and whole. Let simmer for 15 minutes after adding 2 tablespoons of catsup, 1 teaspoon (generous) of Worcestershire sauce, a few drops of Tabasco sauce, discarding the garlic after the simmering. Strain through a fine sieve and return to the saucepan. Add then 2 tablespoons of brandy, 2 tablespoons of butter, 1 tablespoon of flour sprinkled over the sauce, and bring to a boil. Correct the seasoning and pour over the hare. Garnish with a bunch of crisp watercress and quartered lemons.

BRAISED HARE À LA SAINT DENIS

After skinning the hare, clean it through a small hole made in the belly, a hole as small as possible. Remove the head and lard the rabble and the legs with long, narrow strips of fat larding pork. Marinate for 48 hours in MARINADE No. II, page 179, adding to the marinade an extra tablespoon of chives, finely chopped. Lift out and sponge dry. Prepare a stuffing as follows: Chop the liver with the same amount of duck liver, season to taste with salt and black pepper, and add 1 pinch of thyme leaves, 1 small leaflet of tarragon herb, dry or fresh, a blade of nutmeg, a blade of mace, 1 teaspoon of parsley, chopped fine, 1 teaspoon of shallot, chopped fine, and put the mixture through food chopper with 1 tablespoon of butter and 3 egg yolks. The stuffing should be very smooth. Introduce this smooth stuffing through the small hole made for cleaning the hare.

Sew carefully. Blanket the body of the hare thus stuffed with thin slices of fat larding pork, also placing larding slices in the bottom of a braising kettle and over the larding slices, thin slices of lean veal, beaten with the back of a cleaver, while sprinkling coarse black pepper over the veal on both sides; add also 2 small carrots, scraped, then sliced coarsely, 3 small yellow onions, peeled and halved, 6 sprigs of parsley and 6 of chives tied with 1 large bay leaf and a sprig of thyme, 2 whole cloves, and 1 whole bottle of white wine, seasoning to taste with salt. Set the braising kettle in a moderate oven (350°) and forget it for 2 long hours, longer if the hare be old. Lift out, dress on a hot platter, well drained of the unctuous gravy, and brush entirely with beef gelatine slightly melted. Place the kettle over a hot fire and, after removing the excess of fat, allow to boil constantly until the liquid is almost evaporated. Then pour over 2 ladles of Sauce Espagnole (*see* SAUCES). Bring to a rapid boil, and strain, after correcting the seasoning, part of the sauce over the hare and the remainder in a sauceboat. If the sauce should be a little too salty, just before straining, add 2 tablespoons of sweet butter and the juice of a small lemon.

If Spanish sauce is not available, proceed as follows: Brown 2 tablespoons of butter and 2 tablespoons of flour, and when the mixture is thoroughly browned, moisten with the gravy of the braising kettle. In this case the gravy should not be almost entirely reduced, but used as is, straining, of course, through a fine sieve before adding the flour and butter mixture. Serve with a side dish of stewed pears (prepared as indicated under GARNISHINGS).

CURRIED HARE

For this recipe a young hare (or rabbit) is required.

After skinning, cleaning, and sponging a young hare with a damp cloth, cut into serving portions, removing the head, the breast, the heart, and the liver if the family be small, that is 4 persons, or else use the entire animal, except the head, with which make a broth, adding the trimmings. Roll each piece in a mixture of flour, salt, black pepper, and allspice to taste, and sear in ¼ cup of good lard, until thoroughly browned, then transfer the well-drained pieces to a large kettle, pour over either the stock made from the head and the trimmings or enough good beef stock barely to cover to half; then add 4 whole cloves, cover hermetically and bring to a rapid boil; then, reducing the heat to low flame, let simmer for 20 minutes. Meanwhile, heat 1 generous tablespoon of butter in a pan, add to it 1 medium-sized onion, finely minced, and cook for 3 short minutes or until the onion is slightly browned; add then ½ cup of good glazed rice, previously washed and well drained, and stir constantly for 3 long minutes. Then let the rice cook slowly, stirring occasionally, for 20 long minutes. The grains of rice should be whole, and well separated. Sprinkle over the rice, 1 tablespoon of curry powder, more or less according to taste, moisten the rice with a little meat or hare stock and pour the rice over the hare in the kettle. The rice and hare pieces should be covered with the liquid of the kettle. Cover hermetically and set in a hot oven (400°) for 30 long minutes. Dress as follows. Remove the pieces of hare with a two-pronged fork, shaking off the rice, if any, and place on a hot platter (in the center) and draw the rice, using also a two-pronged fork, so as not to break the kernels, on each side of the hare pieces. A side dish of curry sauce may be served.

BEADLE'S PUNCH

1 pinch of cinnamon	2 egg yolks, beaten to
1 pinch clove	a cream
1 small pinch of ginger	1 cup of good red
powder	wine
1 cup granulated sugar	1 full bottle of good
2 cups of boiling water	white wine

A few grains salt

Mix condiments and spices in a saucepan with the sugar and boiling water. Place on a hot fire and bring to a boil. Remove and strain through a fine sieve or a fine cloth and pour this brew, gradually and slowly, over the beaten egg yolks, beating violently and rapidly. Add the red and white wines. Return to the fire, a very low fire, stirring all the while until a white foam appears on the surface. Strain in a crystal punch bowl, and serve in glass cups.

CIVET OF HARE

(*Original Recipe*)

The blood of the hare should be carefully collected, as well as the liver, from which the gall should be very carefully removed as well as the parts which may be contaminated by it. Cut the head in four parts, and cut the remaining part of the hare into serving portions. Place the pieces of hare in a large bowl and add 4 tablespoons of good brandy, 1¾ cups of good olive oil, salt and pepper (black) and a medium-sized onion, cut into thin rings. Allow to marinate for 2 long hours, stirring frequently. Lift out the pieces of hare and sponge dry. Cut into small cubes, ½ lb. of lean fresh pork, and blanch 5 short minutes. Try, that is, brown until delicately colored, lift out and set aside, keeping hot; in the same butter, brown lightly 2 medium-sized onions, cut into quarters. Add 2 generous tablespoons of flour, and cook until flour and butter are thoroughly browned and blended. Add then the pieces of hare and sear on all sides. Moisten to nearly half with enough good red wine, add 7 or 8 sprigs of parsley tied with 1 large bay leaf and a small sprig of thyme, and a small clove of garlic, whole. Cover and allow to simmer gently for 45 minutes. Five minutes before serving, add the blood set aside, slightly heated with a little of the sauce in the kettle, and the liver cut into small cubes. Transfer the hare pieces, lifting them one by one to another kettle, and strain the sauce over. Add then the cubed pork set aside and kept hot, 2 dozen small white onions, parboiled, then glazed in the usual way, and 2 dozen small mushroom caps, peeled, then cooked in butter with the stems (sliced). Dress the whole on a hot, deep platter and garnish the platter with small heart-shaped pieces of bread fried in butter.

HARE CIVET FLEMISH STYLE

Skin, clean, sponge a hare with a cloth dipped in vinegar. Cut the hare in serving portions saving the liver and the blood. Sear the pieces, salted and peppered, in butter, using good judgment as regards the butter, according to size of the hare. When the meat is delicately browned, sprinkle with a tablespoon of flour, and stir, continuing searing a few minutes longer. Pour over a quart of red wine, to which has been added the mashed liver of the hare, then rubbed through a hair sieve with the blood of the beast and ½ scant cup of good vinegar. Then add 1 tablespoon of brown sugar, 8 sprigs parsley tied with a large bay leaf and a sprig of thyme (if thyme in sprig is not available, use ¼ teaspoon of powdered or thyme leaves), 1 lb. of small white onions, peeled and sliced in thin rings, slightly sautéed in butter. Bring this to a rapid boil, reduce the temperature and allow to simmer gently for 1 long hour. Then lift out the pieces of hare and place in an earthenware casserole, in which they will be served. Strain the sauce by rubbing it through a fine hair sieve, onions and all, discarding the parsley and bay leaf (bouquet garni). Pour this strained, smooth, creamy sauce over the pieces of hare, and heat without boiling. You may, if desired, dress the meat and sauce on a deep, hot, round platter, if no earthenware casserole is available, and garnish the edge of the platter with small heart-shaped pieces of bread fried in butter and spread with currant jelly.

This civet must have a sweet-sour flavor. A side dish of plain boiled Brussels sprouts is the usual vegetable which accompanies this delectable dish.

This recipe is a specialty of the Hotel de la Poste, Antwerp, Belgium.

HARE CIVET À LA LYONNAISE

Proceed exactly as indicated in recipe for CIVET OF HARE (*Original Recipe*), page 223, substituting small chestnuts, cooked in meat stock, then glazed, for mushrooms.

HARE CUTLET OR CHOP

IMPORTANT

The preparation of hare cutlets may be made in three ways:

I. As ordinary croquettes, bound with a brown sauce, the base of the sauce being stock made from the trimmings of the hare.

II. Prepared according to the method adapted to HARE CUTLET À LA POJARSKI, as indicated on page 226.

III. Or prepared with a mixture made as indicated in recipe for PARTRIDGE DUMPLINGS, page 54, substituting hare meat for partridge meat, which after all is but a stuffing. These may be molded with the hands, but it is advisable to use a special mold (cutlet mold easily procured in stores) which will be found very practical and handy when making any kind of croquettes, where the same size is required.

The three different methods may be "poached," that is cooked in very little liquid, or sauce, according to indications, over a very gentle fire, as you would for a poached egg; or, breaded, after being rolled in beaten egg. This is called *English Method*. In either case, they are always cooked very slowly to a golden brown (on both sides) in clarified butter, that is, in butter placed in a double boiler and heated, not boiled, slowly until clear, and the whey or little milk has fallen down to the bottom of the boiler. These cutlets are always served with a side dish of the indicated sauce, which may be any one of the hot sauces (*see* SAUCES); or the sauce may be poured directly over the cutlets if directed.

HARE CUTLET DIANA

Use Method No. II, HARE CUTLET À LA POJARSKI. Brown on both sides in clarified butter. Dress crownlike over a hot platter and garnish the center of the crown with mashed chestnuts. Serve with a side dish of Diana sauce (*see* SAUCES).

HARE CUTLET À LA POJARSKI

Remove the meat from the back and legs of a hare. There should be 2 generous cups, and chop finely—do not grind—with ½ cup of butter and ½ cup of bread crumbs, soaked in meat stock (hare stock if possible), then squeeze through a clean cloth, then tossed to loosen. (IMPORTANT. *The loosening of the bread or bread crumbs, after being soaked in the indicated liquid and squeezed through a clean cloth, has a very great importance in every recipe, indicating the use of bread, either for stuffing or stretching the ingredient or ingredients, because of the general heaviness of most stuffing using bread. This has been experimented with several times and in every case when the soaked bread or bread crumbs have not been loosened by tossing, the stuffing has always proved to be heavy and indigestible.*) Season to taste with salt and fine black pepper. Shape in cutlet forms. Dip in melted butter and cook in plenty of butter until golden browned on both sides. Dress on a hot platter covered with a purée of Brussels sprouts, or any other purée according to taste. Garnish the edges with small heart-shaped bread fried in butter and spread with currant jelly. A side dish of your favorite sauce may be served.

HARE CUTLET À LA MELVILLE

The following recipe may appear at a formal luncheon and even dinner, and requires 2 young hares for its preparation.

Skin, clean, reserving the blood of 2 young hares. Rub with a damp cloth. Remove the fillets (placed all along the dorsal bone and on both sides) by placing a sharp knife close to the bone and sliding it all along as far as the legs, then sliding the fingers between the bone and the fillets. Remove the bluish skin carefully. You will then have 4 fillets. Spread them on a clean board, and cut each fillet into 3 pieces. Flatten lightly with the side of a cleaver. Trim neatly, in cutlet shape. Season to taste with salt and black pepper and brush each cutlet lightly with beaten egg yolk, then roll in fine bread crumbs. Now heat ½ cup of butter to the smoking point. Roll each cutlet in it, then roll again in fine bread crumbs, pressing gently with the spatula or the blade of a knife, and sauté slowly over a medium flame in the remaining butter used for dipping, adding a little if necessary. Serve dressed crownlike on a hot platter, the center garnished with a large tuft or bunch of crisp, young green watercress with the following sauce:

Sauce Lord Melville

In a generously buttered earthenware casserole, place 2 medium-sized onions, peeled, then sliced in thin rings. Cover with a thin layer of carrots, grated and sliced thin. Then add all the trimmings from the fillets, and parts of the carcass of the hares (which by the way may be used for a stew if desired), chopped or cut fine. Pour over 1 cup of dry white wine, and add a whole clove of garlic (peeled, but not mashed or chopped), 2 whole cloves and 6 sprigs of parsley tied with a large bay leaf. Add also a pinch of thyme leaves, a blade of mace, 1 crushed juniper berry, 6 whole peppercorns (bruised), and salt to taste. Bring to a slow boil, and let simmer, uncovered, until all the liquid is almost evaporated. Then add 1 generous ladle of good chicken stock; boil once, stirring twice. Turn the whole mixture over a fine-haired sieve, or fine strainer, after letting simmer 15 minutes. Complete the sauce with a good ½ cup of Sauce Espagnole (*see* Sauces) and, when ready to serve, add the blood of the hares.

Recipe Contributed by Chef Legogue, Executive Chef of Lord Melville, Minister of the British Navy.

CHURCHWARDEN'S PUNCH

1 large lemon stuck with 6 whole cloves and roasted in
    a hot oven until dark brown
1 bottle of Bordeaux wine
1 pint (2 cups) of weak tea, unsweetened
¾ lb. granulated sugar (more or less according to taste)

When the lemon has acquired a good dark-brown
color, place it whole in a saucepan with the tea and sugar
and stir well. Add the red Bordeaux wine, cover and
place over a gentle fire to simmer until a white foam appears on the surface. Remove from fire; press the lemon
gently. Serve in glass cups.

FILLET OF YOUNG HARE À LA MILANAISE

Dip 6 fillets of young hares (3 hares are required), lifted as indicated in recipe for HARE CUTLET À LA MELVILLE, above, in highly seasoned Spanish sauce (*see* SAUCES). The fillets should be lightly pounded, and all the nerves and blue skin removed. Roll in a mixture of equal parts of bread crumbs and grated fresh Parmesan cheese. Now roll in eggs beaten as for an omelet, and again roll in bread crumbs and grated Parmesan cheese mixture. Sauté in plenty of clarified butter. Dress in crown on a hot platter. Garnish the center with a large bunch of watercress. Garnish the edges of the platter with small heart-shaped pieces of bread fried in oil, then spread with currant jelly. Serve with a side dish of rich tomato sauce.

JUGGED HARE

(*Southern Method*)

Skin, clean, rub with a damp cloth, and disjoint a full-grown hare or rabbit. Cut the back into 2 pieces and sever every joint. Fry a large sliced onion to a pale brown in hot bacon drippings, then put in the meat, peppered, salted, and floured and cook for 10 long minutes on a hot fire, turning often. Turn the mixture, except the fat, into a large enameled saucepan, containing a layer of salt pork, cut in thin slices, using a good ¼ lb.; sprinkle with 1 medium-sized onion, raw and chopped fine, 1 generous tablespoon of parsley, minced fine, and 1 generous teaspoon of paprika. Top with the ingredients already used for the bottom, using the same amount, adding 3 large tomatoes, peeled and quartered. Pour over a generous ladle of good beef stock, in which a stalk of celery has been boiled with ½ teaspoon of celery seeds. Fit on a tight cover, set the saucepan in a vessel of cold water, and bring slowly to a boil. Keep this up for three hours. Serve the pieces of hare and pork on a deep round hot platter. Keep hot. Thicken the gravy with a generous tablespoon of kneaded butter (equal parts of butter and flour kneaded together), add 1½ tablespoons of red currant jelly, the juice of a small lemon, and ¼ (scant) cup of good sherry wine. Boil once, and turn upon the meat. Garnish with small triangles of fried hominy. Serve at once.

JUGGED (GIBELOTTE OF) HARE À LA PARISIENNE

AUTHOR'S NOTE

For centuries this dish has been made in Europe. In some parts it is not bad, in others middling, but still in others it is delicious. It all depends on the hare, or rabbit, the care in making it, and on the money expended, as well as the recipe. A GIBELOTTE *is a kind of stew and a civet at the same time, to which great care should be brought in its preparation. It is not complicated at all, yet the ingredients must be added in sequence if one wants a real hare or rabbit "En Gibelotte." The animal, be it a hare or a wild or domestic rabbit, should be young, plump, tender, and of white flesh.*

Cut a hare or a wild rabbit into serving pieces, after skinning, cleaning, setting aside the liver and the blood, and rubbing first with a damp cloth and then with lemon juice, after removing all the bluish skin or cellophane covering the meat. Salt and black pepper to taste, then dredge with flour. Keep aside. Now, fry, brown delicately in an iron or earthenware pot, a good ¼ lb. of fresh lean pork, cubed very small. This will give you enough fat, after removing the golden-browned lard cubes, in which to sear the pieces of hare or wild rabbit through and through to a golden brown (fresh rabbit may be pre-pared in the same way) over a hot fire, turning the pieces repeatedly with a wooden spoon. Turn off the gas. Drain all the fat carefully. Sprinkle a scant tablespoon of flour over the meat; add then 1 small clove of garlic (chopped very fine, nearly to a paste), a bouquet garni composed of 8 sprigs of fresh parsley, 1 large bay leaf, and 1 small sprig of thyme tied together, 2 dozen small white onions (peeled), salt and black pepper to taste, and moisten with a generous half cup of good dry white wine, and a generous half cup of good beef stock or more so as barely to cover the ingredients, then the golden-browned cubes of lard, kept hot and aside. Light the gas anew and allow the mixture to come slowly to a boil, stirring gently occasionally with a wooden spoon. Reduce the heat and let your concoction "smile," let simmer gently, imperceptibly. Meanwhile, peel 2 dozen very small new potatoes, or rather place them in a coarse towel with coarse salt, shake forth and back and the thin peel-ing will come off. Sponge the potatoes, do not wash in water at all. Add the potatoes to the gibelotte, smiling gently, pressing down so as to cover them with the liquid, add also 2 large, not too ripe toma-toes, quartered. If your dish is ready before your guests have arrived or are at the table, turn off the gas after exactly 50 minutes of cook-ing. Light it again if necessary. Then you will obtain a gibelotte as it is concocted in the suburb of Paris where all the Parisians go espe-cially on Sunday to enjoy *"une gibelotte de lièvre, de lapin ou de levraut,"* always accompanied with a bottle of good red claret. No mushrooms, no carrots, no pastelike cornstarch, no egg yolk forming the *mise en scène*. Only sequence, and a careful reading of the recipe before starting. That's all. Just before serving, about 3 or 4 minutes, stir in the blood of the animal, mixed slowly with a tablespoon of the gravy, and add the liver, *grainé* (that is, the nerves and skin removed), and mashed with a fork, or rubbed through a fine sieve without any other preparation.

HARE À LA CUILLER À LA MODE
(*Spooned Hare à la Mode*)

The following recipe comes from the famous restaurant Larue of Paris, so well known to Americans. For this supreme delicacy only the rabble, or back of the hare, is used, which may scarcely serve 2 persons. If six are to be served you require 3 young, plump hares.

After skinning, cleaning, sponging a young hare, lift out the back, then the fillets, operating as indicated in recipe for HARE CUTLET À LA MELVILLE, page 226. Insert it (lard it) with narrow strips of fat larding pork, as you would for a Beef à la Mode, previously marinated in good brandy and sprinkled with parsley, minced. Rub the fillet, one for each serving, with salt and freshly ground peppercorns, to taste, mixed with a little nutmeg. Place the meat in an iron skillet with 1 generous tablespoon of bacon drippings and singe it, that is, sear it on both sides, in the skillet. Remove the fat entirely, and add 1 small onion (sliced thin), 1 small carrot (sliced thin), and 1 calf's foot (boned and blanched), then cover and allow to simmer, after a single boil for 5 minutes, then add ½ pony glass of brandy, ¼ cup of MARINADE No. II, page 179, cover again and let simmer 3 minutes, or until the liquid comes to a boil. Then add, 1 scant cup of good red wine, 5 sprigs of parsley tied with 1 small piece of bay leaf, and a pinch of thyme leaves, or a sprig of thyme if available, the size of a pea of garlic, a whole clove and enough salt to taste. Cover tightly and let simmer for 35 long minutes. Turn the mixture into a bread loaf pan, large enough to hold all the contents of the skillet, and having a tight-fitting, thermos-like cover. Wrap the mold in a piece of flannel, doubled or tripled, and let stand in a warm place for 3 long hours. After this lapse of time, the meat is perfectly cooked, steaming hot, tender as dew, delicately aromatized, and ready to be eaten. A spoon is used to eat it. Such a delicacy deserves a wine corresponding, and a bottle of Hermitage is indicated.

HARE LOAF DILL SAUCE
(*Southern Recipe*)

Take a piece of leftover cooked hare and bone thoroughly (there should be 2 cups), 1 goose liver (chicken liver may be substituted if desired, but add 1 teaspoon of good lard), 1 cup of bread crumbs, soaked in milk, squeezed through a cloth, then tossed, 1 small onion (chopped, or still better grated), salt and black pepper to taste, a few thyme leaves, a pinch or blade of sage and an equal amount of clove. Chop and mix all this together, adding alternately, 2 whole eggs. Butter a loaf mold; sprinkle the inside with dry bread crumbs and put half the hare mixture into it; then lay over slices of cooked hare (thin slices), enough to cover, and add the remainder of the hare mixture. Sprinkle with melted lard or bacon drippings and bake in a moderate oven (350°) for 40 minutes, covering top with a buttered paper if browning too fast. Unmold on a hot platter, garnish with crisp watercress and thin slices of lemon, and serve with a side dish of Dill Sauce, made as follows:

DILL SAUCE

Brown lightly, a tablespoon of flour with a generous tablespoon of lard. Add 2 teaspoons of onion, minced fine. Mix well and moisten with 1 cup of stock made with the trimmings of the hare, as well as the bones, stirring constantly while pouring, until mixture thickens. Then season with salt, black pepper to taste, add 1 scant teaspoon of lemon juice, ½ teaspoon of "Fumet" (*see* recipe, How To PREPARE GAME STOCK, page 45), ½ teaspoon brown sugar and 2 tablespoons of finely chopped dill pickles. Boil once, let simmer 5 short minutes, remove the skin which will form on the top, and pour into a sauceboat.

HARE STEW WITH DUMPLINGS
SOUTHERN STYLE

Skin a full-grown hare, clean, rub with a damp cloth, cut into serving portions after setting aside the blood and liver. Roll each piece in salted, black peppered flour, and sear on all sides in 3 tablespoons of bacon drippings. Transfer the pieces to a stewpan and add 1 dozen small white onions (peeled and whole), 1 dozen fresh mushrooms (peeled, caps halved, stems sliced), 8 sprigs of parsley tied with a large bay leaf, 2 whole cloves, 6 peppercorns (bruised gently), a blade of allspice. Cover with good meat stock, preferably beef stock, if available, and add 1 generous tablespoon of good wine vinegar. Bring to a boil and allow to simmer gently for an hour, adding, after 30 minutes of cooking, 1 tablespoon of flour stirred in a little cold water and strained over the stew, the giblets well cleaned and washed, 1 cup of sour cream, to which has been added 2 tablespoons of washed capers. Cover and continue cooking slowly. Ten minutes before serving, add the blood, in which has been stirred the mashed liver, from which all the nerves have been removed, and dumplings made as follows:

DUMPLINGS

1 cup flour	½ cup of milk
⅓ teaspoon salt	2 scant teaspoons baking powder
½ generous teaspoon butter	

Sift the flour, salt, baking powder together and work in the butter. Gradually add the milk. Mix thoroughly. Flour the hands and fold into balls the size of a small walnut. Drop in gravy of the stew, cover closely, and boil 10 minutes without lifting the lid. Serve in a deep, round platter, meat and sauce under, and the dumplings on top. Sprinkle with finely chopped parsley.

CHORISTER'S PUNCH

3 egg yolks beaten with
3 tablespoons of cold water
¼ of a pint of white wine
½ cup sugar (more or less, according to taste)
1 cup cold water

Place in a saucepan the wine, sugar, and ¾ of the cup of cold water. Stir well and place over a gentle fire to simmer slowly until a white foam appears on the surface; remove from the fire and strain over the well-beaten egg yolks in the remaining ¼ cup of cold water, stirring vigorously. Strain over a crystal punch bowl. Serve in glass cups.

PÂTÉ OU TERRINE DE LIÈVRE BOURGEOISE

During the hunting season one often bags a great many hares. Eating hare every day is not pleasing, and one of the best methods of preserving, for several weeks, a delicacy which appears on the table for such a short period is as follows:

Skin a plump full-grown hare, clean, set aside the blood and liver, rub with a damp cloth. Bone thoroughly, and remove the bluish skin and all the nerves. For 3 lbs. of flesh, use 1 lb. of good, fresh, fat pork. Cut the pork in small cubes and try in a deep iron skillet. When very hot, add 1 large bay leaf, ½ scant teaspoon of thyme leaves, and 1 tablespoon of grated onion, then the meat of the hare cut into small pieces, the size of a small white onion, the liver, from which the gall has been carefully removed, as well as all the parts which may have been in contact with it, then the lungs from which the tubes and nerves have been removed, and cut also into small pieces. Sauté rapidly, long enough to stiffen the meat (about 5 short minutes), stirring frequently with a wooden spoon. Pour the whole mixture into a large mixing bowl or earthenware terrine, remove the bay leaf, and let cool. When thoroughly cold, pound in a mortar or still better, put through food chopper. Return to the mixing bowl and add the blood, to which has been added, a few drops of vinegar to prevent curdling, ¼ cup of good brandy, 1 lb. of fine meat sausage, and mix thoroughly. Now line a large earthenware mold, called in French a "terrine," an earthenware pot or mold, either square, or oval, with thin slices of fat larding pork, bottom and sides, the mold having been generously greased or oiled. Turn the hare mixture into the mold. Cover the top and cook in a hot oven (400°), the mold set in a pan of hot water, for 1½ hours. Remove from the oven, and, moving aside the mold, drain all the fat, holding the contents with a clean towel, or opening the mold, sliding it enough to make an opening from which the fat will be drained. Place over the loaf still remaining in the mold, a small board, weighting it. Allow to cool over night. Next day, heat lightly. Unmold, wash the mold and return the loaf to it. Cool again. Pour over, or rather spread over, a layer of fresh lard. Set in a refrigerator. This will keep several weeks.

If the loaf is to be eaten during the week, make a jelly with the bones, the trimmings, ¼ lb. of beef leg, and the outer skin of fresh pork, using about the same amount as that of beef, seasoning to taste with salt, pepper, a bit of bay leaf, tied with 4 or 5 sprigs of parsley, a few thyme leaves, and salt and black pepper to taste. Add then 2 generous cups of good beef stock and bring to a rapid boil, let simmer gently for 2 hours, until the mixture is gelatinous. Strain through a fine cloth, clarify with a few eggshells, and add 1 scant half teaspoon of vinegar. Allow to cool and, when nearly cold, pour over the loaf. This will run on the sides, until the top is covered with a layer of about ¼ to ½ inch. To serve: Slice thin slices as you would bread, dress on crisp green lettuce leaves or watercress, or slaw, red or white, and serve with currant jelly. A fine dish for impromptu luncheon or even dinner.

This loaf cannot be found on the market for less than $15.00, yet, to make at home, it will not cost more than $2.00–$2.50.

VARIATION

If you use all the hare, lift out the fillets; lard through and through with small strips of fat larding pork, rolled in a mixture of parsley, minced fine, allspice, nutmeg, grated onion, or shallots, or chives, the whole mixed thoroughly, using good judgment as to amount necessary for this purpose, the strips of larding pork being previously dipped in a little brandy (optional). Place in a baking dish generously buttered, and season with allspice, salt and pepper to taste. Pour over ¼ (scant) cup of good Madeira wine and let marinate while preparing the smooth mixture as indicated above. Fill the lined mold as indicated, using half the mixture, and, on top of this, place the well-drained fillets, which may be cut in two, lengthwise, if desired, then over the fillets, pour the remainder of the smooth mixture. If desired, you may substitute the meat sausage as follows: To ¾ lb. of meat sausage, add the suet of veal kidneys, using ¼ lb.; the loaf will be a little fatter, which is sometimes desired by certain gourmets and connoisseurs, besides the kidney flavor which is added. With any one of the above preparations, besides the currant jelly, you may serve a side dish of stewed prunes, as in Germany, or stewed prunes with large dried Malaga raisins, stewed with the prunes, as in Holland or grilled chestnuts, as in Poland, or stewed pears, as in France.

HARE STEAK

The back of a full-grown hare may serve two persons, that is, make two steaks.

Skin the number of hares required. Lift out the fillet, by sliding a sharp-pointed knife along, and close to, the backbone. Remove the bluish skin and all the nerves, and cut the fillet in two, lengthwise. Flatten lightly with the side of a cleaver, the meat placed on a wet board, so that the meat does not adhere. Sauté the steaks rapidly in 2 generous tablespoons of butter. Dress on a hot platter, squeeze the juice of half a lemon over and sprinkle with parsley, minced. The remainder of the hare may be used for a civet or a stew.

BLANQUETTE OF YOUNG HARE À LA ZINGARA
(*Turkish Recipe*)

Cut a young, plump hare into serving portions, rather small, skin, clean, and rub with a damp cloth. Place the pieces of meat in fresh water, enough to cover, for 15 long minutes. Then parboil the hare pieces in the very same water in which they were soaked. Drain, and let the cold water run over the pieces placed in a colander. Return the pieces to the kettle, cover with veal or chicken stock, add 1 medium-sized onion, stuck with 2 whole cloves, the heads removed, 7 or 8 sprigs of parsley tied with a large bay leaf, 1 medium-sized carrot, grated, then quartered. Bring to a boil, and skim thoroughly. Allow then to simmer gently for 20 minutes. Season to taste with salt and white pepper, and add 1 generous half cup of well-washed rice, and 1 blade of saffron, more or less according to taste. Let cook 20 minutes longer, until the rice is soft. Remove the parsley and bay leaf, the carrot, and the onion. Dress the hare pieces on a hot deep platter; cover the pieces with the rice. Surround the edge with a narrow circle of melted beef extract. To the sauce left in the kettle, add 4 egg yolks, one at a time, beating vigorously after each addition, and strain over the rice, covering entirely. Serve at once.

HASENPFEFFER
(*A Delicious German Recipe*)

Author's Note

To all casual outward seeming it matters little whether you call any chance long-eared bunny a rabbit or a hare. The hunting hounds always seem to be chasing the hare, in polite sporting phrase, while one going a-hunting usually bags a rabbit. Actually the nomenclature is all mixed up, and the familiar domestic Belgian hare is a rabbit, and the jack rabbit of the plains and the big white rabbits are true hares; the latter species being the northern hare varying its winter dress. And nature's rather definite distinction lies in the fact that the rabbit digs a deep burrow and brings its young into the world naked, blind, and helpless, and the hare makes its home in any convenient, comfortable place, and bears able-bodied children fully clothed, opened-eyed, and ready to run and play at birth.

DIRECTIONS

Skin, clean well, and rub a full-grown hare or rabbit with a damp cloth. Cut into serving portions. Arrange the hare pieces in an earthenware bowl, rather large. Cover with equal parts of vinegar and water. Add 2 or 3 slices of onion, a dozen whole cloves, and 3 large bay leaves, and salt and black pepper, coarsely ground, to taste. Allow this to remain and marinate for 2 long days, turning the pieces of hare, frequently, and seeing to it that they are constantly covered with the liquid. Lift out the pieces of meat and sear in 3 tablespoons of good lard, turning the meat so as to brown on all sides. Remove or, still better, drain the fat, and pour over all the marinade, that is just enough to cover the pieces of meat in the pot. Cover and allow to simmer for 30 long minutes, or until the meat is tender. When ready to serve, stir in a generous cup of heavy sour cream. Bring to a rapid boil. Remove the bay leaves, and dress on a hot platter. Garnish with small triangles of bread fried in lard and serve with a side dish of stewed prunes, or any other kind of stewed fruit.

HARE CIVET AGRA DOLCE
(*Italian Recipe*)
A very ancient Florentine recipe

Skin a plump, young hare, clean, rub with a damp cloth, then cut into serving pieces. Marinate the hare pieces in equal parts of olive oil and red-wine vinegar, adding 1 or 2 cloves of garlic (minced fine), 1 medium-sized onion (peeled, then sliced in thin rings), 3 or 4 branches of sweet basil, salt and coarsely ground black pepper, for 2 long hours, stirring the mixture occasionally. Lift out the hare pieces, sponge and sauté in good olive oil, using 3 generous tablespoons until delicately browned, with 1 medium-sized onion (thinly sliced), 1 medium carrot (thinly sliced after being scraped), 1 bouquet garni (8 sprigs parsley tied with a large bay leaf), ¼ cup of small sticks of white celery (scraped, and of about 2 inches in length), and ½ generous cup of coarsely chopped raw lean ham. Drain the fat entirely, and transfer the whole mixture to a large iron or copper pot. Cover entirely with rich beef stock, adjust the cover, bring to a rapid boil, and let simmer gently for 40 long minutes.

Now for the finishing touches that are a little staggering to French, American, and English lovers of game, although it is one of the most delicious of sauces, the famous ancient.

Agra-Dolce Sauce

To the civet or stew, add ½ cup of brown sugar with a cup of good red Chianti wine, or other dry red wine; add also 1 ounce of GRATED BITTER CHOCOLATE; and when the sauce simmers again, stir in 1 tablespoon of shredded candied orange peel, 1 tablespoon of pignolia nuts, and 1 tablespoon of seedless raisins, previously plumped in hot meat stock, and drained. Let this simmer for 20 long minutes, and complete by thickening the sauce with a scant tablespoon of flour, browned with 1 scant tablespoon of oil. Serve at once, dressed on a hot deep platter, garnished with small triangles of bread fried in olive oil, and spread with currant jelly. This recipe is very popular all over the continent and in fashionable resorts of the Tyrol. Wild boar and venison may be prepared in the same way.

KANGAROO PUNCH
(Very Old Recipe)

12 lumps of sugar	Peel of these lemons,
1 pint of hot water	thinly pared
Juice of 2 medium-sized	2 gills of Jamaica rum
lemons	1 gill of brandy
½ gill of porter or stout	

Mix all the above ingredients in order named in a punch bowl; stir well and serve in glass cups at once.

HARE PIE SALOP METHOD

The hare or rabbit pie of Salop is a famous and succulent delicacy
—and Salop, as all travelers know, is the historical name of the English county of Shropshire. The clever housewives of Salop and the
Welsh border make a rich puff paste and proceed as follows:

Skin, clean, sponge carefully 2 young, plump hares or rabbits.
(Hare or rabbit fur gets into the hair and ears and eyes of the novice.
Even well-prepared meat will show annoying traces of fluffy fur, but
careful wiping with a damp cloth will clear up the situation.) Cut
them into small portion pieces, and dredge in salted and black peppered flour. Arrange the meat in a deep pie dish, lined with rich puff
paste with alternate layer of 2 lbs. fat salt pork, diced small, and a
bouquet garni made of 8 or 10 sprigs of fresh parsley, 1 large bay
leaf, and 1 sprig of thyme, tied securely. Now scald the liver, drain
and put through food chopper, alternately, with an even measure of
fat bacon and a handful (¼ generous cup) of oysters, seasoning as
you go along with salt, black pepper to taste, ¼ teaspoon allspice, ¼
teaspoon of nutmeg, and ¼ teaspoon each of mace and sage. Turn
this paste into a mixing bowl and stir again, then bind with 3 or
4 egg yolks, beaten to a cream. Form this fine and delicious mixture
into small balls, and add to the pie with diced artichoke hearts (using about 6, according to size), and also—in Salop—a few parboiled
cocks' combs. Moisten with 1 generous wineglass of good red wine,
mixed with 1 cup of good game stock made from the trimmings.
Top the pie with a rich puff-paste crust. Prickle here and there with
the tines of a fork to let the steam escape, and bake until done and
golden browned (about 45 to 50 minutes) in a moderate oven (350–
375°). Serve piping hot, without any other accompaniment, but a
side dish of red currant jelly, and plain freshly made toast.

HARE BOUILLI À L'ANGLAISE

Select a young, plump hare or rabbit, skin, clean, and sponge inside and out with a damp cloth, then with lemon juice. Rub inside
and out with salt and black pepper. Prepare a stuffing as follows:

STUFFING

¼ lb. of veal kidneys, skinned,
   scalded, and chopped fine
¼ lb. of veal fat (raw), chopped
   fine separately
1 cup of bread crumbs, soaked in
   milk, squeezed, then tossed
2 whole eggs, well beaten

Salt, pepper to taste
1 blade of thyme leaves
1 blade of allspice
1 blade of mace
1 blade of sage
1 tablespoon of parsley,
   minced fine

1 small white onion, grated

Mix all the above ingredients thoroughly. Fill the belly of the animal, leaving enough space for the swelling, that is, do not fill up too full. Sew carefully, and secure with string as you would a rolled veal breast.

Place the hare or rabbit in enough salt water (cold), bring slowly to a boil, and let simmer gently for at least one long hour. Dress on a hot platter, removing the string. Garnish with parsley or still better with watercress, slices of lemon, seeds removed and serve with:

CAPER SAUCE ENGLISH METHOD

Blend 2 tablespoons of butter and 2 tablespoons of flour thoroughly over a medium fire or flame. Pour in all at once 2 cups of salted boiling water, and beat rapidly with a wire whisk. Remove aside and add gradually, one at a time, 5 egg yolks, beating (using a wire whisk) rapidly after each addition, and add 1 generous tablespoon of heavy cream, previously scalded, and the juice of a small lemon. Then strain through a fine sieve, or, still better, through a fine cloth. Lastly, add 4 tablespoons of capers, well drained. This sauce must not boil any more, lest the egg yolks curdle. Serve at once.

HARE WITH PRUNES
(*German Style*)

Skin a full-grown hare or rabbit, clean, sponge thoroughly with a damp cloth, set aside the liver. Cut into serving portions. Marinate for 2 days, in MARINADE No. I, page 178, seeing to it that the proportion of vinegar is a little more than indicated. Next day, sponge thoroughly and sear the dredged pieces of hare in flour, with 4 generous tablespoons of butter until well browned, for about 10 long minutes, turning often to brown on all sides. Lift out and transfer to a stewpot, cover with some of the strained marinade, season to taste with salt and black pepper, then add the liver, cleaned, gall removed, and whole, and 1 bay leaf tied with 8 sprigs of parsley, ¼ teaspoon thyme leaves, 1 clove, 1 small clove of garlic, 1 small onion (peeled, then sliced), 4 slices of lemon (rather thick), and a blade each of mace, allspice, and nutmeg. Finally, add 1 lb. of small prunes, soaked in water overnight and drained. Cover and let cook slowly for a long hour. Lift out the liver and rub through a fine sieve, add to the sauce in the stewpot 2 or 3 tablespoons of red currant jelly. Serve in a hot, round deep platter, garnish the edges with small triangles of bread fried in butter, then spread with red currant jelly.

A side dish of plain boiled potatoes may be served if desired.

HARE SADDLE GRILLE À L'ANGLAISE

Select a young, plump hare, skin, clean, and sponge carefully with a damp cloth. Marinate for 2 hours in white wine, to which has been added 1 small carrot (peeled, then sliced thin), 1 small bay leaf, 3 rings of onion, 6 sprigs of parsley, and salt, pepper, and allspice to taste. Drain, sponge, and remove the saddle. Sprinkle with melted butter, then roll in fine bread crumbs. Over the bread crumbs, sprinkle more melted butter and place on a well-greased broiler. Set the broiler under the flame of the broiling oven and broil, turning often, until delicately browned and done (about 15 long minutes). Dress on a hot platter. Garnish with strips of broiled bacon, and a mound of shoestring potatoes. Serve with a side dish of Gooseberry sauce (*see* SAUCES).

OLD-FASHIONED CIVET OF HARE À LA SAINTE ANNE

Skin a full-grown hare, clean, reserving the blood and .the liver, sponge carefully. Cut the animal into serving portions. Lard the legs and pieces of rabble with narrow, short strips of ham fat. Place the pieces of hare in a large stewpot containing 4 or 5 tablespoons of heated butter, and sear thoroughly on all sides, for 10 minutes. The pieces should be golden browned to a deep hue, the fire very hot. Then sprinkle a generous tablespoon of flour over the meat, stirring constantly to dredge and allow the flour to brown at the same time. Now add 8 sprigs of parsley tied with 1 large bay leaf, and 1 sprig of thyme, 1 large clove of garlic, whole, a small sprig of wild thyme (serpolet) found in drug stores, 1 large onion, sliced thin after being peeled, and 4 shallots, peeled. Season to taste with salt and coarse black pepper. Pour over all, 2 cups of good red Burgundy wine, and 1 pony glass of good brandy. Cover and let simmer for 1½ hours, very gently, smiling imperceptibly. When ready to serve, parboil the liver separated from the gall, and pound it or, still better, put it through the food chopper. To the liver thus mashed, add the blood of the hare, with a scant teaspoon of good wine vinegar. Let simmer again, but do not allow to boil, for 10 long minutes, to mellow. Lift out the pieces of hare. Dress on a hot platter. Strain the sauce over the pieces. Garnish with small triangles of bread, fried in butter, then spread with red currant jelly, interspersed with large mushrooms, peeled, dipped in seasoned melted butter in which the size of a pea of anchovy paste has been stirred, and broil under the flame of the broiling oven. Serve with a side dish of mashed celery.

MULLED ALE

NOTE—A "mulled" drink is always served hot, in a glass cup. It is a beverage very appropriate for the winter months as it is claimed to stimulate body heat. It is also said to be a good digestive. All beers, wines, and liqueurs, as well as cordials, may be "mulled."

1 pint hot ale	A little piece of cinnamon
Nutmeg to taste	stick
Bruised clove to taste	1 cup boiling water
Sugar to taste	

Infuse in the hot water all the ingredients but the ale. Strain through a fine sieve, add the ale heated to the scalding point, but not boiling. Stir. Serve in glass cups.

RABBLE OF HARE À LA CRÈME

Skin, clean, and rub with a damp cloth a full-grown hare or rabbit. Marinate for 2 hours in ½ generous cup of olive oil, to which is added a large lemon (sliced thin), ½ dozen thin slices of carrots, 6 thin slices of onion, 1 clove (bruised), 8 peppercorns (bruised), 1 large bay leaf tied with 8 sprigs of fresh parsley and 8 sprigs of chives (tied together); turn the animal often. Remove the back, called in culinary terms "Rabble." Sponge thoroughly. Place in a dripping pan after larding with narrow strips of fat larding pork and blanketing with thin slices of fat pork, securing carefully. Place in the dripping pan, 2 tablespoons of butter and roast in a hot oven (400°), basting frequently, for 15 long minutes. The meat should be very rare, *vert-cuit,* as the professional cooks say. Remove the larding slices and the fat from the dripping pan, and add 1 cup of heavy sour cream. Return to the oven and continue roasting 10 long minutes more, basting often with the cream. Dress on a hot platter. Keep hot. Strain the cream through a fine sieve, pressing the solid parts a little. Place the strained cream in a saucepan. Bring to a rapid boil, and add 1 tablespoon of kneaded butter. Taste, and if the cream is not sufficiently sour, add a few drops of lemon juice to taste. Now slice or rather cut the rabble or back crosswise in three portions, and the fillet in three slices. Dress again on a very hot platter, collect all the liquid which may have run when cutting and slicing, add it to the cream sauce, correct the seasoning of the sauce, and pour over the pieces of meat. Garnish simply with small triangles of bread fried in butter and spread with grape jelly, interspersed with thin slices of lemon, each slice topped with a stoned olive enrobed with a sponged anchovy fillet.

RABBLE OF HARE SMITANE
(*Russian Method*)

Follow the directions indicated in recipe for RABBLE OF HARE À LA CRÈME, above, as far as the roasting process is concerned. Slice the meat as indicated and pour over 1½ generous cups of Smitane sauce (*see* SAUCES). Garnish as follows: 6 broiled mushrooms placed on top of a grilled tomato slice, interspersed with a quartered lemon. Dust the cream sauce (Smitane) with paprika mixed with finely minced parsley.

ROAST STUFFED YOUNG HARE
(*English Method*)
Also called "Roasted Hare au Gîte"

Select a young, plump hare. Skin without cutting the bottom parts of the legs, being careful to remove the skin without damaging the paws (the nails are left on). Do not cut the head, but skin carefully, leaving the ears, which should be scalded as is done for young piglings to be served whole. To clean it, make a hole small as possible, remove the lungs, reserve the liver and the blood (the latter should be immediately mixed with 1 scant tablespoon of vinegar stirred in 1 teaspoon of cold water). Remove the gall from the liver, scald it and chop very fine or, still better, put through meat chopper. Soak ¾ cup of bread crumbs in 2 tablespoons of fresh heavy cream. Squeeze, then toss lightly to loosen. Combine with the liver, with as much good butter as there are softened bread crumbs, 4 egg yolks (raw), salt and black pepper to taste, and a blade each of mace, sage, allspice, and nutmeg. Add also 1 teaspoon of parsley (minced fine), 1 teaspoon of onion (minced fine and heated in a little butter for 1 short minute). Mix all the ingredients to a paste and very carefully fill the opening made for cleaning the hare with the stuffing, using a teaspoon, after adding the blood to the stuffing. Sew carefully. Break the bones of the legs. Bring back the hind legs under the belly, secure with small skewers. To the forelegs and the head, give them the attitude as if the animal was at his seat (*au gîte* as the French say). Place carefully in the same position in a dripping pan after blanketing the body with thin slices of larding pork, then surrounding the body with buttered paper. Set in a hot oven (450°) and sear for 10 long minutes without basting; reduce the heat to 375° and continue roasting, basting very often for 20 long minutes. Remove the paper and continue roasting 10 minutes longer. In England, the larding pork surrounding the body of the hare is removed before dressing on a hot, sizzling platter; in Germany, France, and elsewhere, the slices of larding pork are left on, only the strings securing them are removed.

Serve with a side dish of currant jelly, and (optional) a side dish of Poivrade sauce (*see* SAUCES).

SAUTÉED HARE HUNTER STYLE

There are two different methods of preparing this dish.

FIRST METHOD (*Home Style*)

Skin a full-grown hare or rabbit, clean, sponge thoroughly with a damp cloth. Cut off the head and legs up to the second joint, set them aside for other use. Cut the hare into small serving portions, rather small. Heat 2 tablespoons of clarified butter and add the hare pieces. Sear thoroughly, so that the pieces are deep brown, after seasoning them with salt and black pepper. Then add 6 large fresh mushrooms (peeled, caps and stems sliced rather thick), 2 large shallots, coarsely chopped. Cook 3 or 4 minutes, stirring almost constantly, seeing to it that the shallot pieces do not get brown. Drain the butter. Add then 1 generous cup of good dry white wine, as much of game stock made with the trimmings and the head. Cover, after adding a bouquet garni made of 8 sprigs of fresh parsley, 1 large bay leaf, and 1 sprig of thyme. Cook 20 to 25 minutes, over a gentle flame. Then add, off the fire, 1 generous tablespoon of kneaded butter (equal parts of flour and butter kneaded together, which will thicken the sauce), and 1 tablespoon of fresh butter. Heat, but do not boil. Finish with 1 tablespoon of tomato paste, 1 teaspoon of parsley, minced. Dress on a hot platter (deep one) and garnish with small triangles of bread fried with butter, alternately with thin slices of lemon. In some households, the liver, after being mashed, is added to the sauce. This is optional, although it adds much to the flavor.

Second Method

This method is usually employed when hunters have a kitchen at their disposal, either a camp kitchen or the kitchen of the nearest home, and desire to use the product of their bagging at once, right on the spot. In this way, the hare or rabbit has had no time to stiffen, the meat is tender, especially if a young hare or rabbit is selected.

Skin a hare or a rabbit, clean, sponge with a damp cloth, then with another cloth sprinkled with vinegar. Cut into small serving pieces. In a skillet, try ¼ lb. of salt pork, cubed small. Moisten, when delicately brown, with ¼ scant cup of good brandy—brandy from the canteen—and touch with a match; let burn until exhausted, then pour over 1 bottle (a fifth) of good dry white wine; add ½ dozen shallots, peeled and minced, salt to taste and plenty of black, coarsely ground pepper. Place the pot over a bright flame, cover and cook for 20 short minutes. Just before serving, add 1 generous tablespoon of kneaded butter, to which may be added, in equal amounts, parsley, minced fine, or chives also minced fine. Dress sizzling on a hot platter, no garnishing allowed, and bunny is eaten by its captors three-quarters of an hour after being killed.

ALE POSSET

1 pint of rich fresh milk
1 bottle of mild ale
1 slice of toasted bread
Cinnamon, cloves (both ground) to taste

Boil the milk in a saucepan with the piece of toast, whole, and freshly made. Pour the ale into a bowl; sweeten and spice to taste; pour boiling milk over it. A fine beady froth should rise to the surface. Serve hot in glass cups.

SAUTÉED HARE FILLET BERTHA

Skin 2 young, plump hares, clean, sponge with a cloth dipped in wine vinegar. Lift out the fillets. Dust with salt and black pepper and place in a deep platter. Cover them with 1 wineglass of dry white wine, 1 bay leaf tied with 6 sprigs of fresh parsley and a small sprig of thyme, 6 whole peppercorns, gently bruised, 4 thin slices of onion, and 6 slices of carrot. Pour over this ½ cup of good olive oil. Let stand in this marinade for 3 hours. Meanwhile, place in a saucepan, 1½ (generous) tablespoons of grated salt pork, rather lean, 3 tablespoons of butter, ¼ (generous) cup of olive oil, and place over a hot fire, until butter is thoroughly melted, stirring occasionally. Then add 6 tablespoons of fresh mushrooms, peeled and finely ground, then pressed through a cloth. Reduce the flame to moderate and allow this to cook slowly for 15 minutes, stirring frequently with a wooden spoon. Now add 1 generous tablespoon of shallot, finely chopped then squeezed through a cloth to remove part of the acridity or sharpness, and 1 tablespoon of parsley minced fine. Stir well and let simmer very gently over a low flame for a few minutes. Lift out the fillets from their bath. Sponge, cut them in three pieces each, and place in this sauce, seasoning them to taste with salt and black pepper, a tiny blade each of sage, mace, nutmeg, and allspice. Keep them in but a few minutes, just enough to stiffen the meat, or about 5 short minutes. Lift out from the sauce and allow the pieces of fillet to cool a little.

Prepare 6 pieces of oiled paper, large enough to envelop a piece of fillet in each. Place a piece of fillet on each piece of paper, and over it a thin slice of larding pork, the size of the piece of fillet, over this place 1 generous tablespoon of the sauce. Close the paper securely and tie with a string. Repeat likewise with all the other fillets, being careful to tie securely so that the sauce will not escape. When ready to serve, place on a broiler, set the broiler under the flame of the broiling oven until nicely browned on both sides, turning often. Dress as is, that is with the paper on. The guest will have the pleasure of removing it, and taking a good sniff at the delicate aroma of its contents. No sauce, no jelly, nothing else is served with this recipe, created by the Author.

SCALLOP OF HARE FILLET WITH TRUFFLES

Take the fillets of two young hares or rabbits, plump and in the fresh state, after skinning, cleaning, and sponging with a damp cloth. Slice the fillets, scallop style, that is, in thin slices. Place in a large skillet containing ¼ cup of melted and well-heated butter, and cook long enough so as to stiffen the meat; strew over ¼ lb. of black truffles, peeled, then sliced. Cover the skillet with a buttered paper. Lift the meat from the legs, and the mignons as well as the kidneys. With these, make small croquettes in the usual way with which you will garnish the platter when ready to serve. Take the trimmings and bones (cut into small pieces), a small carrot (grated, then sliced thin), 1 medium-sized onion (peeled, then sliced thin), a bouquet garni made with 6 sprigs of fresh parsley tied with 1 bay leaf and 1 sprig of thyme (tied securely), the peeling of the black truffles, ¼ cup of cooked ham (chopped coarsely), 2 cups of beef stock, and 1 cup of Madeira wine. Make this the base of a sauce, by cooking over a hot fire until the liquid is reduced to half, even less. When ready to serve, sauté the fillet pieces rapidly over a hot fire, for a few minutes after removing the buttered paper. To the sauce base, reduced as indicated, and strained through a fine sieve, pressing a little, add ½ cup of rich Sauce Espagnole (*see* Sauces). Bring to a rapid boil and pour over the fillet pieces. Dress on a hot, deep platter, sauce and all. Garnish with the croquettes made with the trimmings as indicated, interspersed with small triangles of rice (cooked, then cooled) fried in butter, and a large bunch of crisp watercress. Serve with a side dish of red currant jelly.

YOUNG HARE VENISON À LA GOMBERVAUX

Author's Note

The following recipe was found and translated by the famous French author Edmond Richardin, Member of the French Academy, from an ancient document of the Honorable Family du Chastelet, and dated 1436, and signed by Dame Pernelle de Lenoncourt, Dame de Gombervaux. A copy was given to the Author by George Claretie, a well-known French attorney, son of Leo Claretie, the President of the Bar Association of France, President du Barreau de Paris, with whom the Author was during the Great War, as interpreter, attached to the British Army, Military Landing Office, in Havre, France.

Take a young hare or young rabbit, skin, clean, and rub with a cloth dipped in vinegar. Bone carefully, reserving the blood and the liver. Lard the hare with narrow strips of cooked ham, roll, and secure with string. Place in a large kettle with 2 medium-sized onions, sliced, 1 clove of garlic, pounded, 10 sprigs of fresh parsley tied with 2 bay leaves and 1 sprig of wild thyme (serpolet), and 2 or 3 sprigs of sweet basil. Pour over, a half bottle of Rhine wine and 1 pony glass of good brandy (the recipe, as regards the wine says textually: ". . . *Adjoutez plantes aromats et pranre la quarte partie d'un hanap de viez vin de Rin; en oult un gobelet de brant vin et selon l'usage laissé trempez du matin jusques à vesprées . . ."* in old and ancient French, meaning ". . . Add aromatic plants and take ¼ bottle of old Rhine wine; plus one goblet of burning brandy [ancient name given to brandy by the British], and according to custom, let marinate from morning until dinner time . . ."). Allow to marinate for 24 hours.

Now take an earthenware terrine or mold. Line the bottom and sides with thin slices of fat larding pork. Over the bottom, arrange, in alternate layers, the pieces of hare and small pieces of lean fresh ham or fresh lean pork. Pour the marinade over the meat pieces, after seasoning to taste with salt and pepper. Chop the liver after removing the gall, with an equal amount of grated lard and a little of the aromatics of the marinade to soften and season, then mix with the blood. Pour this over the meat in the mold, and cover entirely with thin slices of fat larding pork. Set in a slow oven (300–325°) for 4 hours after sealing the mold hermetically.

PUNCH EXTRACT

A good preparation to have on hand, which will keep indefinitely in a cool place.

2 lbs. granulated sugar
2 cups water
   Strained juice of 4 large lemons
1 bottle of spirits such as brandy, rum, whisky, or applejack, according to taste.

Boil the water, adding the sugar. When clear, add the strained lemon juice. Let cool. When cold, add the chosen spirits.

When using, take one part punch extract and two parts boiling water. Serve in glass cups and as hot as possible.

OPOSSUM

This small, haired game is extremely abundant in the fauna of Mississippi as well as of the South. The flavor of its flesh is really delicious and is a cross between pork and hare. All the methods of preparation for hare and pigling may be adapted to it.

RACCOON

The raccoon, a nocturnal carnivore, is related to the bear family. The raccoon may be prepared, like opossum, in all the different methods applied to the hare and pigling.

This animal is more frequently seen on the table in the South than in other parts of the country, but it occasionally makes its appearance in the East. It is in season during the fall and winter months.

The full grown raccoon weighs from seven to twelve pounds, and its flesh is both rank and tough; the young are better, but even these are not good if very fat.

SQUIRREL

The delicious white flesh of this slender rodent may be prepared in all the different and numerous methods of preparations adapted to the hare or rabbit. The skinning is done exactly as that for hare and rabbit, but this little furred animal does not require a long marinating, although a few hours of soaking in the marinades which are used for the hare or rabbit, when the squirrel is old, improves and softens the meat.

ROEBUCK

See DEER.

WAPITI (*Elk*)

This large North American deer, erroneously called elk in the United States, when young and deprived of antlers, may be prepared by all the methods adapted to the deer.

WILD BOAR or WILD HOG or WILD PIG

Actually, the wild boar does not exist in America, although there are found herds of wild pigs or wild hogs in many parts of the United States.

The lusciousness of wild boar roasts (wild pigs, if you prefer) and chops reminds us that the fierce beast has, like Cassius, a lean and hungry look, but all the same a boar's head used to be as important a part of Christmas as the turkey is today, especially in England, Germany, Austria, France, and Belgium.

It all started hundreds of years ago, when a student of Queen's College, Oxford, England, attacked by a wild boar on Christmas Day, saved himself by killing the beast—so the legend says—with a copy of Aristotle which he happened to be studying. He brought back the head, had it served by the college chef for Christmas dinner, and ever since—even to this day—Queen's College commemorates the event by starting Christmas dinner with a mighty boar's head.

In our somewhat softened civilization the once powerful cult of the lovers of rich, high meat and game has faded into obscurity. In the present day of hurry and bustle, there is little serious attention given to the sober study of pleasures of the table; and all matters of the curing and ripening of meats for critical taste are left to the butcher. And it could hardly be otherwise, for where, except in a few country houses, could one find a place to hang a haunch of venison?

WILD BOAR or WILD PIG CUTS
THEIR USES IN COOKERY

As with pork, every part of the wild pig is edible.

BELLY—For blood sausage, braising, baking, broiling, loaves (hot or cold), roasting.

BREAST—For roasting, stuffing, braising, stewing, loaves (cold or hot).

BUTT (*situated behind and on top of the neck above the picnic shoulder*)—For steaks, roasts, broiled, stewed, loaves, braised, boiled, baked, boiled in loaf, hot or cold.

EARS—For jauling, Southern method.

FEET—For broiling, stewing (when boned).

HAM—For roast, haunch, venison, boiling, baking, steaks, cutlets, stuffed.

HEAD—For loaf, prepared in mock turtle, in sour cream, in stew forms.

KIDNEYS—For all the preparations adapted to kidneys of other edible animals.

LIVER—For all preparations of the beef, calf's, lamb, mutton, and pork.

LOIN, FILLET—For venison, haunch, roast, braising, steaks, mignons, scallops, fricassee, kernels (called *noix* in French, and usually braised), cutlets (when pounded), sautéing, fine loaves (individual or large ones), fricandeau, aspic, etc.

NECK—Stewed, braised, boiled, baked, and in loaf, hot or cold.

RIBS—For chops, roasts (boned and rolled), braised, roasted, baked, stewed, broiled.

TONGUE—For pickling, braising, roasting.

IMPORTANT—*When roasting or braising a piece of boar or wild pig, it is of the utmost importance that the rind should be left on all throughout the cooking process, then removed before dressing on the platter. This adds much to the flavor. This does not apply when larding is indicated.*

MARINADES

The MARINADES Nos. I, II, and III, respectively, indicated at the beginning of the FURRED GAME RECIPES, pages 178–179, may be used for marinating wild pig, which is almost obligatory; the length of marinating regulated according to size of the pieces. Usually, for a large piece, 4 to 5 days are required. For small pieces, according to directions.

Besides being marinated, the meat of wild pig must be larded, the large pieces through and through with narrow strips of fat larding pork, the small ones with shorter strips, sometimes seasoned with spices and condiments according to directions.

OPTIONAL SIDE DISHES

Besides the traditional applesauce, which is almost obligatory, a side dish of red currant jelly, grape jelly, or cranberry jelly or molded whole cranberries may be served also. The meat of the wild boar or wild pig demands a thorough searing, and well done as for pork. This rule applies to all the different methods of preparation, unless otherwise indicated, which is very seldom, lest the meat be indigestible.

BREAST OF WILD BOAR
(*Hungarian Method*)

Marinate a neatly trimmed breast of wild boar in MARINADE No. III, page 179, for 4 long days. Sponge and place, after larding it through and through with fat larding pork fat, in a roasting pan with 1 large carrot (grated, then sliced), 1 celery stalk (scraped, then cut into small pieces), 1 parsnip—small one—(grated, then split in two, core removed, discarded, and sliced—outside—thinly), 1 large bouquet garni composed of: the tender green leaves of the celery stalk, tied with 10 sprigs of parsley, 2 large bay leaves, and 1 sprig of thyme, 1 medium-sized onion, peeled, then sliced thin, 3 whole cloves, 10 whole peppercorns, and pour over ½ (generous) cup of the marinade. Set the pan in a hot oven (450°) for 20 long minutes, turning the meat after 10 minutes of searing, reduce the temperature to 350°, and continue roasting, allowing 20 long minutes for each pound of meat. Dress the meat on a hot platter, prick it with the tines of a long fork, to let the whitish-pinkish blood come out (this helps ascertain the point of cooking, that is one can see if the meat is done to the point, that is done). Drain this liquid into the roasting pan. Place the pan on a hot fire. Bring to a boil, stirring from the bottom of the pan to loosen all the gelatinous particles which may adhere; then sprinkle over a tablespoon of flour, continue stirring, while pressing the vegetables so as to mash them coarsely. Now pour over a glass of good red wine, then as much sour cream, and 1 generous tablespoon of good paprika, stirring meanwhile, until the mixture thickens. Strain through a fine sieve, pressing a little so as to extract all the vegetable pulp available. Heat to the boiling point, stir in, after correcting the seasoning, 1 generous tablespoon of good butter. Stir and pour into a hot sauceboat. Garnish the platter simply with a large bunch of watercress and quartered lemon. Serve at once.

BISCHOFF BOURGUIGNON

Grate 2 medium-sized lemons and squeeze the juice from both. Place the grated peel in a punch bowl, and strain the lemon juice over. Place in an enameled saucepan, 2 bottles of Chablis-Moutonne (Burgundy wine) with a 2-inch stick of cinnamon, and 2 or 3 whole cloves, from which the heads have been removed. Place over a moderate fire and when the wine begins to foam on the surface, pour over the lemon grating and juice. Sweeten to taste. Now to the most interesting part of the preparation:

Pour in a long-handled spoon, 2 tablespoons of good brandy with a lump of sugar; touch with a match and let it flame awhile. Meanwhile, you will have turned off all the lights in the dining room, after pouring 1 cupful of good brandy over the punch in the bowl. The brandy flaming in the spoon should be constantly fed with more brandy, until altogether 2 cupfuls have been used, stirring the mixture in the punch bowl occasionally. The brandy flame will die out by itself, imparting a fine flavor to the already delicious white Burgundy wine. It is advisable to wait a few minutes before pouring into glass cups, lest the cups suffer. Other white Burgundy wine, such as Pouilly, Chablis (ordinary), and so forth may be substituted. Sauternes wine also makes an excellent Bischoff, as well as the Arbois and the Volicheres.

BRAISED SHOULDER OF WILD BOAR RUSSIAN STYLE

Entirely bone a shoulder of wild boar. Lay flat over a wet board and pound with the side of a cleaver, turning while sprinkling with black pepper, salt, and 3 juniper berries, pounded. Cover the beaten meat entirely with a slice or several slices of thin larding pork. Over this place a thin, or several thin, slices of cooked ham, coated on both sides with a mixture made as follows: parsley, chives, allspice, olives, in equal parts and chopped fine, then bound with butter so as to form a paste. Roll then as tightly as possible, securing with string and place in MARINADE No. III, page 179. Place the meat thus prepared in a braising kettle, the bottom of which is lined with 1½ (generous) cups of "braise" or mirepoix as indicated in recipe for GROUSE IN AUSBRUCHE, page 29. Pour over 1½ cups of good red wine. Cover the braising kettle hermetically and set in a moderate oven (375°), allowing 20 long minutes for each pound of meat of which there should be 5 lbs., plus 20 minutes extra allowance to start the braising process. Dress the meat on a hot platter, slicing enough to go around for the first helping. Keep hot. Remove all the fat from the braising kettle. Pour the contents in a small flat-bottomed pan; bring to a boil, while pounding all the solid parts. Strain through a fine sieve. Return to the fire and bring to a boil (there should be 1½ cups of sauce, or gravy). Remove from the fire and gradually beat in ¼ lb. of good, sweet butter, added bit by bit, beating vigorously after each addition. The sauce should be foamy, creamy, unctuous, and a dark-brown color. Correct the seasoning, pour part of the sauce over the cut slices, and serve the remainder aside with a side dish of thick unsweetened applesauce.

A side dish of Corn Custard may be served, made as follows:

CORN CUSTARD

Combine the following ingredients:

2 cups of scalded milk	2 egg yolks and 3 egg whites,
½ green pepper, chopped fine and	beaten together slightly
blanched	1½ cups of fresh corn, cut
1 pimento, chopped fine	neatly from the cob
1 tablespoon of minced onion	Salt, pepper, and nutmeg
½ cup chopped celery, parboiled	to taste

Pour into a shallow baking dish. Place the dish in a pan of hot water, and bake in moderate oven (325–350°) for a good half hour. May be baked in individual custard cups if desired.

BRAISED SHOULDER OF WILD BOAR WITH JUNIPER

Marinate a whole shoulder of wild boar or wild pig in MARINADE No. III, page 179, for 4 long days, turning the piece of meat occasionally, and stirring the marinade frequently. Place the well-drained shoulder in a braising kettle, and add: 1 large carrot (grated, then coarsely cut), 1 large onion (peeled, then quartered), 1 large stalk of celery (scraped, then cut into pieces of about 2 inches in length), 2 celery roots (grated), 2 bay leaves, 1 teaspoon of whole peppercorns, as much juniper berries, 3 whole cloves, and add enough marinade, strained, mixed with equal parts of red wine, to cover the meat. Cover the braising kettle hermetically and set in a moderate oven (375°) for 3 long hours, without disturbing but once after 2 hours of cooking process. As already said, the wild pig or boar meat should be well done, lest it be indigestible. Lift out the meat and dress on a hot platter. Keep hot. Turn the entire mixture left in the braising kettle into a fine sieve, after removing the excess of fat, and press through all you can, forcing well. Return the sauce to the fire and allow to reduce over a hot fire until there are about 1½ cups, less than more. Add 2 tablespoons of red currant jelly or an equal amount of brown sugar. Garnish the platter with roasted potatoes, and serve with the sauce aside, besides the traditional stiff apple-sauce.

BRAISED HAUNCH OF WILD BOAR IN BURGUNDY WINE

This fine dish was served for the first time and prepared by J. De Gouy, father of the writer, who was Chef de Bouche (Esquire de Cuisine) to their Royal Highnesses the Archiduc Rodolphe and Archiduchesse Stephanie, at a banquet given at the Imperial Palace of Vienna, March 1, 1884, in honor of the late Emperor Francis Joseph of Austria, the King of Naples II, the King of Serbia, Milan I, since assassinated, and all the archiducs and their consorts. The dish was also much relished by the ex-Emperor of Germany, then King of Prussia, and was often prepared by Maître Urbain Dubois, then Chef de Bouche of the ex-Emperor, and co-author with Maître Escoffier of the immortal cook book Le Guide Culinaire.

The recipe follows; ordinary ham, Virginia ham may be prepared in the same way.

Saw the protruding bone off the hind leg of a wild boar, weighing from 8 to 10 pounds. Rub with a damp cloth, retaining the rind, then marinate in MARINADE No. III, page 179, for 4 long days. Eight hours before dinner time, plunge the piece of meat into a large kettle containing rapidly and violently boiling salt water (salt to be omitted if using a ham) to which has been added 1 teaspoon of whole peppercorns. Reduce the temperature, and allow to cook for 4½ to 5 hours, simmering gently, imperceptibly. Remove the kettle from the fire and allow the piece of meat to cool in the broth. Lift out and place in a braising kettle after removing the rind, and trimming the fat neatly. Do not add any seasoning or braise or mirepoix, but pour over 1 full bottle of very good red Burgundy wine. Do not cover. Place in a moderate oven (325–350°) and let simmer gently until the meat takes on a dark reddish-brown hue. Meanwhile, with highly spiced meat stock made with the trimmings and bones, using 2 cups, make a thick sauce with roux (2 tablespoons of butter and 2 tablespoons of flour, blended to a dark brown over a gentle fire). Add to the sauce thus prepared all the spices available, such as: allspice, sage, nutmeg, mace, thyme leaves, 1 bay leaf, and 10 sprigs of parsley tied with the bay leaf, and an equal amount of tender green leaves from the top of a bunch of celery. Place all this over a hot fire and allow to reduce to nearly nothing. Then pour over 1¾ cups of the wine from the braising kettle, after removing the fat. Salt then to taste. Slice enough portions to go around for the first helping. Reshape, pour part of the sauce over the sliced part and serve the remainder aside. Serve a side dish of plain boiled spinach, seasoned to taste and generously buttered, or glazed carrots, glazed onions. However, besides the chosen side dish, a dish of sauerkraut and mulberry sauce (Preiselbeer), a compote of stewed pears is obligatory.

BRAISED HAUNCH OF WILD BOAR
PRINCE DE CHIMAY

The wild boar or wild pig should be young, plump (*marcassin* in French, meaning a baby one). *Remove the rind* of a hind leg of wild young boar or pig. Lard it through and through with narrow strips of fat larding pork, dipped in brandy, using about 2 dozen strips. Place in a flat-bottomed vessel, which should be of earthenware. (IMPORTANT—*Do not use any metal, lest the marinade decompose. This applies to every marinaded edible food.*) Pour over 1 pint of vinegar and a full bottle of good old red wine, then add: 10 sprigs of parsley tied with a sprig of thyme, 6 tender green leaves of celery, and 2 large bay leaves (3 will not be amiss), 1 large onion (peeled, then sliced thin), 3 cloves of garlic (mashed), 2 medium-sized carrots (grated, then sliced thin), salt, and 1 scant teaspoon of whole peppercorns (bruised). Allow to marinate for 4 long days. Lift out, sponge carefully, and place in a braising kettle over a hot fire, the braising kettle containing ¾ cup of lard, well heated. Sear on all sides until browned. Lift out and keep hot. To the fat in the braising kettle, add 4 tablespoons of flour and let brown thoroughly, stirring all the while. When well browned, pour in gradually, while stirring constantly, 3 (generous) cups of strained marinade. Return the haunch to the sauce and set, hermetically closed, in a moderate oven (350°) for 3 hours, turning the meat twice during the cooking process, adding, ½ hour before serving, 3 tablespoons of good brandy. Dress the meat on a hot platter. Cut enough slices to go around for the first helping. Remove the excess of fat, pour part of it over the slices and serve the remainder aside with another side dish of mashed potatoes, garnishing the platter with apple rings (*see* GARNISHINGS).

BRAISED FILLET OF WILD BOAR
IN CIDER

Lard through and through a whole fillet of wild boar with narrow strips of fat larding pork, rolled in salt, black pepper, and a pinch of nutmeg, using good judgment, the strips at a distance of 2 inches apart. Marinate overnight in MARINADE No. II, page 179. Lift out, sponge, and place in a small braising kettle, the bottom of which is covered with a cupful of "braise" or mirepoix, made as indicated in recipe for GROUSE IN AUSBRUCHE, page 29. Cover with good cider, and add 1 pony glass of good applejack. Cover hermetically and set the kettle in a moderate oven (375°), allowing 20 long minutes for each pound of meat, plus 15 minutes to allow the cooking process to start. Remove the meat. Dress on a hot platter. Keep hot. Place the contents of the kettle in a saucepan, add 2 tablespoons of kneaded butter (equal parts of butter and flour kneaded), and allow to boil until the mixture is reduced to a good full cup. Pour a little of the sauce over the meat, after correcting the seasoning. Serve the remainder aside with applesauce, and a side dish of sauerkraut generously greased with the excess of fat removed from the sauce.

ALT BERLIN SCHLOSS PUNCH
(German Recipe)

2 lbs. granulated sugar	4 cups cold water
2 bottles of Rhine wine	A few lumps of sugar
1 pint of good rum	

Make a syrup with the water and granulated sugar and when boiling point is reached, let boil twice, then reduce the flame and allow to simmer gently for 10 long minutes; then remove from the fire and add the Rhine wine. Stir. Pour into a crystal punch bowl. Place 2 or 3 lumps of sugar in a silver ladle held over the punch and set it afire after having poured a tablespoon of rum over the sugar. As it burns, pour slowly and carefully the remaining rum, allowing it to drop burning into the punch bowl. Let the flame die out; wait a few minutes before pouring into glass cups, lest the glass suffer.

BRAISED HIND LEG OF WILD BOAR
(German Method)

Prepare, cook a hind leg of wild boar or wild pig as indicated in recipe for BRAISED HAUNCH OF WILD BOAR PRINCE DE CHIMAY, page 260, for 3 long hours. Lift out. Remove the rind, leaving a little fat. Make two incisions, lengthwise, from end to end and as far as the bone, one up to 2 inches from the end bone, the other way down to the bottom of the leg. Slide a sharp-pointed knife along the bone and remove it. Then slice the leg in thin slices, then reshape in its natural form, without the bone of course. Keep hot. In a saucepan, put 1 tablespoon of butter, 2 tablespoons of brown sugar, and ¾ cup of fresh brown-bread crumbs, season to taste with salt and a pinch of powdered cinnamon. Stir this mixture over a low flame, so as to obtain a rather thick paste, adding more brown-bread crumbs if necessary. Spread this mixture all over the leg. Return the leg to a dripping pan, generously greased, using lard, pour in the pan ½ cup of the gravy from the braising kettle, fat removed, and allow to brown delicately in a moderate oven (350°). Meanwhile, remove all the fat from the gravy in the braising kettle. Bring the gravy to a boil and strain without pressing at all. There should be 2 scant cups. Add now 1½ tablespoons of kneaded butter (equal parts of butter and flour kneaded to a paste). Boil once over a hot fire, skim carefully, and finish with 3 tablespoons of red currant jelly (in Germany, instead of currant jelly "Hägebutte" is used, but this kind of yellow berry does not exist in America). The fillet, the loin, may be prepared in this way. A very fine dish, especially when served with a side dish of generously greased sauerkraut, cooked with 4 or 5 pigs' knuckles, and a side dish of French fried potatoes in batter made as follows:

FRENCH FRIED POTATOES IN BATTER

You may use either boiled potatoes in their skins, then peeled and sliced, or raw potatoes, cut as for French fried potatoes, but smaller, and fried halfway in hot fat then cooled.

When ready to serve, dip the potatoe sliced or in strips in a frying batter, place in a wire basket, and plunge the basket in hot boiling deep fat. Drain and serve on a hot platter covered with a fancy folded napkin.

GRILLED FILLET OF WILD BOAR MOSCOVITE

Cut from the leg of a wild boar or wild pig, thin slices; pound mercilessly with the back of a cleaver, sprinkling, as you go along, coarsely ground black pepper. The slices should be reduced to a wafer-like thinness. Dip in melted lard after seasoning to taste with salt, and grill on both sides until delicately browned. Dress on a hot platter. Garnish the platter with small pancakes (as small as possible), rolled, after being spread with cottage cheese. Serve a side dish of Moscovite sauce, and a side dish of stewed apple, unsweetened, and highly seasoned with nutmeg and cloves to taste.

JUGGED SHOULDER OF WILD BOAR IN RED WINE

Marinate for 3 long days, in MARINADE No. II, page 179, a shoulder of wild boar, neatly trimmed. Drain and sponge thoroughly and sear the meat in ½ cup of bacon drippings over a medium flame. Lift out and transfer the meat to a large kettle; then add ½ lb. of small white onions (peeled and whole), 1 large green pepper (seeds removed, and coarsely chopped), ¼ lb. of fresh mushrooms (peeled and stems sliced, caps quartered or halved, according to size), 1 small bottle of green olives (drained), 1 large bay leaf tied with 8 sprigs parsley and 7 sprigs of tender green leaves of the top of a bunch of celery. Salt to taste and add ½ (generous) teaspoon of whole peppercorns, as well as a pinch of thyme leaves. Pour over, 1 cup of the marinade and 2 cups of good red wine, then add 1 teaspoon of flour stirred in a little water. Cover, bring to a boil, and allow to simmer for 2¾ hours over a gentle fire. Dress the piece of meat on a hot platter, the vegetables around and well drained. Now reduce the sauce to a generous half cup. Correct the seasoning and stir in 2 tablespoons of red currant jelly, and 1 scant tablespoon of horseradish (prepared), well drained. Garnish the platter with thick slices of green tomatoes, dipped in olive oil, then seasoned with salt and pepper to taste and broiled under the flame of the broiling oven, each slice of tomato placed on a round piece of bread fried in butter, and at both ends a small bunch of green watercress. Serve the sauce aside with a side dish of stewed corn.

PUNCH À LA VICTORIA

Take the juice of 6 lemons, grate 2 of them, and the juice of 2 large oranges, 1 quart of water and 2¾ cups of sugar, more or less, according to taste. Stir until the sugar is entirely melted. Turn the mixture into a hand freezer and freeze firm. Open the freezer and add 1 pony glass of good rum, same amount of curaçao, same amount of brandy. Close the freezer and turn for 2 or 3 minutes. Place the mixture in a large punch bowl, in which there is a large piece of ice. The alcohol will melt the ice. Beat 3 or 4 egg whites until stiff, and add enough powdered sugar as if making a meringue, gradually, while beating constantly. When the ice has melted return the mixture to the freezer, after folding in the egg whites, and freeze for 5 short minutes. Serve in sherbet glasses.

WILD BOAR LOAF ARDENNOISE

Grind 2 lbs. of wild boar or wild pig meat either from the shoulder or the breast, after marinating the meat overnight. Also 1 lb. each of lean veal, and lean salt pork. Grind also ½ cup of beef suet, then melt it over a very low flame, until it smokes. Drain into another pan and in it fry, golden browning, 2 medium-sized onions, thinly minced. To the onions, add 2 large peeled tomatoes, breaking up the pulp. Set aside. Prepare 1 lb. of fresh string beans and cut them lengthwise. Then chop them with a sharp knife on a cutting board, but do not mince or crush them. Cut up and slice thinly 6 stalks of fresh and tender celery, including some of the tenderest leaves; and peel ½ lb. of fresh mushrooms and sauté the caps and stems in 2 tablespoons of butter for 5 short minutes, then slice the caps thinly and mince the stems. Grate 2 small carrots coarsely, and finely mince enough washed, sponged parsley to make a generous tablespoonful. Now gather all the ingredients together in a mixing bowl and stir them up lightly with wooden salad spoon and fork, tossing them over and over till they are thoroughly mixed; season with salt and coarsely ground black pepper, a good pinch of thyme, ½ teaspoon of dry mustard, and 2 tablespoons of Worcestershire sauce. Separate the yolks and whites of 2 eggs and beat the yolks slightly with half a cup of milk, then add to the mixture. Line a loaf mold, bottom and sides previously brushed with lard, with very thin slices of the best bacon. Lastly whip the whites of the eggs till they are stiff, but not dry, and fold them gently into the mixture. Turn the mixture into the bacon lined loaf pan. Adjust the cover of the loaf pan, which should fit tightly, if not, brush the edge of the mold (pan) with a mixture of flour and water, and press the cover over so that it will stick to the edge of the mold, and seal hermetically. Envelop the loaf pan thus sealed in a kitchen towel, and secure with string. Place this delicious bundle in a large kettle containing rapidly and violently boiling water, let boil 10 to 15 minutes over a hot fire, then transfer the kettle and its contents to a hot oven (450°). Boil the water for 30 long minutes, but do not boil away; then reduce the temperature to 375°, and let simmer for 1½ hours.

When you first disrobe the loaf pan, then remove the tight-fitting cover, you will see that the loaf has shrunk away from the sides and is almost floating in a sea of rich and delicious sauce. Do not be alarmed, it should be just so. Carefully drain off the sauce and thicken it with a roux, and a tablespoon of good tomato paste. Turn out the loaf on a fireproof hot platter, peel off the strips of bacon and arrange them around the loaf, and put the dish into a very hot oven (450°), or under the flame of the broiling oven, and brown the surface quickly without drying it. The bacon will be dried off and crisped at the same time. Place the fireproof platter over a larger one, covered with a napkin, to prevent its slipping, garnish the platter edge with small heart-shaped pieces of bread fried in butter, interspersed with large mushrooms, peeled, broiled, and garnish with fine-cooked peas generously seasoned and buttered. Pour part of the sauce over the loaf and serve the remainder aside with a side dish of French fried potatoes.

Deer, hare, and in fact all the furred game may be prepared in this method.

FIVE O'CLOCK PUNCH

Select 1 medium-sized fresh pineapple, ripe to the point; peel, slice as thin as possible, and core, using an apple corer. Arrange the thin slices in a deep flat-bottomed crystal punch bowl, sprinkling each layer with powdered sugar to taste. Allow to mellow overnight, thus drawing the liquid from the slices, keeping the bowl covered and in a cool place (a refrigerator may be used). Next day, pour over a full bottle of champagne (other sweet wine such as Sauternes, or a Saint Émilion, such as Château de Brown; or a Martillac, such as Château Ferrand, a wine endorsed by thousands of wine lovers. It has a wonderful aroma, a fine fragrance, and a delicate bouquet. Rather sweetish, its light sweetness leaves a pleasing aftertaste; or a Loupiac wine, such as a Cru du Haut Loupiac, cheering, bouqueted, and deliciously sweet; so is the wine Domaine de Loupiac.

Early in the morning, prepare ½ (generous) lb. of small, perfumed wild strawberries (garden strawberries may be used if the wild ones are not available). Throw them carefully hulled, washed, then rolled in powdered sugar, over the pineapple slices, in the sweet juice mixed with champagne, or other selected wine, which should be a sweet white wine, at any rate, and allow them to bathe in this ambrosia for at least 6 long hours, still keeping the bowl and its contents in a cool place. Fifteen minutes before serving, take a glass pitcher and pour into it ½ bottle of champagne (or the sweet white wine substituted for it), and a large piece of ice weighing about ¾ lb. Put also the same amount of ice, cut into 5 or 6 pieces in a punch bowl. Bring all these, punch bowl and pitcher with their contents into the parlor, or the dining room. The hostess herself serves these delicacies, using a silver fork and a silver ladle as follows:

Place in the bottom of each glass *coupe* a little of the strawberries over a slice of pineapple, then fill each *coupe* with the liquid.

This preparation is easy to make, economical, and rather delicious. Canned pineapple may be substituted for fresh pineapple, champagne may be omitted and a sparkling wine substituted.

Recipe contributed by Madame Lods de Wegmann, of Paris.

WILD BOAR LEG AGRA DOLCE
(*Italian Recipe*)

Braise a larded wild boar leg, marinated for 4 long days in MARI-NADE No. II, page 179, as indicated in recipe for BRAISED SHOULDER OF WILD BOAR RUSSIAN STYLE, page 257, using a hind leg instead of a shoulder, and continuing the braising process for 3 long hours. Serve with a sauce made as indicated in recipe for HARE CIVET AGRA DOLCE, page 238, adding 2 or 3 tablespoons of pignolia nuts to the sauce, 1 tablespoon of grated orange rind, and 1 tablespoon of grated or chopped fine lemon peel just before serving.

WILD BOAR CUTLET
(*Flemish Method*)

Cut 6 slices of wild boar or wild pig, from the leg, each slice weighing 8 ounces. Pound each slice with the side of a cleaver, sprinkling as you go along with a mixture of dry mustard and black pepper. Turn it over and season again with the mixture, pounding meanwhile. The fiber will be broken down and the cutlet will expand under the punishment, which should not cease till the thickness has been reduced to ⅜ inch. Melt 4 tablespoons of lard—good pork lard—in a large baking sheet and place over the wild boar cutlets, sprinkled with salt to taste. Sauté rapidly over a very hot flame, turning frequently, so as to brown on both sides. Dress on a very hot platter and garnish the platter with cooked, sliced, and sautéed sweet potatoes. Serve with a side dish of thick, unsweetened applesauce.

WILD BOAR CUTLET À LA MOLDAVE

Cut 6 cutlets from the hind leg of a young wild boar, each weighing 8 ounces. Marinate overnight in MARINADE No. II, page 179. Drain. Sponge, lard each cutlet lengthwise with 4 narrow strips of fat larding pork. Flatten a little, but gently, and sauté in melted butter, using about 3 tablespoons, in a large skillet, turning frequently. When half done, sprinkle over 4 generous tablespoons of onions, minced and blanched in butter for 1 long minute. Pour over 6 tablespoons of sour grape juice, stirring gently but thoroughly from the bottom of the skillet; then add 1 cup of Poivrade sauce (*see* SAUCES). Cover and allow to simmer very gently for 10 long minutes; then add 1 tablespoon (generous) of fennel, chopped fine, and 3 tablespoons of capers. Let simmer again 3 long minutes, to mellow. Dress the cutlets in circles on a hot platter, overlapped and interspersed with small heart-shaped small pieces of bread fried in butter. Fill the center with Potato Croquettes Dauphine, made as indicated below, and pour the sauce over the cutlets, serving the remainder aside, if any.

POTATO CROQUETTE DAUPHINE

Peel 1 lb. of potatoes. Cut into quarters and boil in cold salted water in the usual way. Drain. Dry the potatoes over the flame of the range, and put through ricer. Place the potatoes in a mixing bowl and add 3 generous tablespoons of butter, salt and white pepper to taste, a few grains of nutmeg and beat thoroughly as if making ordinary mashed potatoes, adding 1 whole egg and 3 egg yolks, alternately, and beating vigorously after each addition.

Have a cup of boiling water on the fire, boiling rapidly, to which add ½ cup of butter, let boil until the butter is melted, then add 1 cup of bread flour, all at once and stir vigorously over the heat until a ball forms in the center of the pan. Cool slightly, then add 4 fresh eggs, unbeaten, one at a time, beating well after each addition. The mixture should be very stiff, of a light golden color. Add this paste to the mashed potatoes and mix thoroughly. Divide the mixture into small parts each one the size of a small egg, shape, corklike, dip into beaten egg, then in very fine bread crumbs and place in a wire basket. When ready to serve, plunge the basket into hot, boiling deep fat for 3 or 4 long minutes or until the small croquettes are delicately golden browned.

Serve the dish immediately, as it should be eaten very hot.

WILD BOAR CUTLET SAUTÉ À LA VIARD

Cut 6 thin slices from the leg of a wild boar, each slice weighing 7 ounces. Pound very lightly, sprinkling the cutlets as you go along with salt and pepper on both sides. Trim the cutlets neatly, and sauté in 2 tablespoons of melted butter. Immediately pour over the cutlets 4 tablespoons of hot butter and cook over a very hot fire, turning once. Both sides should be very brown. Set the pan in a moderate oven for 3 long minutes to finish cooking. Dress the cutlets on a hot platter, a sizzling platter, in circle, leaving the center open. Keep hot. Put in a saucepan ½ cup of Spanish sauce (*see* SAUCES) and ½ cup of good white wine. Heat slowly. To the pan in which the cutlets were cooked, add ¼ cup of white wine and bring to a boil, stirring from the bottom of the pan to loosen all the gelatinous particles which may adhere. Turn this into the saucepan containing the Spanish sauce and the white wine. Bring to a boil and allow to reduce to half. Correct the seasoning and pour the sauce over the cutlets. Garnish the center with a large bunch of watercress. Serve a side dish of apple rings, made as indicated under GARNISHINGS.

WILD BOAR CUTLET ROMAN SAUCE

Sauté 6 wild boar cutlets prepared as indicated above, using olive oil instead of butter. Serve with a side dish of Roman sauce (*see* SAUCES) and a side dish of mashed chestnuts, celery, or lentils.

WILD BOAR CUTLET SAINT MARC

Cut 6 cutlets as indicated in recipe for WILD BOAR CUTLET SAUTÉ À LA VIARD, above. Lard with narrow strips of fat larding pork, using 6 strips for each cutlet. Place in the bottom of a braising kettle, 1½ cups of "braise" or mirepoix, made as indicated in recipe for GROUSE IN AUSBRUCHE, page 29. Top with the larded cutlets and pour over ½ cup of good meat stock and ¼ cup of white wine. Set in a moderate oven (375°) for 40 long minutes, covered tightly. Lift out the cutlets and dress in circle on a hot platter, leaving the center open. Garnish the center with small balls of chestnut purée, the size of a large marble and very hot. Garnish with a bunch of watercress and small triangles of bread fried in butter, interspersed with thin slices of lemon. Serve aside the gravy from the kettle, as is, after removing the excess of fat, in a sauceboat and a side dish of cranberry jelly.

HURE DE SANGLIER
(*Wild Boar Head in Loaf*)

AUTHOR'S NOTE

This delicious dish, suitable for an impromptu luncheon, is usually served as hors d'oeuvres (appetizers). When cut in small pieces and dressed on a piece of fresh brown bread, it then constitutes a substantial dish. It may be prepared easily at home and keeps long in a good refrigerator. The head of a pork may be prepared in the same way.

INITIAL PREPARATION

Bone a wild boar or wild pig head (the butcher will do it if asked), exactly as for a calf's head. Wash well. Save the tongue. The head should be cut off way down to the neck, and a little below the ears. Place the head in fresh cold water, to wash thoroughly, in a large kettle. Drain, and discard the water. Return the boned head to the kettle and cover with equal parts of cold water and white wine and add the following ingredients: 1 onion, quartered (large one), 12 sprigs parsley tied with 3 bay leaves and 1 sprig of thyme (10 sprigs of tender leaves of the top of celery may be added to the parsley if desired), 2 carrots, 4 whole cloves, 2 cloves of garlic, peeled, but left whole, 1 generous teaspoon of whole peppercorns.

Cook this, covered, on a low fire for 6 long hours, according to size of the head. The head will be done when a straw may easily pierce the rind of the head, which should be left on.

Now, drain the head. Place on a large platter, let cool a little. Remove the rind and place it on a well-buttered square, deep earthenware dish, which will be the mold. Cut the tongue which has been soaked in salted water for several hours and cooked separately for one long hour, over a very low fire, into 1-inch pieces. Remove the thin skin around the brain, which has been cooked separately, that is blanched in salted water, and dice small. Place the meat in a large platter as you go along cutting. Season with salt, a little pepper if necessary, remembering that the meat was cooked with peppercorns, a few grains of cayenne, ½ teaspoon of sage, and ¼ teaspoon each of allspice, mace, and nutmeg. Mix this thoroughly, but carefully. You may add a little of the flesh of the wild boar, previously boiled, and diced very small if desired. Now pour over this 1 scant cup of the strained cooking broth, and a pony glass of good brandy. Mix again. Now pack the meat into the square earthenware deep dish over the pieces of rind. Pack solid, pressing hard, as hard as possible, to prevent any air pockets. Cover the top with a small board, fitting snugly over the meat, and place upon it a heavy weight. Set in the refrigerator and do not use for 48 hours at least.

Chopped truffles, or cooked fresh mushrooms, or green pistachio nuts, or part of each, may be added, if desired.

ROAST CHESTNUT-STUFFED BABY
WILD BOAR

For many years tender young marcassins—young wild boar or pigs—have been traditional in England and in America, where the wild ones, not known, except those imported, were replaced by young piglets, long before the turkey won honors as our national bird of feast days.

It is important to select a fat and short little wild pig as it is much finer and more tender. Different stuffings may be used according to taste, such as the American sage stuffing, or the English stuffing, or the apple stuffing, or yet the Russian stuffing, all of them to be found under DRESSINGS AND STUFFINGS in the Contents.

First you must proceed to its cleaning, trussing, and washing. Then rub its inside with plenty of lemon juice, first, then plenty of lard mixed with salt and black pepper. Following comes the stuffing which should be deliciously scented with herbs that give another tang to the wild meat, add brightness to the flavor, and make enjoyment of food an art instead of a gesture, and the process of eating such a regal preparation, not merely mechanical but tinctured with imagination. For this recipe I would suggest the following mixture: 1 lb. of fresh mushrooms (peeled, then ground), 1 large black truffle (cooked 5 short minutes in Madeira wine, after being peeled, then ground), ¼ cup of blanched almonds (ground), ½ cup of parsley (minced fine), ¼ cup of chives (minced fine), ¼ teaspoon each of allspice, sage, thyme, marjoram, and mace in powder form, 1 cup of cooked ham (ground), 1 cup of meat sausage, 2 cups of bread crumbs (soaked in cream, then squeezed, and spread a few minutes over a colander to remove the excess of moisture), salt and coarsely ground black pepper, using good judgment as to quantities.

Place all these ingredients in a mixing bowl, and mix while adding 1 egg white, beaten stiff, and 2 egg yolks, beaten to a cream, gradually and alternately. Mix thoroughly, then stuff San Antonio's little wild companion. Sew up its little belly, containing this tempting stuffing. Tie him up after rubbing with plenty of good olive oil. Now make four parallel gashes 3 inches long through the skin on each side of the backbone, and put on rack in a long, narrow dripping pan. Sprinkle with salt and pour 2 generous cups of stock made from the trimmings around the little one, and cover with a large buttered, or oiled paper. Roast—searing the piglet for 20 long minutes in a hot oven (500°); then reduce the temperature rapidly to 300–325° (maximum), and continue roasting, allowing 25 long minutes to the pound, because of the scented stuffing which requires a thorough cooking, basting every 10 minutes with the liquid in the pan. Remove the oiled or buttered paper 30 minutes before the piglet is done, that is approximately after 2½ hours of slow roasting, and brush over with heavy sour cream.

Have ready a small red apple (raw) for the mouth. Fill the cavities of the eyes with large cranberries. Put a necklace of crisp young watercress around its neck to "dress up." Place apple cups filled with applesauce, or with half applesauce and half cranberry sauce, thoroughly mixed, or whatever combination you may desire, such as baked apples topped with a large plump prune, stuffed with a few cranberries (cooked), and garnish all around with watercress, of which a small serving will go along on each plate. A side dish of Hunter sauce (*see* SAUCES) is usually served aside.

Brussels sprouts, smothered white cabbage, mashed potatoes, or candied yams are often served with this dish, way down in the South.

NOËL RED CLARET PUNCH
(*A Christmas Punch*)

1 quart of strong camomile infusion, linden tea, or ordinary tea, according to taste
1 bottle of good red Bordeaux wine
The juice of a small lemon, strained
1 lb. of loaf or lump sugar
1 pint of best rum

Brew the chosen infusion and strain carefully through a fine cloth or fine strainer, better twice than once to ensure clearness. Pour this into a large porcelain bowl or heat-proof glass dish or bowl; add the red Bordeaux wine and the juice of lemon (the addition of the juice of an orange adds to the flavor). Heat thoroughly, but do not boil. Place over the salad bowl or glass bowl a pair of fire tongs and on it the sugar loaf. Pour over the sugar a wineglass of the rum. Set afire, feeding the flame constantly with the remainder of the rum, pouring it very slowly and carefully over the melting and flaming sugar.

Meanwhile, you'll have turned out all the lights in the dining room. The alcohol fades away in the blue flame and the punch is then served by the hostess, in glass cups.

GAME SAUCES

". . . Food is a subject so deep, so tremen-
dously large in scope that whoever attempt
to write on it, find it impossible of conden-
sation. . . ."

BRILLAT-SAVARIN

SAUCES

A perfect sauce is always a triumph. A bit of this, a sprinkle of that, a dash of imagination, and the most prosaic food is "saucily served."

The preparation of foods so that the most is made of natural flavors and textures, that's good cooking. The enhancement of natural flavors and textures through the addition of contrasting flavors and textures, generally in sauce form, that's fine cooking.

Nearly all sauces are derived from three basic types: White, brown, and butter. For the white you may use cream, milk, or white stock; the brown sauces are made with dark stocks or meat drippings; from butter is made the light sauce, such as Hollandaise.

The famous Bechamel sauce—created by the Marquis Louis de Bechamel, during the reign of Louis XIV of France, during ". . . the grand and even gigantic era of the culinary art period, when the science of culinary artists began to be admired. . . ." (quotation of Brillat-Savarin)—is merely a rich cream sauce seasoned with a bit of carrot, a slice of onion, a bay leaf, a parsley sprig, and some white pepper. The whole simmered gently and strained. The cream base can then be varied at service time by adding a little whipped cream (½ cup to each cup of sauce), the beaten yolks of 2 eggs, some chopped green herbs, cooked shrimps, minced sautéed mushrooms, grated cheese, tomato purée, or nearly any combination of these ingredients.

Brown sauce is the base for most highly spiced sauces; the tomato and green pepper combinations are richer if made with this brown sauce, also called "espagnole"; the flour must be browned in the butter before the liquid is added. This is called a roux. The liquid for the base of many sauces is always a rich stock which may be combined with tomato purée, fruit juices, or vegetable stock, essence of meat (or fish), of game, and highly seasoned. If minced vegetables are added, it is then called "jardiniere"; if minced ham, vegetables, and herbs, it is called "italienne," and so forth.

Other hot sauces which are in a class by themselves are those which are made with a vinegar or sour base. The most common of these is the well-known mint sauce. Sliced onion and whole spices, heated slowly in vinegar with a little sugar, give a piquant flavor, and is usually used with fish, ham, and game.

The butter sauces cannot be generally classified as either hot or cold, although they are usually served with hot food. Softened butter may be flavored with lemon juice, minced parsley and onion, or chives. These are usually spread over cooked fish or on top of steak. The butter may be melted and browned or melted and flavored with lemon juice or vinegar.

Hollandaise sauce, one of the most popular of the fine warm sauces, is one of the easiest sauces to make if the recipe is followed properly. The eggs (yolks), lemon juice, and half the butter should be put into a small saucepan, which should be held over hot water, while the butter is melting and the sauce thickening, and while you stir vigorously and constantly. The rest of the butter should then be stirred in and the sauce beaten mercilessly, although gently, until it again thickens. *Never Use a Double Boiler for This Sauce,* unless you are very careful not to allow the water to boil in the lower part. When the sauce has thickened, set it aside if you are not ready to use it at once, and reheat it, stirring constantly, just before serving.

APPLE CURRY SAUCE

(Suitable for Leftover Cooked Game of Any Kind)

⅓ cup minced onion
1 cup diced, pared, cored, tart cooking apple
3 tablespoons of fat
3 tablespoons flour
½ teaspoon salt and pepper to taste

1½ (more or less) teaspoons curry powder
1½ cups game or meat stock (milk may be substituted for game or meat stock if desired)

Cook the onion and diced apple in the fat until tender. Add seasonings, including curry powder, then pour on, gradually, while stirring constantly, the chosen liquid in which the flour has been stirred. Place over boiling water and let cook, stirring constantly until mixture has thickened. Cover and allow to simmer gently, always over hot water, 15 minutes longer, stirring occasionally.

BROWN SAUCE SPECIAL FOR GAME

(*Master Recipe*)

(*Suitable for Any Kind of Game, Bird or Furred*)

1 tablespoon of dried mushrooms	1 tablespoon of Worcestershire sauce
2 tablespoons of bacon, diced small	1 small bay leaf
	6 sprigs parsley tied with the bay leaf
2 tablespoons of onion, minced fine	1 small sprig of thyme
2 tablespoons of carrot, chopped fine	Salt and pepper to taste
2 tablespoons of flour	1 teaspoon of "Fumet" (*see* recipe, How To PREPARE
1½ cups of game stock, meat stock, or bouillon	GAME STOCK, page 45)

Barely cover the dried mushrooms with boiling water and allow to stand for 15 minutes. Cook the diced bacon until brown and crisp. Lift out, and in the fat left in the pan cook the onion and carrot until lightly browned. Then remove from the pan. To the fat in the pan, add the flour (add more fat if necessary so as to have 2 tablespoons of fat) and blend until well browned. When thoroughly browned, pour in the game stock, or meat stock, or bouillon, gradually, while stirring constantly, from the bottom of the pan, until thick and smooth. Return the onion and carrot to the sauce together with the mushrooms, drained and chopped fine, and add all the remaining ingredients. Stir and allow to simmer gently for 15 minutes, skimming the top occasionally to remove the film coming to the surface. Strain through a very fine sieve. Keep hot until wanted. This sauce may be the foundation of several other sauces calling for a brown sauce base, or may be used as is, simply adding, for furred game, 1 or 2 tablespoons of red currant jelly, or whatever ingredient, or ingredients are indicated.

BARBECUE SAUCE I

(Hot) (Suitable for Furred Game. May Be Also Used for Cold or Hot Wild Hen, Turkey, and the Like)

To 1 generous tablespoon of butter or drippings, heated to the smoking point, add: ⅓ cup of minced onion and ⅓ cup of minced celery, and a bit of garlic, and cook slowly, stirring meanwhile, for 3 long minutes; then sprinkle over 2 tablespoons of brown sugar, and 2 generous tablespoons of cider vinegar. Stir until the sugar is melted and mixture is well blended, then add: 1½ tablespoons prepared mustard, 2 tablespoons of Worcestershire sauce, a pinch of salt, cayenne, and coarsely ground black pepper to taste, stir well and pour over 1 cup of tomato catsup stirred in 1 cup of hot stock (game or meat). Stir and allow to simmer gently for 25 long minutes, over a very low flame. Just before removing from the fire, add 1 generous tablespoon of lemon juice. This sauce should be served very hot.

BARBECUE SAUCE II

(Hot) (Alabama Method) (Especially Suited for Wild Hen, but May Be Used for Furred Game)

Heat 1 cup of apple vinegar, and stir in ¼ lb. of butter. Bring to the boiling point. Then add 1 cup of tomato catsup, mixed with 3 tablespoons of Worcestershire sauce, salt, black pepper, and cayenne to taste, 1 pinch nutmeg, 1 pinch of sage, 1 pinch of allspice, 12 sprigs parsley tied with 1 large bay leaf and 1 sprig of wild thyme (serpolet), juice of 1 large onion, and juice of 2 lemons with the grated peel of half a lemon. Cook slowly for 30 long minutes, over a low flame, stirring occasionally.

Down South this sauce is largely used for chicken as well as game.

BARBECUE SAUCE III
(*Hot*) (*Mississippi Method*)

Melt 2½ lbs. of butter, and add the juice of 8 lemons, stir well, then add ¼ cup of tomato catsup, mixed with 3 tablespoons of Worcestershire sauce and 1 scant teaspoon of Tabasco sauce. Stir thoroughly, the pan still on the fire, then add 2 small cloves of garlic, whole, salt and black pepper to taste. Finally, add ¼ cup of ground sweet-sour pickles. Let simmer very gently for 30 long minutes. Discard the cloves of garlic. Serve with wild hen, wild furred game. May also be served with turkey, chicken, and guinea hen.

BECHAMEL SAUCE
(*Master Recipe for Game*) (*Suitable for Base of Any Cream Sauce Used for Game Bird or Furred Game*)

Stir 2 tablespoons of flour with 2 tablespoons of butter until thoroughly blended, but not browned (this is called a brown roux, in culinary terms). Then pour over, gradually, while stirring constantly, 1½ cups of scalded milk, alternating with 1 cup of strained game stock, until mixture begins to thicken. Turn mixture into a saucepan, the bottom of which is lined with ½ cup of lean veal (diced small, previously sautéed in butter, but not browned), 1 small leek (cut into small pieces, and thoroughly washed in several waters), 1 small carrot (grated, then sliced), 2 thin slices of lemon (seeded), 1 medium or, still better, 2 small white onions (peeled, then sliced thin), 6 sprigs parsley tied with 1 large bay leaf and 1 small sprig thyme, salt, white pepper, and nutmeg to taste. Bring rapidly to a boil, stirring occasionally, then reduce the temperature and allow to simmer very gently for 30 long minutes. Strain the sauce through a very fine sieve, pressing lightly. If the sauce is to be used at once, then add 2 egg yolks, one at a time, beating well after each addition, and, just before serving, add 1 cup of rich cream, and 1 tablespoon of butter.

This method is applied to game sauce only and does not leave the sauce snow white, as it should be for other preparations; it is a little brownish, but much more delicious.

If the sauce is not to be used at once, but later on, remove from the fire and let cool, placing a piece of wood or other material under the saucepan, to allow the air to circulate under and hasten the cooling process. When wanted, simply heat and add the finishing ingredients as indicated above, plus those indicated in the recipe. This sauce is much finer than the ordinary cream sauce made of flour, milk, butter, and salt and pepper.

IMPORTANT POINTS ABOUT MAKING AND KEEPING SAUCES

IMPORTANT

Sauces for which butter is called for as a finishing touch, will always curdle when the butter is added too soon, or too long in advance. If the sauces do not curdle, they always lose part of their fineness.

If a sauce calls for aromatization of Madeira, sherry wine, or liqueur, the wine or spirit should be added just before serving unless otherwise indicated.

As far as possible, do not use iron spoons when preparing sauce. Wooden spoons alone should be used. Iron imparts a bad flavor when used in cookery.

Sauces prepared too far in advance, and remaining in too large pans, take on the flavor of fat.

Leftover sauces should be kept in either earthenware or enameled bowls, and set in refrigerator only when thoroughly cooled. They may be used for loaves (meat or fish) or for preparing leftover meat, fish, game, or vegetables.

SAUCE ESPAGNOLE

(Master Recipe) (Suitable for Game Birds and Furred Game)

Because this sauce is often used in cookery, it is important to read the recipe carefully, and it is advisable always to have some of it on hand, as it may be used for fish, eggs, any kind of meat, and all sorts of game. In fact, it is really the brown sauce used universally where good cooking is appreciated. It may seem elaborate, difficult, and costly, but it is not. If one wants to enjoy good cooking, healthful cooking, the best ingredients are necessary. It is much wiser to follow a recipe that calls for only one egg, for instance, than to skimp an egg in a recipe that calls for two. It is folly to make a recipe calling for even one egg when the one you have on hand is of doubtful quality. In other words, "one cannot make a silk purse from a sow's ear."

RECIPE

Melt in a saucepan which may hold 2 generous quarts, 3 tablespoons of butter which has been clarified, that is, that has been melted over hot water, slowly, so as to allow the particles of solid matter to fall at the bottom of the pan; add 3 generous tablespoons of flour, always a little more flour than butter is advisable. Let cook slowly over a low flame, stirring occasionally until thoroughly blended. If the recipe calls for a dark blending, let brown to the right hue; if the recipe calls for a light-brown blending, as for Bechamel sauce, cream sauce, white sauce, do not overcook. For sauce espagnole the browning should be of a deep hue. Cooking slowly will give a nutty flavor, cooking too fast will give a bitter taste to the sauce. Moisten, gradually with good meat juice or meat stock, stirring constantly until the pan is filled to 2 inches from the top. Allow to boil without ceasing to stir from the bottom of the pan; then let simmer gently for 50 long minutes, stirring occasionally. Then remove all the fat, using a spoon. Strain through a fine sieve into another pan.

When this sauce is completed, if not used at once, set aside and let cool and whenever wanted, take the necessary amount and add the different essences or reductions to make other sauces, such as Madeira sauce, Poivrade sauce, venaison, piquante, and so forth. Then let reduce according to directions and strain. By this method of preparing a sauce espagnole or Spanish sauce—whichever way you prefer—in preparing a dinner where several sauces are required, those having as a base brown sauce, the work is very much simplified.

SAUCE VELOUTE
(*Master Recipe*)

Proceed as for the sauce espagnole, but an enameled saucepan should be used preferably to any other, unless the one used has been freshly soldered. The *roux,* or blending of butter and flour should not be colored, or browned. The liquid used for moistening should be either chicken or veal stock. The cooking process is the same as for sauce espagnole, only the liquid is different.

With this sauce on hand, all you have to do is add the essences or reductions called for in the recipe, such as Hungarian sauce, Ivory sauce, Nantua sauce, Soubise sauce, etc., unless a Bechamel sauce is indicated.

BUTTER SAUCE
(*Master Recipe*)

In general, the butter sauces cannot be classified as either hot or cold, although they are usually served with hot foods.

Blend together 1 tablespoon of clarified butter and 1 tablespoon of flour, but do not brown. Gradually add 1 cup of water, stirring constantly, over a hot fire. At the first boil, remove from the fire and add 2 or 3 egg yolks, one at a time, beating vigorously and constantly after each addition, using a wire whisk. Do not allow the mixture to boil any more, lest the egg yolks curdle. Season to taste with salt and white pepper, and finish by beating in 2 tablespoons of butter, added bit by bit, and a few drops of lemon juice. With this sauce as a base, different variations may be made, such as Maltaise sauce, Mousseline sauce, Mustard sauce, Egg sauce, English method, Anchovy sauce, and so forth.

BREAD SAUCE I
(*Suitable for All Kinds of Game Birds*)

To a cup of boiling milk, add 1 generous cup of bread crumbs, 1 small white onion stuck with a small whole clove, from which the head has been removed, and 1 tablespoon of butter. Season to taste with salt and white pepper—the latter may be omitted—and let simmer very gently for 15 long minutes. Remove the onion, beat gently with a wire whisk, and finish, off the fire, with ½ (scant) cup of scalded heavy cream.

BREAD SAUCE (FRIED) II
(*Suitable for All Kinds of Game Birds*)

To 1 cup of good game stock, or clear meat stock add, 2 tablespoons of very lean cooked ham, diced very small and 2 small shallots, minced fine. Let simmer very gently for 15 minutes. Meanwhile, fry in 2 tablespoons of butter, 6 tablespoons (or more if the sauce is desired thick) of freshly made bread crumbs, until slightly browned. Add to the game stock mixture with 1 teaspoon of parsley, minced, and a few drops of lemon juice.

BIGARADE SAUCE
(*Suitable for Domestic and Wild Ducks*)

Two methods to prepare this delicious sauce are used; one for braised ducks, and the other for panned ducks.

FIRST METHOD
Remove entirely the fat from the gravy in the braising kettle, strain through a fine sieve, and reduce the sauce to 1 cup. Strain again through a fine sieve or through a fine cloth and add a few drops of lemon juice. The addition of a tablespoon of butter to

enrich the sauce enhances the flavor, when added just before serving the sauce, and 1 tablespoon of grated orange peel.

SECOND METHOD

Remove all the fat from the pan in which the duck has been panned, sprinkle ½ teaspoon of flour, or still better the same amount of arrowroot, and stir thoroughly until the flour or arrowroot is cooked and assimilated. Add then 2 teaspoons of sugar caramelized over a low fire, and moistened with 1 generous tablespoon of good wine vinegar. Finish with the juice of half an orange (lemon juice may be used, or both). Just before serving add 1 tablespoon of grated orange and 1 teaspoon of grated lemon peels.

CAMBRIDGE SAUCE

(Cold) *(Suitable for Any Kind of Cold Cooked Furred Game)*

Pound together 4 egg yolks, hard-cooked, 2 sponged anchovy fillets, 1 teaspoon of capers, ¼ generous teaspoon of chervil, 2 small leaves of tarragon herbs (dry or fresh), ½ generous teaspoon of chives, moistening with ¼ (good) teaspoon of prepared mustard, stirred in ¼ cup of olive oil and 2 teaspoons of wine vinegar. Beat rapidly until the mixture is a paste. Season with a few grains of cayenne but no salt nor pepper. When ready to serve, add ½ teaspoon of very finely minced parsley.

CUMBERLAND SAUCE

(Cold) *(Suitable for Any Kind of Cold Cooked Furred Game)*

Melt 3 tablespoons of currant jelly. Cool, then add 1 tablespoon of red or white wine, 2 tablespoons of orange juice, 1 (scant) teaspoon of prepared mustard, 1 (scant) teaspoon paprika, ½ teaspoon ground ginger, and 1½ tablespoons each of shredded lemon and orange peel. The orange and lemon rind should first be covered with cold water, brought to a rapid boil, drained, then cooled before being added to the mixture.

CHAMPAGNE SAUCE

(Expensive but Delicious for Game Birds of Delicate Texture)

Pour into a saucepan, a pint bottle of champagne (imitation champagne may be used, because of the expense) and add 3 tablespoons of ground mushrooms, caps and stems, ½ teaspoon of finely minced shallots, and 5 sprigs parsley tied with a small piece of bay leaf. Cook over a hot fire until mixture is reduced to half. In a little cold game stock, stir ½ teaspoon of cornstarch and pour slowly into the champagne sauce, stirring rapidly. Season highly with salt, white pepper, and a pinch of allspice. Boil 5 short minutes, and strain through a fine sieve.

CHÂTEAUBRIAND SAUCE

*(Usually Served with Broiled Dark Meat, This Sauce Is
Very Suitable for Large Furred Game)*

On a hot fire, reduce 1 cup of white wine to which has been added 2 shallots, minced, a pinch of thyme leaves, and a small piece of bay leaf, to ¼ cup. Then add 1½ cups of veal stock, and reduce again to half. Strain through a very fine sieve and finish, off the fire, with 3 generous tablespoons of maître d'hôtel butter (*see* COMPOUNDED BUTTERS in Volume II, *Fish Book*) and ½ teaspoon of fresh tarragon leaves, minced fine.

CHERRY SAUCE

*(Suitable for Duck and Venison Game, Especially
Hare and Wild Pig)*

Reduce to half, 1 cup of good port wine, to which has been added: 1 whole clove, a pinch of nutmeg, a pinch of allspice, and 4 or 5 small leaves of thyme, mixed with ¼ teaspoon of grated rind of orange. Then add 4 tablespoons of game stock and ¼ cup of red currant jelly. Finish, just when ready to serve, with the juice of half an orange and 1 tablespoon of butter.

CRANBERRY SAUCE

(Suitable for Wild Turkey, Duck, and Almost All Furred Game)

Pick, wash 1 lb. of cranberries. Cover with game or meat stock, strained, add a dash of salt and 3 whole cloves. Cook until tender. Strain, remove the cloves and rub through a fine sieve. Return to the saucepan and add enough strained juice (in which the berries have been cooked), so as to obtain a thick mixture. Sweeten very lightly, as the flavor of the fruit, natural flavor, should be very prominent. Pour into a mold or small individual molds and let cool. When ready to serve, unmold and serve. With game, it is the special cranberry sauce, and should always be served very cold to contrast with the sizzling hot game, thus enhancing the flavor of the fruit.

CREAM GIBLET GRAVY

(American Recipe)

(Suitable with Any Kind of Large Game Bird)

Simmer the giblets in enough water to cover, adding 3 thin slices of onion, 6 peppercorns, 1 small bay leaf, 1 tablespoon of celery leaves, chopped fine, a pinch of thyme and salt to taste, until tender, over a very gentle fire. This should be done while the game bird is cooking. Strain off the liquid; chop the giblets or, still better, put through food chopper and add to the liquid. There should be ½ (generous) cup of liquid. Heat to the boiling point and add 1 cup of Bechamel sauce, stirring until the Bechamel sauce is thoroughly mixed. Allow to boil once and let simmer very gently for 15 long minutes, stirring occasionally.

CURRANT MINT SAUCE

(Cold) *(Suitable with Any Kind of Preparation of Wild Boar; also Wild Duck, Woodcock and Pheasant and Wild Hen)*

Empty a jar of red currant jelly into a mixing bowl and break into small pieces with a fork. Do not beat. Add 1½ tablespoons of finely chopped fresh mint leaves, 1 tablespoon of grated orange rind, and 1 teaspoon of grated lemon rind. Instead of fresh mint, you may combine equal parts of red currant jelly with equal parts of mint jelly. In either case, grated orange and lemon peels should be added.

DEMIGLACÉ SAUCE

If the meat for which this sauce is intended has been braised or roasted, strain and remove all the fat. Place in a saucepan with 1 cup of Sauce Espagnole, page 285, ½ (scant) cup of white wine, and 4 tablespoons of tomato purée. Bring to a rapid boil and allow to reduce to half volume over a hot fire; then add the indicated amount to the other indicated sauce, seasoning to taste with salt and pepper.

DEVILED SAUCE

Place in a small saucepan, 1 shallot, minced very fine, and 1 tablespoon of vinegar. Allow this to reduce to half, over a hot fire. Then add, 1 scant cup of good meat stock or game stock, using the game stock from the trimmings of the animal for which the sauce is intended, 2 tablespoons of tomato paste, 1 whole clove, head removed, and cook for 10 long minutes. Meanwhile, mix on a plate or saucer, 1 tablespoon of flour, as much butter and a few grains of cayenne pepper to taste, and add to the sauce. Heat well without letting boil, stirring occasionally.

DIANA SAUCE

(Suitable Especially for Furred Game. May Be Used for Game Birds)

To 2 cups of Sauce Espagnole (*Master Recipe*), page 285, add 2 tablespoons of vinegar, ½ teaspoon of whole pepper corns, bruised, and reduce to half over a hot fire. Add then ¼ cup of the marinade, in which the meat has been soaked, strain, and allow to simmer very gently for 25 long minutes. When the meat is ready, add ¼ cup of the gravy, strained and thoroughly cleared of all the fat. Place then over a medium flame and add 1 teaspoon of kneaded butter (equal parts of butter and flour kneaded together). Boil once, and strain through a fine sieve. Just before serving, stir in 2 or 3 tablespoons of fresh cream, whipped stiff, and 1 tablespoon of hard-cooked egg white, coarsely chopped.

DUCK SAUCE

(*Suitable for Wild Duck*)

Reduce 2 cups of broth, made from the giblets, to 1 cup. Place the pan in which the bird has been cooked, over a hot fire after removing all the fat. Sprinkle over 1 tablespoon of flour, and stir from the bottom of the pan, so as to remove all the particles of ingredients which may adhere, until the mixture is well browned; then pour over the reduced broth slowly, while stirring constantly, until mixture thickens. Strain over a saucepan. Let the fat come to the top, and remove carefully. Allow this to reduce to half, then add ¾ cup of SAUCE ESPAGNOLE (*Master Recipe*), page 285. Boil once, remove from the fire, and add 2 tablespoons of orange peelings, cut into narrow strips, and 1 cup of sections of orange, from which the skin and seeds have been removed.

FRUCTIDOR SAUCE

(*Suitable Especially for Duck, but May Be Served with Any Kind of Game Bird*)

Remove ⅔ of the fat from the pan in which the bird has been cooked. Set over a medium flame and pour in ½ wineglass of curaçao liqueur, a scant ¾ cup of orange juice, and stir from the bottom of the pan until the mixture is thoroughly mixed; then let reduce to half. Strain through a fine sieve, and add 2 tablespoons of orange jam, and 1 generous tablespoon of shredded orange peel and ½ teaspoon of grated lemon peel. Correct the seasoning before pouring into a sauceboat.

GIBLET GRAVY

(American Method)

(Suitable for Large Game Birds, Such as Hen, Goose, Duck, Turkey, Etc.)

Clean the giblets and cut into large pieces. Place in a saucepan and cover with boiling water (meat stock, especially chicken, or still better game stock made from the trimmings, may be used if desired); add 1 small grated carrot, sliced thin, 1 small peeled onion, quartered, 5 or 6 tender leaves of celery top, 6 sprigs parsley tied with a bit of bay leaf, 1 whole clove and a pinch of thyme, and cook until the giblets are tender, replenishing the chosen liquid when necessary. Remove from the fire, strain, reserve the liquor, and grind the giblets. After removing the bird from the cooking pan, remove all the fat, reserving about 1 generous tablespoon and the remaining gravy from the cooking process. Place the pan, in which the bird was cooked, over a hot fire, sprinkle 1 scant tablespoon of flour over and stir from the bottom of the pan, until the mixture thickens. Allow to simmer gently until delicately browned, then pour over 1 cup of the liquor of the giblets. Boil once, strain and season to taste with salt and pepper. Reduce the sauce so that there are 1½ cups, add the ground giblets, sprinkle with ½ teaspoon of parsley, minced. Serve.

GLOUCESTER SAUCE

(Cold) (Suitable for Any Kind of Cold Cooked Furred Game)

To a cup of stiff mayonnaise, add ⅓ cup of heavy sour cream, to which has been added a few drops of lemon juice, 1 pinch of fennel, minced fine, and 1 teaspoon of Derby sauce (a cold bottled sauce found in commerce), but if not available Worcestershire sauce may be substituted.

GOOSEBERRY SAUCE
(Suitable with Almost Any Kind of Dark-Fleshed Furred Game)

Throw ½ scant cup of gooseberries, previously cleaned, then split in two, but not separated, seeds removed, in 1 generous cup of slightly salted boiling water, let stand 4 long minutes. Drain and add to 1 cup of BUTTER SAUCE *(Master Recipe)*, page 286. Just before serving, add a few drops of lemon juice.

GRAND VENEUR SAUCE
(Suitable with Any Kind of Furred Game)

The only difference between this sauce and the sauce called Venaison sauce, is that the latter is slightly clearer.

To 2 generous cups of SAUCE ESPAGNOLE *(Master Recipe)*, page 285, reduced to 1 cup over a hot fire, add ½ teaspoon of peppercorns, coarsely pounded, 1 tablespoon of vinegar, and again allow to reduce to half, over a hot fire. Add then ½ generous cup of the gravy from the cooking pan, the fat of which has been carefully removed and strained, and 2 tablespoons of the strained marinade. Allow to simmer gently for 30 long minutes, strain, serve. Using this method, it is not necessary to thicken the sauce with flour.

ITALIAN SAUCE
(Suitable for Any Kind of Furred Game)

Mince very fine, 2 large fresh mushrooms, peeled, 1 shallot, and 1 tablespoon of raw, lean ham (fresh lean pork may be substituted). Cook this mixture in a scant tablespoon of butter for 2 long minutes, stirring constantly and over a hot fire. Sprinkle over 2 teaspoons of flour, stir and cook 2 minutes longer, stirring all the while. Gradually pour in ½ (scant) cup of white wine, and ½ (generous) cup of the gravy from the pan in which the meat has been cooked, alternately and stirring constantly. Allow to cook slowly for 20 long minutes. Remove all the fat carefully, and add 1 pinch of chervil, 1 pinch of parsley, both minced fine, and 2 small leaves of fresh or dried tarragon herbs, also minced fine. Correct the seasoning. Serve.

HORSERADISH AND RED CURRANT SAUCE

(Suitable with Any Kind of Game, Feathered or Furred)

On a hot fire, reduce ½ cup of port wine, to which has been added a pinch of nutmeg, cinnamon, salt and pepper to taste, to one-third. Stir in 2 small jars of red currant jelly, and stir occasionally until thoroughly mixed and the jelly is melted. Boil once. Serve.

HUSSARDE SAUCE

(This Delicious Sauce, Usually Made To Accompany Dark Butcher's Meat, May Advantageously Be Served with Any Kind of Furred Game)

Very lightly brown, 1 medium-sized onion and 1 shallot, very finely minced, in 1 tablespoon of butter, over a gentle fire. Be careful not to brown, then pour over 1 cup of white wine. Stir and let reduce to half. Then add 1 cup of SAUCE ESPAGNOLE (*Master Recipe*), page 285, in which has been stirred, 1 scant tablespoon of tomato purée and ⅓ generous cup of good chicken or veal stock. Add also 2 generous tablespoons of lean raw ham, in large cubes, or still better a 5-ounce piece of lean raw ham, ½ small clove of garlic, mashed, and 5 sprigs of fresh parsley tied with a small piece of bay leaf and a small sprig of thyme. Let this mixture cook for 30 minutes. Then remove the ham and strain through a very fine sieve or through a fine cloth. Return to the fire. Season to taste with salt and pepper; then add the already removed ham, cut either into small cubes or in narrow strips, julienne-like, ½ teaspoon of prepared horseradish, well drained, and tossed to loosen, and 1 teaspoon of parsley, minced very fine.

HUNTER SAUCE

(Suitable for Any Kind of Furred Game)

Sauté in 2 tablespoons of butter, ¼ lb. of fresh mushrooms

(peeled, sliced, using caps and stems), and 1 generous tablespoon of shallot (minced fine), for 3 long minutes, stirring constantly but gently, using a wooden spoon. Pour over 1 cup of good white wine, stir, and allow to reduce to half (the liquid). Then add ½ cup of good tomato sauce, and ½ cup of SAUCE ESPAGNOLE (*Master Recipe*), page 285. Bring slowly to a boil, and let simmer for 5 long minutes. Just before serving, add 2 scant tablespoons of butter, 1 teaspoon of chervil, minced fine, and 2 leaves of fresh tarragon herbs.

MADEIRA WINE SAUCE

(Suitable with Any Kind of Small or Large Furred Game)

After removing the meat from the pan, strain and remove the fat carefully from the pan (roasting or braising pan). Place the sauce in a saucepan. There should be a good half cup, and add ½ cup of good white wine, and 2 generous tablespoons of tomato paste. Reduce this to half over a hot fire, stirring constantly with a wooden spoon (about 5 long minutes), then add 4 tablespoons of good Madeira wine, stirred in ¾ cup of SAUCE ESPAGNOLE (*Master Recipe*), page 285.

MORNAY SAUCE

(Not Often Used Today, but Delicious with Game Birds)

To a cup of BECHAMEL SAUCE, page 283, add ¼ cup of the cooking gravy of the bird, thoroughly cleared of fat and strained, 2 tablespoons of grated Parmesan cheese mixed with an equal amount of grated Swiss cheese. Add then 1 tablespoon of butter and stir rapidly until the cheese and butter are melted.

MOSCOVITE SAUCE

(Russian Recipe) (Suitable for All Venison)

To ¾ cup of very hot POIVRADE SAUCE, page 297, add 4 tablespoons of Malaga wine, 3 tablespoons of juniper-berry infusion, strained, and 1 generous tablespoon of blanched, then grilled, almonds, cut into small strips, 1 generous tablespoon of raisins, plumped in hot meat stock, and well drained. Stir well and serve as hot as possible.

ORANGE MINT SAUCE

(*Cold*) (*Suitable for Bird and Furred Game*)

Pour 1 cup of game stock, strained, over ¾ cup of loosely packed mint leaves (dry or fresh). Cover closely and allow to infuse until thoroughly cooled. Then add ½ generous cup of orange marmalade, and 1 teaspoon of grated lemon peel. You may sweeten to taste if desired, as sometimes the orange marmalade is a trifle bitter.

ORANGE AND WINE SAUCE

(*Especially Appropriate for Ducks, Wild or Domestic*)

Cook the finely chopped, not grated, peel of a large orange in ½ generous cup of water, 10 short minutes. Drain and discard the water. Return the orange peel to a saucepan and add 1 (generous) cup of white wine, and the duck giblets, and cook slowly for 35 long minutes. Brown 2 tablespoons of flour in two tablespoons of butter, and add to the wine and giblet mixture, plus 1 orange, cooked in the orange cavity, during the process of cooking, either roasting or braising. Cook 5 long minutes over a medium flame and strain, pressing a little, through a fine sieve. Season with salt and black pepper as well as a pinch of nutmeg to taste. Serve as hot as possible.

OXFORD SAUCE

(*Cold*) (*Suitable for Any Kind of Furred, Cooked, Cold Game*)

Operate exactly as indicated for CUMBERLAND SAUCE, page 288, except that the orange and lemon used should be grated.

POIVRADE SAUCE

(Suitable for Any Kind of Furred Game)

Heat 2 generous tablespoons of olive oil and add 2 tablespoons of carrot, as much onion, coarsely cut, 6 sprigs of fresh parsley tied with 1 small bay leaf and a small sprig of thyme, and ½ cup each of trimmings of furred game and ham until all is delicately browned, stirring frequently with a wooden spoon. Drain all the oil, then add 1 generous tablespoon of vinegar and ½ cup of good white wine. Stir and let the liquid reduce completely, but do not burn the vegetables and ham. Now add 1 scant cup of SAUCE ESPAGNOLE *(Master Recipe)*, page 285, and ½ cup of rich game stock, rather thick, and ½ cup of the strained marinade. Cook very slowly, covered, and until the sauce is reduced to half. Strain and let simmer, for 10 short minutes, over water after adding 6 whole peppercorns, coarsely ground. Just before serving, strain through a very fine sieve, pressing a little. Serve this very *"hot"* sauce as hot as possible.

POLISH SAUCE

(Suitable for Any Kind of Furred Game)

Operate exactly as indicated for recipe above, adding, just before serving, 2 tablespoons of blanched, grilled almonds, cut into small strips, and 1 teaspoon of brown sugar. (*This sauce is very popular in Poland and in Germany.*)

PORT WINE SAUCE

(English Method) *(Suitable for Any Kind of Game Birds, Especially with Wild Ducks)*

Over a hot fire, reduce to half, 1 generous cup of port wine, to which has been added 1 teaspoon of shallot, minced very fine, and a very small sprig of thyme, the juice of 2 oranges (small), and a few drops of lemon juice, ¼ teaspoon of grated orange rind, and a few grains of salt and cayenne to taste. Strain this through a fine cloth, return to the fire and add 1 cup of good veal stock, to which has been added, 1 scant tablespoon of flour, stirred in a little water. Boil once, skim, and let simmer 5 long minutes before straining again into a sauceboat.

ROEBUCK SAUCE

(English Recipe) *(Suitable for Any Kind of Preparation of Furred Game, Especially Deer and Venison)*

Mince fine one medium onion, and 2 tablespoons of raw ham, and sauté in heated butter until delicately browned. Pour over ½ scant cup of good vinegar, stir and add 6 sprigs parsley tied with 4 sprigs of tender leaves of top celery, and 1 small bay leaf as well as 1 sprig of thyme. Boil and allow this to reduce to almost nothing. Then add 1½ cups of SAUCE ESPAGNOLE *(Master Recipe)*, page 285, stir and allow to simmer very gently for 15 long minutes. Now remove the parsley bunch (bouquet garni), season to taste with salt and black pepper, and add 1 small glass of port wine, and stir in 1 generous tablespoon of red currant jelly.

ROMAN SAUCE

(Also Called Raisin Sauce)

(Especially for Venison, but May Be Adapted to Any Kind of Furred Game)

Cook to a caramel brown, 1 generous teaspoon of sugar, and pour over 5 tablespoons of vinegar, stirring until dissolved, then pour over 1 cup of SAUCE ESPAGNOLE *(Master Recipe)*, page 285, and 4 generous tablespoons of game stock, procured from 1 cup of game stock, reduced to 4 tablespoons. Allow this to reduce to a scant half. Strain through a fine cloth, return to a saucepan, season with salt and black pepper to taste, and add 1 teaspoon of pignolia nuts, grilled, 2 tablespoons of seedless raisins, plumped in hot game stock, and well drained.

SALMIS SAUCE

AUTHOR'S NOTE

According to Escoffier and other masters of cookery, this sauce, which resembles a coulis, has but one method of preparation. Only the liquid used varies according to the kind of game—bird or furred game—to which it is added, and according to the plumpness or leanness of the game used.

Sauté very gently, ¾ cup of "braise" or mirepoix, made as indicated in recipe for GROUSE IN AUSBRUCHE, page 29, in 3 scant tablespoons of butter, adding all the trimmings available, which of course should be of the same kind as those of the bird or furred animal for which the sauce is prepared, until delicately browned. Pour over 1 cup (generous) of white wine, stir and allow to reduce to two-thirds, over a hot fire. Then add 1½ cups of SAUCE ESPAGNOLE (*Master Recipe*), page 285. Allow to cook slowly for 30 long minutes. Strain through a fine sieve, pressing hard so as to obtain all the essence from the solid parts and ingredients. Just before serving, add 1 tablespoon of butter. Stir and serve.

SAINT HUBERT SAUCE

(*Cold*) (*Especially Appropriate for Hure de Sanglier—Wild Boar Head Loaf—but Suitable for Any Kind of Furred, Cooked, Cold Game*)

Cut into small dices, 1 jar of red currant jelly, rather stiff, and add, using a fork, 3 tablespoons of vinegar, in which a scant teaspoon of dry mustard has been stirred; finally add 3 tablespoons of olive oil.

SMITANE SAUCE

(*Russian Recipe*)

(*Suitable for Any Kind of Game, Bird and Furred, Especially Sautéed and Casserole Preparations*)

Sauté in 1 generous tablespoon of butter, 2 small onions, finely minced, until soft, but not browned, stirring constantly, over a gentle fire; moisten then with ½ cup of white wine, stir and allow the liquid to reduce completely. Add 1 generous cup of heavy sour cream, previously scalded, stirring all the while, until the mixture is well blended; allow to simmer gently for 5 long minutes; strain through a fine sieve or a fine cloth. Then, and only then, season with salt and pepper. Just before serving, if a sharp sourness is desired, add a little lemon juice to taste.

SOUR CREAM SAUCE

(Suitable for Any Kind of Cooked Game, Furred or Bird)

Blend 1 tablespoon of flour with 1 tablespoon of butter over a hot fire, but do not brown, moisten with ¾ cup of heavy sour cream, stirring constantly until mixture thickens. Then place over hot water. Keep hot. Beat well, 4 egg yolks with 2 tablespoons of cold meat stock, until foamy, seasoning to taste with salt, white pepper, and a few grains of nutmeg. Pour the egg mixture gradually over the sour cream, placed over hot water, stirring rapidly and constantly. Remove from the hot water and beat in 3 tablespoons of butter, added bit by bit, and using a wire whisk.

SULTANA SAUCE

(Suitable for Any Kind of Cooked Furred Game)

Bring to the boiling point, 1 generous cup of strained game stock, to which has been added ½ cup of good white wine, 2 thin slices of lemon (seeds and rind removed), 2 whole cloves (heads removed), 1 small clove of garlic (whole), 1 small bay leaf tied with 5 sprigs of parsley, 5 sprigs of chives, and 1 very small white onion, and allow to continue boiling for 15 minutes; then reduce the fire and let simmer for 20 long minutes, or until the mixture is reduced (the liquid) to ⅓ cup or thereabouts. Strain into another saucepan, place over a low fire, and add ¾ cup of SAUCE ESPAGNOLE (*Master Recipe*), page 285. Just before serving, stir in 2 egg yolks, and 1 teaspoon of finely chopped parsley, after correcting the seasoning.

TYROLIAN SAUCE

(Cold) (Suitable for Cold, Cooked Furred Game)

To a cup of mayonnaise, add ¾ teaspoon of capers, minced fine, 2 tablespoons of tomato paste, 1 teaspoon of finely chopped parsley, and 1 tablespoon of finely chopped sour gherkins. Mix well.

VENAISON SAUCE

See GRAND VENEUR SAUCE, page 294.

GAME GARNISHINGS

APPLE SURPRISE

Core and halve 3 apples of the same size, and cook until red in a syrup made of equal parts of water and sugar, and candied cinnamon. Lift out carefully and fill each apple cavity with cranberry sauce, mixed with equal part of strained, prepared horseradish.

APPLE RINGS

Wash, do not peel, but core 3 red apples; cut in 1-inch slices. Melt butter, using 4 tablespoons, in a skillet, add ½ cup of water and 1 cup of sugar mixed with a dash of salt, and cook to boiling point. Then place the rings carefully in the syrup, and allow to simmer very slowly until tender. Remove the apples to the platter on which the game meat is dressed, and fill the center of each slice with either red currant jelly, a plump stewed prune, or whatever fancy or taste may dictate.

BAKED PEAR FERMIÈRE

Select 3 large, not quite ripe pears, peel, do not core, and cook in 1 cup of water seasoned with nutmeg, salt, and 3 tablespoons of sugar, until the pears are tender, but not soft. Lift out carefully, then remove the core, and in its place, arrange a plump stewed prune or apricot, filled with red currant or any other kind of jam desired.

BROILED GRAPEFRUIT

Slice or segment peeled grapefruit, sprinkle with salt to taste, and place under the flame of the broiler for just enough time to allow the fruit to brown delicately, turning often.

BAKED ORANGES

Wash 6 whole small oranges and cover with water in a saucepan; boil gently until orange skin is tender and can be pierced with a toothpick; lift out and cool. Cut a thin slice off the blossom end of each orange and carefully remove the core. Fill each orange with 1 teaspoon of butter, 1 teaspoon of sugar and a few grains of nutmeg mixed together. Place the oranges in a tight-fitting covered dish, filled ⅔ full of water; set in a moderate oven (350°) and bake for 1 long hour.

BROILED PEACHES

Remove halves of canned peaches from the syrup, drain and sponge carefully; arrange the peaches cut side up in a shallow baking dish. Brush with butter to which has been added a little nutmeg and broil under moderate heat until the peaches are delicately browned. Fill each cavity with either a plump stewed prune, stone removed, and filled with a little cranberry jelly, or a whole large cranberry.

CANDIED BANANAS

Peel 3 large bananas, and cut in two crosswise. Arrange in a shallow oiled or buttered baking dish. Mix 2 tablespoons of water and ¼ cup of corn syrup and pour over bananas. Dot with butter and bake in a hot oven (450°) 10 long minutes, basting often with the sauce in the baking dish. Banana may also be broiled, if desired. Pears or oranges may be prepared in the same way.

CANDIED KUMQUATS

Cook ½ quart of kumquats, carefully washed in tepid water, for 30 short minutes with enough water to cover. Drain. Repeat, that is, cover again with water and allow to simmer slowly until tender. Drain; cut the kumquats in halves, crosswise, carefully remove the seeds, and cook very gently in a syrup made of 1 cup of water, 1 cup of sugar, and a pinch of salt to taste, for a short hour or until the kumquats are translucent.

CURRIED APPLES

Wash, do not peel, but core 6 small apples (red and tart apples should be selected). Cut in half, crosswise, and spread the cut surface with a paste made as follows: 2 generous tablespoons of curry (more or less according to taste), 1 pinch of salt to taste, ⅓ cup of brown sugar, and ⅓ cup of butter. Bake or broil in a shallow baking dish under moderate heat until the apples are tender. A fine garnishing.

FRIED BANANAS

Cut 3 bananas (peeled) into halves, lengthwise. Roll in flour and pan fry in 4 or 5 tablespoons of butter till delicately browned on both sides. Just before serving, dip into melted red currant jelly, drain, and arrange around the game.

GLAZED CRANBERRY APPLES

Core, after washing, but do not peel, 3 nice red apples and cut in halves, crosswise. In a skillet, mix 1 generous cup of water, 3 whole cloves, a pinch of nutmeg, a pinch of salt, and cook to boiling. Add then the apple halves and simmer gently for 5 short minutes. Lift out and let drain. Boil the syrup until very thick, then add the cranberries (there should be a cup), previously washed and sponged, reduce the heat and remove from the stove as soon as the cranberries begin to pop open. Heap the cranberries in center of apple rings, and arrange around the game.

FRENCH FRIED GREEN PEPPER RINGS

Wash 3 or 4 green peppers. Cut a slice at both ends, and carefully remove the seeds and white parts. Cut in slices, as for French fried onions. Roll in flour, then in milk, and again in flour. Fry in hot deep fat, as you would French fried potatoes, until golden brown. Drain thoroughly and garnish around the game.

PINEAPPLE RINGS

Proceed as indicated for FRIED BANANAS, page 307, substituting pineapple rings, cut in two, crosswise, for bananas.

SIRNIKI (*Pancakes*)
(*Russian Recipe*)

Rub through a fine sieve 1 lb. of dry cottage cheese. Break 2 whole eggs over the cheese, add salt, white pepper, and enough flour to bind (you may add 2 tablespoons of chives, minced fine, if desired). Shape on a floured board in little round patties about 2 to 3 inches in diameter and fry in heated butter till golden brown on both sides. A side dish of sour cream is the usual accompaniment.

WINE JELLY

Soak 2 tablespoons of granulated gelatine in ½ cup of cold water, then add 1½ cups boiling water. Stir, then add 1 scant cup of sugar, stirring until sugar is dissolved. Now add the chosen wine either sherry, Madeira, red or white wine—there should be 1 scant cup—to which add ¼ cup of strained orange and lemon juice, all together. Pour this mixture into a flat-bottomed dish. Chill, unmold, and cut in whatever shape desired, using small French fancy cutters.